The Living Religion

THE

Living Religion

JEAN VIEUJEAN

Translated from the French by David Heimann

THE NEWMAN PRESS • WESTMINSTER, MARYLAND

1964

Nihil obstat: JOHN F. DEDE, S.S., J.C.D.
      Censor Deputatus

Imprimatur: LAWRENCE J. SHEHAN, D.D.
      Archbishop of Baltimore
      March 25, 1963

The *nihil obstat* and the *imprimatur* are official declarations that a book or pamphlet is free of doctrinal and moral error. No implication is contained therein that those who have granted the *nihil obstat* and the *imprimatur* agree with the views expressed.

Foreword

"TRUTH EXISTS . . . and if we do what we should to come to the truth, it will not flee from us in an everlasting flight" (Ollé Laprune). The whole problem is to do what we should. This is true already in the acquisition of the natural virtues of the world. And it is infinitely more true in a consideration of religious truth.

Here we are considering the truth which concerns the foundations, the totality, the destiny, the mystery of the person. We are treating of the meaning of life. We are treating of the discovery, through the evidence of outer appearances, of the one Being who truly *is,* the Being who creates everything, gives everything, asks everything—"invisible by the very reason that he is present."

It would be very strange if truth like this could be acquired "quickly or at a bargain," as Malègue says. That is the fundamental error that blinds so many men, whether they are Christians or unbelievers. Although they know that the sciences cannot be acquired without assiduous and tiresome effort, they suppose that the knowledge of God can be got at with little difficulty. The unbeliever says that God will have to come to find him, if there is a God. He forgets that God cannot be discovered except by those who ask, who seek, and who knock, and that if man is not humbly waiting within his heart, the great Visitor will knock on the door in vain. Then there are the legions of formal and lukewarm believers who think they have found God and take no further interest in him. They forget that it is not God whom they have learned to know, if, thinking they have already found him, they no longer look for him.

But there is another equivocation which is even more dangerous. It supposes that God and the mystery of Christianity in which God has given himself to the world can be discovered only by reason, and that a clever manipulation of propositions and speculations is all that is needed to demonstrate the truth of his existence.

"God being a person," says Rivière, "every conversion is a question of meeting God. That is a terrible mystery."

It is a terrible mystery because it means putting into action everything that is most spiritual within us, this basic self which is made up, as we shall soon see, of something infinitely more subtle than reason.

Still we have to admit that most of the time men neglect, or even ignore, the most promising of the powers that they have within them. They allow themselves to continue in their slumber. That is the basic reason for the mediocrity of so many lives. "Blessed are the drowsy," says Nietzsche, ironically. And William James laments the fact that we "are really digging the grave for our most beautiful potentialities," while Alexis Carrel thunders forth with the fearful sentence that the "atrophy of our fundamental activities makes man a spiritually blind being."

Man must be aroused from this slumber. That is the painstaking preoccupation of every man who has discovered the riches that money cannot measure, the riches that the life of the spirit produces in great abundance once it rises from its torpor. "My whole effort," says Gabriel Marcel, "can be understood as aimed towards the production . . . of the currents by which life is re-born in certain regions of my spirit which seemed to be condemned to torpor and abandoned to decay." No wonder that Christ himself, above all others, insists upon the necessity of keeping watch. "Blessed is the servant whom the master, when he comes, finds watching. He will set him over all the goods of his house." What he means are those who keep their spirit active and alert.

Elsewhere he insists upon the necessity of doing the truth if we want to come to the truth. And that brings us to a third equivocation which keeps many men from discovering the true values, especially religious values, and making them the nourishment of their lives.

Values can be discovered only by being experienced. It does not help merely to read even the most detailed books on physical education. The reader will never know whether they are right or wrong as long as he does not spend the prescribed time carrying out the exercises that are suggested. We cannot discover God in books on apologetics or religion. They can only point out the route and invite us to make the voyage. If we remain sitting down or lounging in the comfort of our homes, we will never know how bracing and how stimulating the fresh clean air can be upon an open hilltop.

Values—and the highest of all values, which is God—are given only to those who give themselves. Whoever is terrified or recoils at the thought of effort is condemned to a stalemate. Each individual person has to question himself in order to know whether he really wants to pay the price for what is beyond all price.

The conditions we have just outlined are severe, but they cannot be got around. They are the conditions that inspire every page of this book. We all know only too well how the ignorance of these conditions keeps many believers in lukewarmness and indifference, and holds unbelievers fast in their inactivity and, sometimes, even in their scorn. This introduction to the problem of religion is addressed to the loyalty and courage of believer and unbeliever alike. They will not find the answers to all their questions in this book. We will never be finished asking questions. But they will find a brotherly call to everything that is best within them: their intimate self, their sincerity, their spiritual energies, their will. They will find in it everything that is most mysterious and most beautiful within their will: liberty, attention and love, waiting, open to the world and to its final secrets. What remains is the work of God. If they do what they should, they can be sure that he will not fail them and that some day he will reveal himself in all his magnificence to everyone who knows how to wait for him—actively—without growing tired of waiting. Then they will know the meaning of this new birth of which the Gospel speaks, the passage from darkness to the light.

This work is intended primarily for the university student and the educated adult. Still, it should not be beyond the grasp of the student who has completed his course in the humanities and who might derive some principles from it that are indispensable if he wants to survive the religious crises that are so common among young students and which are only aggravated by the specialized scientific studies of the university.

And it is our wish that the unbeliever find nothing but light and sympathy in these pages. What we have to say—as will soon be very apparent—concerns the discovery of the loftiest worldly values as well as those of the Christian religion. For both sets of values lead equally well to the consideration of the laws which regulate the basic, intimate ego of the human person. We can never arrive at this fundamental ego with any real sincerity and not rub shoulders with the absolute.

Contents

[ix]

The Living Religion

CHAPTER I

Sincerity and Religion

I. Sincerity Towards Self

The First Duty

THE FIRST DUTY we have is complete sincerity with our-selves. We must learn to know more and more what our nature is, our mystery, our meaning. We must realize all our individual duties more and more perfectly. These are the basic conditions we must accept if we deserve to be called men.

In the course of our life we pass through much that is shadowy; we experience many doubts; we deny a great many things. But before the obligation of being sincere with ourselves we cannot hesitate. That would be lying to ourselves, denying our very own selves, betraying our own nature. In the presence of men who do not admit this fundamental duty there can be no argument. Nothing is to be expected from them as long as they remain fixed in this internal contradiction of being and not wanting to recognize what they are or become what they are supposed to become.

As for those who admit this fundamental imperative and make a serious effort to bring their lives into subjection to it, we might say that they have loyally accepted their human calling, that they deserve to be called men. They are certain of working out their destiny, no matter what their ideas on the subject might be at the moment, no matter how confused or incomplete or false they are.

Deformed Sincerity

As we shall see later, all human values, especially the higher ones, tend to lower themselves in the thought and life of men. Sincerity is no exception to this gradual degradation.

Sincerity must not, of course, be confused with cynicism. The cynic finds his pleasure in unpleasant witticisms about life, the world, himself and, more often still, other men. What attracts him is not the element of truth that his statements might contain. It is rather the fact that they are unpleasant. He speaks them out without respect and without charity; that already disfigures the truth. Usually he sees only one side of existence and men, the worst side. His perspective is thrown off balance by the baseness of his spirit. What is base drags other things down, says Saint-Exupéry.

On the other hand, we must recognize that sincerity is not easily realized in its full purity. False sincerity is current in the world. Man is very apt to lie to himself. Perfect sincerity is a summit towards which man must aim without ceasing, without growing weary. As soon as his effort falters, the powers of falsehood and dissimulation within him return to action and work their evil effects. Sincerity is an active virtue, and the effort must not stop as long as there is life.

Another danger which we constantly meet is the temptation to rest content with forms of sincerity that are real, but superficial. To be sincere is to know self just as self really is. But the human person is made up of different strata, some more on the surface, some lying at a greater depth. Too often our examination stops with one of our secondary egos and does not penetrate to the fundamental ego. This confusion is so frequent and its consequences are so serious that we must take great pains to avoid it. These pains are the price of sincerity. There are three secondary aspects of the human ego which must be examined briefly before we can attempt any description of the real fundamental ego.

The Social Ego

The first form of the ego that we distinguish is what we might call the social ego. It is made up of the sum total of ideas, acquisitions, aspirations, impressions, feelings, aptitudes and tastes which we have in common with those who live together with us. By way of example we might mention our scientific conversations, our political or social ideas, our judgments concerning men and happenings, our feelings towards certain persons—in short, everything that is concerned with the normal surface changes of our everyday life, everything that we can communicate without really discovering ourselves, without betraying the secret of our fundamental personality.[1]

The Liminal Ego

A second ego, more hidden than the first, has been called a waking dream. It can also be called the liminal ego, because it is encountered on the border between conscious and unconscious. The unconscious is a great storehouse of little known energies and especially all kinds of instincts deep within us. At any given moment—everyone has had the experience—this unconscious can beat against the door of the conscious and awake a whole crowd of impulses, aspirations, images, ideas. These then flood chaotically into consciousness, where they pause for the briefest moment, occasionally implanting themselves there, but more often disappearing to make room for others. It can be compared to a fantastic film which is being run off within our marginal consciousness[2] without our control and even without our direct perception. Some of these impulses are noble, generous, heroic. Others are inconsistent, comical, ridiculous, absurd. And some of them belong to the evil cesspool that can exist even in the most pure men and which contains a disorderly confusion of emotions of pride, vanity, disgust, hate, vengeance, cruelty, avarice, disturbed thoughts, perverse desires, and sometimes even absolutely monstrous day-dreams.

Can this liminal ego be called the authentic ego? Yes and no. These impulses are *in us;* that much is true. But they are not really *ours.* And they do not become ours unless we capitulate to them, unless we willingly make them the collaborators and accomplices of our activity. We cannot simply deny their existence.

[5]

It is even useful to look them in the face from time to time, for they can give us information about the semiconscious motives of our activity.[3] At any rate, they reveal an aspect of our activity with which we have to be familiar. But most of the time we only have to smile and abandon them to their own fleeting disappearance. Our truth is not to be found there. Nor is it in their rapid display of ideas before our own eyes or the eyes of someone else that our true sincerity lies hidden. "Nothing is more deceitful than what is spontaneous," writes Rivière; "nothing is more foreign to the real self."

The Character Ego

There is still a third ego to be distinguished. We might call it the character ego. Every one of us actually has a psychic structure which is peculiar to himself. That is what is called character. It is the synthesis of numerous elements that can be classified within two general categories, *endowment* and *volition*. Endowment comprises the innate qualities, often grouped under the name of temperament, and all the internal dispositions that result from the thousand influences that people and things exercise upon us without our knowing it, and which help to fashion what we are without our consciousness perceiving them all clearly and admitting them deliberately. Volition comprises all the psychic elements for which we are responsible and which come from influences that we seek or accept voluntarily: effort deliberately put forth or omitted, habits, good or evil, which are contracted through the free cooperation of the will.

It is this character ego that the science of character study attempts to penetrate, describe and classify by means of the many different methods of investigation it has created: observation, comportment tests, interview, graphology, morpho-psychology, and many others. Certain elements of the character ego are readily accessible to investigation; others are less so. Some are conscious, others unconscious.

[6]

There is no doubt that the recognition of the character ego is of the utmost importance for sincerity and self-control. Still, character is not identical with the personal ego of man. It can change, whereas the person remains the same. It is quite true to say with Pascal that "my psychism is not I myself."[4] There is something farther down than character.

The Personal Ego

Beyond the social ego, the liminal ego, and the character ego, which can all be analyzed and described, which can form the object of phychological research, there exists in every one of us a mysterious reality which is secret and fundamental. It forms the true sanctuary of the human personality.

It is difficult to analyze precisely because it is singular and unique; it cannot be compared with any other person. We shall call it the personal ego, the metaphysical ego, the foundation of being, the "I." Futher than that it cannot be described because of its radical simplicity. It is without form, without color, without dimensions, without parts, without succession in time or place.

It is not reasoning or analysis that gives us an insight into this knowledge. It is a spiritual intuition,[5] the immediate grasp of consciousness itself without the intermediary of any image or concept.

Most of the time, we have only a marginal consciousness of this fundamental ego. We are always present to ourselves, constantly, but in a veiled and clumsy manner, always more or less implicit. Our ego is overcast and drowsy. Its voice—for that is what it is, a voice, a call, a summons—is more or less stifled by the interference that the other psychic egos constantly set up: ideas, reasoning, images, emotions, drives—all constantly rising up within us.

And yet from time to time this ego does command our attention, sometimes only in passing, then again for several moments at a time, sometimes only timidly, then again with great insistence. When it does, that is when we are explicitly face to face with ourselves, confronted by ourselves.[6]

To accomplish this meeting with our real self, we do not need any subtle or mysterious effort such as could not be expended by a man whose mind has not been trained by years of philosophical discipline. This self-experience is within the grasp of everyone. Far from being the result of clever dialectics or a skillful process of abstraction, it is the fruit of great interior attention and intense spiritual examination. It is to be grasped in the concrete, and it requires, above all else, great recollection of soul. That is how we suddenly come face to face with ourselves, in the naked mystery of our own existence.

The Appearance of the Fundamental Ego

When this basic meeting actually takes place, I have more to do with regard to my own self than simply to confirm the fact that I exist. I see myself as a summons, a demand, a duty. I am, and I must become, and this becoming depends upon me. I have been entrusted to myself as work to be finished, as a job to be done.

It is a gripping discovery, for at the same time I become aware of the personal effort that this work will mean for me. It is a fundamental, a basic job. It is a job at which I will spend the whole of my life: becoming what I am supposed to become, being faithful to the exigencies of my fundamental ego.

At the same time, too, I am aware of a further truth: I *can* accomplish this task. Together with the duty, I have the power and the ability. At the same time that I see myself as a being that exists and thinks, I understand that I am free. I can[7] orientate my life towards the realization of my fundamental ego or I can take another direction. I can respond to its summons or I can refuse it, stifle it.

It is all up to me: I can make myself or I can break myself. I alone, once and for all. I am responsible for myself and for my destiny. No one can make the slightest act of will in my place. I myself have charge of myself. Face to face with my fundamental ego and my destiny, I am, and I can see that I am completely alone.[8]

Authentic Sincerity

Being sincere means first of all stopping to examine this fundamental ego. It means meeting the obligation of looking it squarely in the face when it gives us a call, instead of turning sharply away from it and taking flight. Moreover, it means setting the scene for this meeting with self from time to time, being willing to meet the conditions which prepare for this experience: silence, solitude, recollection, attention. Being sincere means having the courage to enter within self and spend some time there in quiet, serious conversation. It means daring to face self, to look self in the eye, with final and authentic truth.

Being sincere means working towards a constantly greater clarity of intellect and consciousness. The man who really wants to answer his human calling has to become more and more genuine and true. He has to make his life fulfill all the necessary conditions in order to arrive at a more and more perfect perception of truth in all its domains, but particularly on the moral and spiritual plane. For these two planes are of the greatest interest and importance to the lot of the personal ego.

For this purpose it is essential not only to be sure of the proper functioning of reason. We must also make a deliberate effort to clarify and purify our fundamental ego, so that it will be able to respond to the most illuminating and fertile intuitions. That is why it is so important to keep purifying it from everything that tends to darken it and slow it down. There are many factors constantly exerting their influence upon it, trying to distract it and make it lose its way, to weaken and darken it, to deceive it. Some of these powers that blind our spirit are part of ourselves, the passions and instincts.[9] Others besiege us from without. They are the great currents of thought that influence all of humanity: ideologies, politico-social movements, and in general everything that goes to make up the emotional, intellectual, and moral atmosphere which surrounds our existence. Everything is to be found there: true and false, good and evil. That is why, insofar as we can, we must examine and probe and control everything, unless we want to become the plaything of every popular new idea. Being sincere means working with an ever-mounting obstinancy to preserve interior righteousness and the innate ability to see things clearly.

Being sincere, finally, means being faithful to the call of the fundamental ego,[10] to the imperatives of conscience. It means allowing them to be heard, to raise their voices more and more powerfully, instead of trying to avoid or stifle them as we are inclined to do. It means to keep challenging our passions and instincts. It means to subject the opinions current in our society to a pitiless scrutiny, where we often discover that they are only mediocre or even sordid. It means to withdraw to the center of our fundamental ego—purified and enlightened now—in silence, with attention.

That is when the call will rise up within us, more and more explicit, urging us to become true and just and good men; men who not only welcome truth when it presents itself, but even make a deliberate search after truth; men who want justice for everyone, even for their enemies, and not only for themselves; men whose only thought in this world is to do something good on every possible occasion, to work for the advantage of everyone on earth, even those by whom they have been wronged.

This sincerity with self is the exact opposite of a romantic and narcissistic self-contemplation. It would be the greatest self-deceit to confuse it with a purely emotional preoccupation with self, with self-satisfaction in the enjoyment of our own states of soul, with a sensual and morbid taste for self-scrutiny and examination. There is only one kind of self-knowledge which deserves the name of sincerity, and it can be recognized by the fact that it is humble, despoiled of all that is misty and cloudy;

that it is manly, full of challenge, aimed at constantly and courageously outstripping self.

It is just as different from pure "introspection." Introspection consists rather in exploring the secondary egos which have been discussed above. Its object is to draw up an inventory of our resources and weaknesses, our good qualities and our defects, our assets and our liabilities. It is a useful effort for controlling our conduct, but it is not enough for the man who wants to be completely sincere with himself.

Clarity and Faithfulness

From everything that has been said up to this point it is easy to see that the drama of sincerity is enacted within the heart of man's secret self, in his soul, where the roots of both intelligence and will are intermingled to effect one common task.

Certainly we can distinguish between intellectual sincerity and moral sincerity. The first type consists in actively searching for truth[11] and in recognizing it when it has been discovered. The second consists in living in accord with this truth, "doing" the truth to the limit of personal ability. But these two forms of sincerity should never be separated. Each one depends upon the other. They are like two sisters who cannot make any progress without leaning upon each other. Truth cannot be seen well unless it is lived. And it cannot be lived well without an effort to throw a new and brighter light upon its essence.

That is why the work of becoming sincere is never really complete. Every light is a path to follow out, a call to be answered, a demand to be realized. And each step brings us to the discovery of a new light, a new call, a new demand, a more and more compelling realization of what our conscience is demanding.

There is nothing surprising about this. The whole life of man is becoming, growth, slow ripening, living dialectics. A perfectly pure soul and a clear-sighted spirit and an open mind cannot be acquired in a day, no more than the virtue of faithfulness to duty. No man can ever say that he is completely true and entirely faithful. But everyone is under obligation at least to be aiming towards it, to take at least one step forward every day.

That is not an easy task; there is no denying it. But no one ever said that the profession of being a man was open to an upstart or a social climber.

Fear of Self

The question can be asked whether men are willing to give the necessary attention to this search for a constant increase in illumination and faithfulness in the mastery of self. All the evidence points to a negative answer. The great majority of men are inclined towards the outside world. All their efforts are aimed at understanding this world by means of science and organizing it by various technical skills. And not infrequently they lose all sight of the world within them—their fundamental, intimate personality.

If we examine the matter more closely, we will discover that many men are afraid of this bold meeting face to face with self. They are running away from themselves, not always by seeking distractions of a sordid nature, but more generally by giving themselves over to continuous hard work so that there will be no time left for silence and recollection, for interior life and prayer.

Many men remain hidden to themselves. Many men sink into a spiritual darkness that grows deeper every day. Without being directly and clearly aware of the fact, they slip gradually into a sort of bad faith regarding themselves and life. They no longer make any effort whatsoever to look boldly upon the truth and they grow less and less interested in avoiding the continual betrayal that every man is tempted to become guilty of in the sphere of truth and justice and charity. Finally they reach the point where they want to judge everything according to the dictates of their first uncontrolled impulse and their immediate short-range interests, or on the scale of a very callous and hardened system of thought.[12] Without really knowing it, they have become counterfeits of manhood.

When do they become culpable? And how great is their sin? No one can know that except God, who examines the hearts and souls of men. This brings us to the secret of personality, the problem of individual responsibility face to face with self. No one can know what is going on in another man's conscience. He cannot know the answers that another man is making to the call of his own interior voices. Every man must know himself; every man must judge himself; every man must see to his own destiny. He has to keep watch over himself, over his own sincerity, over his own good faith. He is alone.

Sincerity, the Secret of Life

Sincerity is something that must be insisted upon, for without it, without constantly returning to our interior sources of activity, without this never-ending struggle for truth, for clarity, for faithfulness and interior awareness, everything in man grows cold and callous, and finally ends in degradation and corruption. The avenues that lead to what is real, especially what is real for his moral and social and religious being, are closed to him. Even if he does accept some certain truths, such as God and duty and justice, these truths run the risk of remaining abstract formulae in his mind instead of becoming the seeds of his new life.

We are constantly verifying this fact by our experience with everything that concerns religion. If our fundamental and intimate self, or what we call our faculties of communion, do not enter into action, none of the religious realities which are supposed to transform and control the whole of our life can have their true form or appear in their proper dimensions. What is more, we cannot even arrive at the discovery of these realities. We remain deaf and blind to them because we have not taken the one path that is capable of bringing us into contact with them.

[13]

But it is not only religion that depends upon our constant effort to purify and enlighten our personalities. There is our moral life as well, our human relations and our basic contacts with creation.

All of these relations become superficial, conventional, formalistic. Every form of human activity grows mechanical. The whole man changes into a robot, unless he continually keeps his thoughts and words and acts alive by plunging them deep into his fundamental self and making their roots stronger there every day of his life. And he must keep this fundamental ego awake by the careful cultivation of a true interior spirit and a faithful sincerity. It is in this activity that the one real secret of human life lies hidden.

II. Sincerity Towards the Problem of Religion

Sincerity and the Basic Problem

The most immediate result of being sincere with ourselves is that we find ourselves face to face with the first of all our problems, the problem of our destiny.

At every moment of our lives there are countless problems to demand our examination and solution. There are big problems and little problems. We have to decide what we will eat, what we will wear, where we will find a home. We have to find a state of life that satisfies us. We have to decide whether we will marry and whom we will marry, what profession we will enter, how we will bring up our children, what schools we will send them to. Some of us even have to settle the problem of what country we will live in, or what world.

There is no one who, if he reflects for even a moment, will fail to realize that all these problems, no matter how difficult they might be, are only secondary, partial, passing problems. If they are solved poorly, there are obstacles to be met, sometimes even great suffering. But still we realize that not everything is lost. And if these problems can be settled by a solution that turns out well for us, we do feel a real sense of satisfaction. But still we are well aware of the fact that not everything is saved or accomplished. We remain unfinished beings, beings who are waiting, beings with hunger and thirst. These problems all interest certain aspects of our existence, important aspects perhaps. But the whole of our life, the total destiny of our person, is not called into play.

All these partial problems lead every one of us to inquire into the fundamental problem of self in its totality. What is this self? How did it get here? Where does it belong and what is its role among the beings that surround it? What is it really supposed to do upon this planet? Is there going to be some future for it beyond the gates of death? Is there some hope of complete self-realization? Or is it rather, despite its intense desire and long waiting, condemned to disappear someday without leaving any more tangible trace upon this world than a soap bubble when it bursts and evaporates into the air?

That is the first problem, the problem that calls the totality of our person into play. It is a problem that involves the whole of man. It is a question of determining individual destiny, not in one or the other individual point of difficulty, not for this or that small problem, not for tomorrow or the day after tomorrow, but absolutely, beyond all the contingencies of space and time. Is there for me, for any one, for everyone, some hope of realizing the whole of self?

If we make a superficial examination of most men, we might readily believe that the greater number of them do not even ask themselves this fundamental question. Their lives are completely taken up with secondary, lesser problems.

For that matter, it is true that very many men only rarely become directly and clearly conscious of the question and really reflect upon it with attention for any length of time. And this is to be explained by the same reasons that prevent them from entering into the presence of their fundamental self and staying there a while. The forum of their interior attention is constantly occupied by secondary problems, a contract to draw up, some work to finish, some business to settle. Their conscious attention is always monopolized. They live carried along by the passing tide of the present.

But still they constantly have some consciousness of their first and foremost problem, even though it is a veiled and indirect and marginal consciousness. This problem exists side by side with the spiritual intuition of self. We come to know ourselves, as we have said, as existing, responsible, free. We might add that we learn to know ourselves as a question to be answered, as *the* question. But frequently, all too frequently, we lie to ourselves and run away from the answer. The same reasons that turn us away from the inspection of what is fundamental in our personalities also turn us away from boldly facing our most fundamental problem. The more sincere we are with ourselves, the more we shall pose the essential problem of human personality.

Sincerity and the Problem of Religion

The problem of human destiny implies the problem of religion. We might even say that it can be identified with the problem of religion. If there is a possibility of total self-realization for man, for his personal ego, he cannot find it except in another personal ego, an infinite one, God. This leads to a living relationship between him and God, a living relationship that we call religion.

Sincerity towards self naturally leads man to the threshold of the problem of religion. It prepares him to meet with God, no matter what the time and manner of this discovery might be.

These two affirmations are, properly speaking, indemonstrable. They cannot be admitted except by those who have had the experience in their own lives. To the unbeliever and the agnostic we can say only this:

"Persevere in your effort and your sincerity. Strive constantly to detach yourself from every prejudice you meet, from ready-made ideologies, from systems that are like an iron fetter upon your intelligence and your life. Try to put yourself in the circumstances that are prerequisite for a new and clearer discovery of the demands of your conscience. And be most generous in doing everything you can to accomplish all your duties.

"As far as religion is concerned, never be satisfied with a superficial familiarity. In religion, most of all, be careful to overcome prejudice and the ready answer and indifference. Do not give in too readily to the hostility or contempt you might feel spontaneously in the examination of religious truths. These feelings might very well be only the result of some secret resentment deep within you or the influence of the atmosphere you breathe.

"At the same time, search deep within yourself in your examination of the problem of religion. Within yourself first of all, so that your spirit will be open to every truth and ready to accept the highest values. Otherwise the words that describe them will remain so many empty expressions for you, without sense or value.

"But also examine the problem of religion itself. Find out exactly what religion is, and if you end up by rejecting it, at least have a very clear knowledge of what it is you are rejecting. For there are very many people who confuse authentic religion with one of its disfigured imitations and finally cast off what is true out of open contempt for the counterfeits they have already explored.

"If you are faithful in this twofold task, even if you conclude that you do better to persist in a state of doubt or denial, you are still perfectly in order, first of all with yourself, then with the Absolute, with him whom we call God. You will be saved."

Sincerity and Salvation

Is this what the Catholic Church really teaches? Beyond a doubt it is. God does not refuse his grace to anyone who does his best. That is the constant teaching of Catholic theology. It would be an unheard-of injustice for a man to be lost without being responsible for it.[13]

Sertillanges has put this well in his *Catechism for Unbelievers*. in the section that explains the well-known maxim "Outside the Church, no salvation." What happens to unbelievers, then? Can they possibly have grace, that is, the supernatural life necessary for salvation? This is his answer:

"Answer: Unbelievers *can* have grace, even atheists, even apparent persecutors, who are really only confused.

"Question: What must they do to receive grace?

"Answer: They must have the proper dispositions to obey the truth that they do not know or are even fighting against. They must make a sincere effort to understand it as long as they are in a state of doubt, and they must fulfill the important duties that they already recognize while they are waiting.

"Question: But that is not faith; and you say that when grace takes possession of the depths of a person's soul, it produces faith in that person's mind.

"Answer: These unbelievers of whom we are speaking do have the faith. In their hearts they really adhere to what they do not know, implicitly, potentially. Baptized infants really have the Faith and they cannot know anything. The poor unbeliever thinks that he knows something different; he thinks that he is denying error. But God can see through everything that his mind denies and can understand that his heart is faithful. In the spirit of such a person God can see the proper orientation even though its proper object is not recognized. And he is present to that heart by his grace, which is the fountainhead of supernatural charity. He is present to that spirit by the mysterious and supernatural virtue of faith.

"Question: And do these people belong to the Church?

"Answer: Yes, insofar as we understand the Church as a society that is predominately spiritual, that is, an intimate union

with Christ and the Holy Spirit—no matter how hidden or unconscious the knowledge of this union may be."

The Demands of Sincerity

It is sincerity that saves. But we must not entertain the illusion that this sincerity is something easy. Quite the contrary; it is one of the most difficult conquests that man can make.

Too often we consider sincerity as a passive virtue. Let truth show itself, we say, and I will gladly open my door. We forget that on every plane, but especially on the moral and religious planes, truth demands to be sought out. It is like a treasure buried in a field. We have to dig before we can find it. Sincerity has to be active. According to his own potentialities and opportunities every man must study, consult competent authority, reflect. And he has to spend some time in being quiet and recollected, in fostering a spirit of interior attention. For light comes only to open minds. Truth does not give itself to anyone unless he has first given himself to truth.

One of the biggest dangers which threaten our sincerity is unconscious bad faith. It is of much more frequent occurrence among men than conscious bad faith, that is, than deliberate falsehood.

Unconscious bad faith is the state of spiritual blindness or darkness which develops progressively within our mind when we do not put up a strong enough struggle against all the causes of error which are constantly assaulting us and which we have outlined above. These are, on the one hand, the various instincts which play an immense role in the structure and conduct of our personality, and, on the other hand, the events, the current ideas, the persons, the institutions, the customs—the whole social surroundings, in a word, in which we live our lives.

Religious Sincerity and the Modern World

If we want to form some estimate of the sincerity of modern

[19]

man with regard to the problem of religion, we shall have to be careful and refrain from passing judgment on particular cases. This judgment belongs to God alone. But, on the other hand, if we look at modern incredulity and the agnosticism of our day taken as a whole, there are certain comments we can make that seem to get quite close to things as they really are.

We can note first of all that a good number of the unbelievers have been brought up in an atmosphere of religious indifference, sometimes neutral, sometimes openly scornful. During their childhood and their adolescence, the surroundings of both family and school life have kept them carefully sheltered from the problem of religion. Religion has been presented to them as a sign of decline, beyond, if not against, the teachings of science, and consequently not a worth-while object of interest for the modern intelligence.

When they arrive at the age of personal reflection, they have no acquaintance with religion except in the light of some unfavorable prejudices which have crystallized within their minds. They notice only the most exterior manifestations of religion, those which take place right before their eyes—processions and pilgrimages—or the most crying disfigurations or, finally, even partial presentations, often caricatures of the truth that they find in certain popularizations or quasi-scientific books or distorted religious pamphlets. Their teachers in religion are Anatole France, André Gide, Romain-Rolland, Alain or Sartre, and Camus, or even Proudhon, Marx, and Nietzsche.

Very few of them take the trouble to examine the fatally oversimplified views which they have carried along from childhood and adolescence and their reading of the popular writers. Very few of them go back to the authentic sources of religious knowledge. That is why it is hard to say that their attitude is really serious and sincere, worthy of a true intellectual, worthy of a man who wants to assure truth a place of primary importance in his life.

Others, during their childhood and adolescence, have been

brought up in an atmosphere of more or less fervent, more or less enlightened Catholicism. When they reach the age at which they really begin to think for themselves, that is, between eighteen and twenty-five, they are no longer concerned with keeping up their culture and their religious life. This last has fallen victim to the moral and intellectual crisis which flares up during adolescence and the late teens. Besides that, it has been stifled and robbed of its values by the specialized studies which have overrun the whole field of research and investigation, limiting the spiritual sense and the powers of communion in favor of purely scientific activities.

Other diversions, generally with a materializing and secularizing influence, have served to aggravate this religious and spiritual anemia. Finally, there are professional tasks which quickly take over the whole horizon of life. The result of this atrophying process is fatal—an impoverished religion, open to doubt, to fault-finding, and to skepticism, religious indifference and finally the loss of the Faith. Who could dare to say that such a state of ignorance and doubt is the fruit of a really sincere life, a really sincere search for truth?

In order to arrive at more precise conclusions and to realize what the situation actually is, it would be well to enumerate the most frequent forms of skepticism and agnosticism in the world about us today.

1. *"Active" Skeptics.* These are men of constant activity, completely absorbed in their earthly task of being intellectuals, physicians, professors, conquerors, ministers. From time to time the question rises: Just what good is all this activity really doing? They avoid the problem and rush off to throw themselves into a new whirlwind of activity. They are men who gain the whole universe—at least for a time—but lose sight of their souls, their intimate personalities, their destiny.[14]

2. *"Passive" Skeptics or Epicureans.* There are two types of these. The first is composed of men whose whole life consists in play, alcohol, good cheer and sex. The second includes the sort

of person whom we currently refer to as "lower middle class." They are the people whose ideal is a very peaceful life, far withdrawn from every kind of responsibility, carefully safeguarded against every risk. Generally they are so closely bound and bounded by the "comfortable" that the problem of life's real meaning, if it ever even comes up in their lives, never meets with enough initiative to become a source of uneasiness within their minds.

3. *Scientific Skeptics.* These are the men—very numerous at the end of the nineteenth century and even in our own day—who do not recognize any values except those discovered by scientific research and technical progress. Religion, just like metaphysics, is a primitive mode of thought in their eyes. Now it has been left behind by science.

4. *Resentful Skeptics.* These are the men who are revolted at the sight of suffering and who cannot admit that it is compatible with the existence of an infinitely wise and good being.

5. *Autonomous Skeptics.* These are the men who see man as the supreme being in the universe, absolutely independent. Religion is only an "alienation," that is, a tendency by which man projects into an imaginary being all that is best within himself: wisdom, strength, power. Man cannot really become what he is supposed to be except by restoring all these attributes to himself and proclaiming himself absolutely autonomous. This is the intellectual position of those who are called atheistic humanists. Their principal leaders were Feuerbach, Nietzsche, and Auguste Comte.

6. *Social Skeptics.* These thinkers usually start from the same position as the autonomous skeptics, but they examine the social aspect rather than the philosophic aspect of life. They are active men, doers, fascinated by the thought of social justice, frequently quite selfless and sincere. They think that "religion is the opiate of the people," that it is an anaesthetic poured out upon the masses by a controlling class which is trying to keep the masses from achieving economic and social equality.

7. *Dilettantes.* These are the men who spend their time on earth playing with every form of life, without ever really settling upon any one definitely: artists, esthetes, often pure snobs, disciples first of Anatole France and then of André Gide. Everything that ties man down, especially his family, morality and religion, must be rejected as a threat against his liberty. Liberty, for them, is synonomous with aloofness.

8. *Atheistic Existentialists.* These are the men who proclaim that the idea of God is contradictory, and that man is "a coarse and absurd being, a being that is overdone, in excess of itself," that he "is what he is stupidly," and that we can never really come to know him without an experience of nausea. He is a being "without meaning, without past, without future, face to face with nothingness and the death that will put an end to this absurd adventure which cannot be supported except by means of unjustifiable decisions." In France, they are Jean Paul Sartre and his school.

9. *Intellectual Skeptics.* These are the men who have sincerely examined the claims of religion but have decided that they must persist in their doubt, "out of faithfulness to reason." Without in the least suspecting their sincerity, we believe that in a good many cases they are conducting their religious researches by methods that are valid only for the material sciences, and that, on the plane of faith, they are unconsciously looking for the same kind of certitude they can find in the positive sciences. Thus they put themselves, as we shall later see, in an impossible position.

Many of this last group of skeptics are very upright from a moral point of view. They are real lay saints and they merit our respect. In some of them there gradually arises a quiet state of mind, removed from eternal disturbances, a peaceful occupation with the earthly, an almost total absence of all sense of the divine.[15] Others have a restless soul. They cannot resign themselves to a life that has nothing before it and nothing after it, for anything, for anybody.

CHAPTER II

Religion as the Peak and Synthesis of Human Activity

THE FIRST DUTY of sincerity is objectivity; that is, sustained effort to learn to know things as they really are, in their truth, in their essence, in their respective values. Failing to make this effort is proof positive of intellectual weakness and lack of maturity.

We have to admit that a good many men in the world today pay only the most superficial attention to religion. Most of the time they have only a poor and deformed notion of it. They have no real understanding of its bearing or its nature. They do not put it in its proper place in the over-all scale of human activities.

There are many reasons for this ignorance and injustice. One of them, and not the least of them, is that the man of today is much more enchanted by scientific and technical values than the man of yesterday. They take up all his time, all his intelligence, all his energy. He can touch them with his hands, see them with his eyes. He can understand their immediate reality and results. They make a thousand improvements and comforts for his daily life. In our own century they have taken great strides forward, and we are fascinated by them. We have become slaves to their illusive spell.

When this intoxication settles upon him, man loses contact with other values that are more important, but more profound, more secret, slower to produce any tangible results and on that account less inviting. That is why he only rarely gives his attention, and even then distractedly, to the impartial contemplation of nature and art, or to a deliberate effort to develop a high degree of moral consciousness. And he is even less concerned with God and religious values. Intellectual leaders like Alexis Carrel have not ceased to denounce and lament the almost total neglect which has become the sorry lot of "moral sense, the sense of beauty, and above all the sense of the sacred."

That is why it is absolutely necessary to devote a chapter to the study of the various activities that are proper to men, so that we can understand the nature and bearing of each. Then we will be able to arrange them in a certain hierarchy as well, after we have examined their relationship to each other. Finally, we will be in a position to say exactly what religion consists in and how important a place it occupies in life.[1]

We are treating, as we have said, the activities that are proper to man. Man is the stage for a great many activities that he performs in common with the animal world, the plant world, even the material world. But there are certain activities that are proper to him alone, and they are not difficult to discover.

They can be classified in four main groups:

1. Scientific and philosophical activities.
2. Technical activities.
3. Moral activities.
4. "Communion" activities.

After examining each of these groups in order, we shall be in a position to define religious activity.

I. Scientific and Philosophical Activity

Man is a being who seeks to know, to understand, to explain everything he sees: the world, man, himself. This search for knowledge is spontaneous. It is a response to the natural bent of his intelligence.

In this effort to learn and understand, we can distinguish three stages or phases: empirical knowledge, scientific knowledge, and philosophical knowledge.

Empirical Knowledge

By means of the obvious everyday observations that he makes, every man acquires the knowledge of a great many facts of which he is not even fully conscious. But they are of great use to him for the organization of his individual and social life. He learns that things fall, fire burns, the sun reappears every morning, the ground is hard, water is not, his body seems lighter when he goes swimming, things freeze when it is cold. . . .

That is what is called common, popular, or empirical knowledge. It springs up all by itself, like uncultivated plant growth. It varies from one individual to another depending upon natural powers of observation, instinctive curiosity, and a greater or lesser ability to retain what has been learned from these spontaneous experiences. This kind of knowledge is relatively unconscious knowledge. We all know a great many things without even knowing that we know them. It is a poorly organized and confused knowledge which contains a little bit of everything: material and spiritual, concrete and abstract, useful and merely cultural. It is always of the greatest importance and has a big role to play both in our private lives and in our social relations. This is the kind of knowledge we have of most of the people that we meet, not at all systematic, neither clear nor conscious, but purely empirical. It is confused and not reflex; but still it is very sure and very rich.

Scientific Knowledge

This empirical knowledge naturally seeks to increase its depth and bearing. Impelled by necessity or merely by utility or perhaps even only by the natural dynamism of his intelligence, man is led to make a deeper investigation of the world that surrounds him. This is what gives rise to science.

Science seeks to know systematically and consciously. It makes one observation after the other; it fashions new procedures, new methods, new instruments which are better adapted to examine into reality—for example, the telescope or the microscope. It sets up artificial processes and conditions in order to observe the phenomena of nature with greater attention and detail. This is what we call scientific experience. Its purpose is to draw up an increasingly complete inventory of both the organic and the inorganic world.

In order to make greater progress in this work, science becomes specialized. That is, it cuts off a section of the universe and makes it the exclusive object of its research. Or else it limits its examinations to one or the other aspect of things and produces different branches of scientific investigation, such as physics, chemistry, astronomy, biology, in a word, the whole constantly increasing system of specialized sciences which man has developed to complete his cataloguing of the universe.

But science is not content with merely accumulating materials. It tries to classify them according to their similarities, their causal dependencies, and their various interrelationships in view either of their composition or the effects which they produce. That is how it arrives, first at generalizations and abstractions, and then finally at "laws," for example, the law of Archimedes stating that every body immersed in liquid suffers a loss in weight equal to the weight of the volume of liquid it displaces. Or the law of Newton, which states that bodies attract each other in direct proportion to their relative masses and in inverse proportion to the square of the distance between them.

Scientific laws are actually individual experiences which have been grouped into a system or drawn together by some flash of genius and whose essential relationship is expressed by means of a short formula which allows us to retain them more easily and make better use of them in our encounters with the realities they express. Actually in many sciences these "constant" phenomena which have been discovered and proved by observation and experience are expressed in an even more precise system of formulae based upon mathematical equations.

These laws are not to be regarded as something inherent in nature, a sort of half-veiled imprint existing in the individual facts which the scientist is able to bring to light by isolating it from the thousand unimportant details which conceal it from the eyes of the ordinary observer. These laws are only constant relations in nature discovered by scientific observation and expressed by means of symbolical formulae in order to make them easier to retain, so that the scientists can use them in speaking among themselves and making a practical application of them to the problems of everyday life.

In keeping with the natural bent which leads human intelligence to reduce everything to some form of unity, science combines all the phenomena it examines in the form of hypotheses and systems and theories. These theories are all intended to represent a large complexus of individual laws—and an even larger complexus of individual phenomena—as simply and as surely and as exactly as possible. We need only mention the series of systems successively developed by men like Ptolemy, Copernicus, Newton, Laplace and Lemaitre in an attempt to give a more and more precise explanation of the formation of the world and the gravitation of heavenly bodies.

These theories are not explanations properly so called. Nor are they "a complexus of general laws whose truth is established by experience and induction." They are rather a product of the human mind, a sort of "synoptic background or schematic arrangement intended to sum up and classify the laws arrived at by observation." They constitute a more or less successful *representation* of the facts. The best theory is the one that best explains the order within nature. Even though theories are always open to modification and reform, always provisional and unverifiable, they are still excellent working procedures and they set up an orientation for future research that is often very fertile, provided that they do no tend to limit the advance of human reason by making it less ready to abandon a good theory for a better one.

The Extent and the Limitations of Science

It would be absurd—and surely no one would think of doing it—for anyone to challenge the fact that science has produced some really marvelous results.

"No one with any sense," writes Sertillanges, "would even think of minimizing science itself. Even if it were absolutely without use, and even if it were opposed to some of our fondest desires, we would still have to honor it and practice it for the sake of the truth it contains and for the nobility of mind that it creates, willing to seek out the truth in everything.

"It is a wonderful experience," he says, "to reconstruct the order of the universe within your own head: to take the position of the astronomer and see yourself standing unmoved against the awe-inspiring background of universal motion, flooded with new thoughts, raising the horizon of your knowledge to distances that must be measured by tens of thousands of light years, feeling the worlds revolve upon their axes, learning of the life that sprouts upon their surface and the phases of evolution that follow one upon the other, each of them bursting forth in a fever of activity and then slowly dying out once its work is done; or, turning to the other extreme, to the lesser firmament of atoms, a universe within itself, moving and joining together and breaking off, reaching farther and farther down into reality until it attains a depth of being so infinitesimal that man's mind no longer knows how to represent it all in words."[2]

This is the same "joy of learning" that Peter Termier had so much to say about.

And it is true. If we draw up a catalogue of all the inventions and improvements produced by science even within the last fifty years, we cannot deny the fact that its services in behalf of mankind have been considerable and that it shows the greatest promise for the future.

But even though it has shown itself to be useful in all these planes—not only in the exploration and subjection of the material world, but even in the study of man and society, morality and religion—it still cannot pretend to be the ultimate answer in itself. It is still not enough.

To believe that it can attain the whole domain of truth, to believe that someday, by means of new and more perfect methods, it will succeed in giving the final explanation of everything that exists, to think, finally, that science alone, left to itself, can supply everything that man has need of—these are the dangerous illusions we call scientism.

To say that science is everything is, in the words of Sertillanges, a gross pretense that can only frighten the man who thinks and who has had some experience of life and the order of human affairs.[3]

Left to its own resources, science can never succeed in making the least advance in the knowledge of the universe in its first beginnings, its basic laws and goals. These are the questions that never cease to haunt mankind and they are always the most important and interesting in this life.

Science is, of course, quite capable of enumerating material facts and making an analysis of the elements that go to make them up. It can even grasp the relationships between these things, discover the laws that govern them, and draw the practical conclusions. That is its proper domain. That is where it has made really remarkable progress and is on the point of advancing even further. But, unless it goes beyond itself, it will never succeed in discovering the basic reality of things, their essence, the stable metaphysical basis which serves as a hard, unalterable reality beneath the manifold changes that take place in things. Science can never understand the value that these beings contain within themselves by the very fact that they exist, independently of any analysis that science can make or any practical utility they might have.

Finally, even though science contributes to the progress and liberation of man, it is still not the only cause or even the principal factor in his progress. And when it does presume to take the whole leadership, as is frequently the case, when it relegates moral or religious values to a place of secondary importance, or even tries to annihilate them, then it becomes a terrible danger for mankind. Then civilization loses its equilibrium and threatens to collapse. Science threatens to falsify everything, to lead things astray and bewilder them, to destroy whatever it has created. In isolating itself, in pretending to become the one solitary directing force for the destiny of mankind, it tends to "engulf all of civilization within a narrow funnel of its own making, by gradually shrinking the scope of human interest and activity."[4]

This danger has never been more evident than it is at present.

Science has its place, its mission, its value. Let it put forth its maximum effort, let it advance from conquest to conquest, and that is all well and good. But may it always please God to give us more and more intellectuals in the pattern of Bergson, Carrel, Lecomte du Noüy, who try to restore the highest human activities in demanding room for morality, for the spiritual, for what is sacred.

Philosophy

Scientific knowledge does manage to introduce us to the real in a certain sense. But despite its immense progress, it remains on the surface of things; it can never penetrate to the ultimate substrata of being.

But the human spirit is made in such a way that it desires to know the ultimate elements that make up reality, the ultimate explanation of being, the most intimate elements and the most hidden causes of existence.

Thus it is that man, continuing along his path of investigation into the real, goes beyond science and arrives at philosophy.

Beneath the illusive mobility of external phenomena that he discovers in the material world, man seeks to uncover the substantial, essential foundation that lies beneath all the accidental changes. He gives himself over to the philosophy of nature.

Beneath and beyond the biological and psychic phenomena that he had discovered within man, he wants to know the fundamental element, the first principle that explains them and holds them together. What is this factor, this self, this I, that animates and unites and expresses everything that it experiences? Is it spiritual, free, responsible, imperishable? That is the philosophy of man with all its branches and subdivisions.

Finally, beyond even the realm of visible being, beyond all the worlds whose mutual gravitation holds the universe in place, man wants to know if there is not some Being who explains all these other beings, a Being who combines within himself all the perfections of all the other beings and towards whom all the other beings tend, some unconsciously, others freely in the light of their final end. That is the philosophy of being, the Being whom we call God.

These are the three great orientations of philosophical research. All the other problems of philosophy can be grouped beneath these three heads.

Philosophy is a science just like the others; but it goes much further than those branches of material investigation that commonly go by the name of science. It is an attempt on the part of man to grasp and express reality in the elements that make it up, in its causes, in what really are its final principles.

But even philosophy has its limitations. It is an activity that must be respected and prompted among men, just as science must be respected and prompted. For it extends and surpasses the range of science by advancing further into the intimate heart of being and its meaning. Still, it is not enough for man. It is a form of pure knowledge and it aims at a more or less complete satisfaction of his reason. But man does not live by knowledge and reason alone.

II. Technical Activity

Science and Technical Activity

In scientific and philosophic research there is always a great joy that the real scientist and intellectual never tires of praising.

We have already spoken of Peter Termier and what he had to say about the "joy of learning."

But it would be a great mistake to believe that this research is always aimed at the discovery of knowledge purely for its own sake, purely disinterested. When a man applies himself to research, he is certainly impelled by a passion for knowledge, but at the same time he is animated by a certain opportunism either conscious or unconscious. When he wants to penetrate deeper and deeper into the secret of material reality, it is ultimately in order to be able to cope with it, to control it, to harness it and make it serve. And when he studies individual psychology and the social conduct of man, it is in order to organize the world more rationally and more methodically.

There is nothing surprising about this. Man is not pure spirit. He surpasses the world of matter by the gift of his mind, but he is still immersed within it by the weight of his body. He is always bound up partly with the material. Either it will be matter that overcomes and dominates man, or it will be man who conquers the force of matter and reduces it to his own service and the service of mankind in general. That is one of the missions of mankind. Man, says the Book of Genesis (2:15), was placed in the Garden of Eden to cultivate and develop it.

Pure, detached, disinterested knowledge is not the proper end of man. And woe to the science that does not aim at loving, at serving, at working, for the good of man.

Side by side with the activities of learning—or, to be more precise, developing from the activities of investigation as the fruit develops from the branch—the life of man is taken up with activities of invention and creation. Science has its grandeur; but technical activity has a nobility about it as well. An individual man might be better at the one than he is at the other. But in general the two branches are closely bound together and they depend one upon the other for the most basic necessities.

The Vast Field of Technical Activity

Technical activity can be defined as the activities by which

[34]

man creates things outside his own person either for his utility or for his comfort.

This word *create* has to be understood in a human sense. Man can never make anything out of nothing: he can only modify what already exists. But he shows himself so masterful in this work of transforming what already exists that we can see in man a beautiful reflection of the divine creative power. "God has created creators," says Bergson.

The field of these technical activities is immense.

The ancients called them arts, a complex of practical rules by means of which man's *intelligence,* together with the aid of his *hands*—those wonderful instruments which play such an important role in our life—can mould and change and reorganize the world.

The ancients distinguished arts of the useful and arts of the beautiful. The first group was subdivided into the servile arts (those which were formerly practiced by slaves or servants and which depend more upon the hands than the intelligence) and the liberal arts (those which were practiced more by free men and in which the intelligence plays a greater role than the hands).

Their arts of the beautiful comprised the whole gamut of artistic creation that we still know today as the fine arts: poetry, music, painting, architecture. . . .

The only real importance of this or any other classification of the arts is that it makes us aware of the immense diversity of technical activities and gives us some idea of their hierarchy. These activities all occupy a position of great importance in the life of man.

The housewife who puts a room of furniture in order, the foundry worker at his machine, the farmer sowing and reaping, all the workers that we call manual laborers are all engaged in technical activity.

The engineer who invents or perfects a machine, the industrialist who puts up a plant, the merchant who opens a store, the architect who draws the plans for a house or office building, the professor who communicates his knowledge, the doctor and the nurse whose work is to restore their patients to health, the social worker who devotes her time to a thousand different occupations, the priest who consecrates himself to the work of the apostolate, the politician who works for the common good in trying to organize a province, a country, or the whole world, the lawyer who prepares or interprets or contributes to the prestige of the law, the leader upon whom the supreme responsibility for the whole nation depend, parents who are bringing up a family—they are all, each in his own way and measure, technicians, artisans of the well-being of humanity, creators of order within human life.

As for the literary artists, the painters, the musicians, they too exercise a technical activity: they create beauty for the joy of the human heart and soul.

There is a hierarchy of importance and value among all these different technical activities. Some are more noble than others because of their object; but that is only a relative point of view and of secondary interest.

What we must try to discover in each of them is its essence, its intrinsic worth, its relation to the life of man. The work of the washerwoman must be treated with respect just as the work of the artist or the statesman is treated with respect. All these technical activities are necessary or at least very useful in the formation of a civilized society. If any one of these branches—even if it were the lowliest among them, for instance, the work of the dishwasher or the janitor or the laundry man—were to refuse its services to the world, there would be a universal catastrophe and a frightening regression towards barbarism. We must not look down upon any profession; we must see the worth of each man; we must be filled with gratitude towards all of them because they all cooperate for the good of the whole human race. That is the only attitude that is worthy of a man.

The Extent and Limitations of Technical Activity

After what has been said, we do not have to insist upon the importance and wide extent of technical activities. What has to be stressed here is rather the eminent dignity of work, every kind of work: whether the constant, persevering effort to understand nature and harness it to human needs; or some secular pursuit in the political or social order, on a national or even universal level, learning how to be more and more active in the liberation of man and the creation of peace and order and harmony in the world; or, finally, the effort of an elite group which has received a whole firmament of special gifts to use in the creation of beauty, in order to play upon the deepest and most mysterious fibres of our souls.

Creation is a tendency that is born into man. To produce something like himself outside himself, a child, a piece of work, a statue that bears his own image and likeness; to leave his mark upon a soul, an era, a world; or, something of lesser importance, to forge a good tool, to prepare a good meal, to keep a house in beautiful order; in a word, every piece of work that is done well, from the lowliest to the highest—these are all activities proper to man, signs of his greatness. They are among his supreme callings, the functions that place him as close as possible to the Creator. It is not only fatherhood and motherhood that place man in the immediate neighborhood of God; every creative work does this, every technical activity.

But if we look at technical activities in their results, it is not hard to see that they form an important element of civilization and a powerful tool for the liberation of mankind. They are not, in themselves, the whole of human life. They are only one aspect. They need to be completed by something else, as we shall see. But, nonetheless, they represent a very important element. Their providential aim is to remove man from the slavery of his primitive needs and make it constantly easier for him to develop his intellectual and moral spiritual life. "The conditions of the spiritual life are material," writes Sertillanges. "Every development of the true, the beautiful as a whole, social development, their universal development by civilization, is made possible by various technical activities in which science takes the initiative."[5]

Thus, technical activities form one of the most marvelous

instruments for the spread of altruism and charity. They open the way for all the human social relations that can unite the family of man.

Science and technical activity well deserve a great share of praise and recognition. But only on the condition that they remain in their place, in order. Technical activities, especially those whose immediate object is the world of matter—the less noble ones if we really stop to consider, those which furnish us with airplanes, railroads, automobiles, elevators, refrigerators, central heating, gas, electricity, even nuclear energy—these activities show an alarming penchant for stealing the limelight, for monopolizing the whole of man's effort, for growing drunk with their own power, for looking down on all the other kinds of activity, for failing to recognize or even for denying the existence of moral and spiritual values.

There is another aspect of scientism: absolute and exclusive faith in technology. A classic expression of this ideology can be found in these naïve lines written by a devotee of technology around 1880: "We will have industry to thank, some day, when we have all become enlightened and upright men. Technology will produce men without prejudice and without vice, just as it has produced bulls without horns: the miracle involved is certainly no greater."

This myth of science and technology has now lost the greater part of its enthusiasts, especially among the circles of true scientists.

We have only to take one, good, thorough look at our world to understand the shortcomings of technology when it tries to set itself up as the sovereign and exclusive master of human destiny. That is when it becomes, in the words of Sertillanges, the supreme form of barbarism, civilized barbarism, of course, systematized barbarism, armed barbarism, and on that account more dangerous to the human race as it continues to grow more powerful. It is never safe to compress steam without a safety valve. We cannot save civilization by developing all the forces which could destroy it unless we have some counterbalance to hold them in check. It is good to be able to set the entire engine of natural forces in motion, but only if we can be sure that it will not end up by destroying us.[6]

All the great minds who have remained level in this matter admit with real alarm that modern man has become like the conjurer in Goethe who had succeeded in harnessing all the elements of matter but had lost the formula for stopping them or using them the way he had planned.

True human progress, writes Lecomte du Noüy, consists solely in the perfection and amelioration of man himself, not in the perfection of the tools he uses or the promotion of his physical well-being. This is the attitude of the materialist and it is insulting to human dignity, because it systematically neglects the most noble human qualities, the only ones which are in a position to assure him the happiness he deserves, happiness of a higher order than that of the cow who is content to chew its cud.

The learned biologist goes on to say that this problem of human perfection has arrived at an urgency that concerns everyone, now that man has discovered the secret of nuclear energy. "For the first time in the history of mankind the conflict between pure intelligence and the moral values has become a question of life and death."[7]

III. Moral Activity

The Moral Life

To learn to understand the world, to make it serve our needs, to organize it into a more and more comfortable place for everyone to live in—this is beyond all doubt one of the vocations of man.

But it is not the most important one. There is a higher and more precious law written in the very depths of his soul. He is called to create himself, to rule himself, to perfect himself, to make a more interior, a freer and more spiritual being of himself.

This work, this self-conquest, this creation of self is what we call moral life, moral activity.

In speaking of sincerity we said that, when we come to a full and deep realization of our own consciousness, we do not only come face to face with ourselves as existing, but we see that we are incomplete beings, entrusted to our own care, a task to be finished, something proposed, even something imposed upon our own responsibility. We are a given factor and an unknown factor at the same time. Every one who becomes even a little conscious of his basic personality discovers this direction inscribed upon it: "You are left completely in your own hands. You are to be your own master. You have the power to dispose of yourself, and you must use this power, not according to the vagaries of your imagination, but intelligently. You must try to make a more loyal creature of yourself, purer, more just. You must turn into a force and a light for other men and a ray of glory for God. You have been created already, but now you must become your own creator. You have been begotten already, but now you must become your own father. You are like a block of marble which must be turned into a beautiful statue— and you are to be your own sculptor."

The Principal Components of the Moral Life

In order to realize this harmonious whole which is the object of the moral life, there are many different tasks a man must meet. To neglect even one of them would be to expose our moral life to anemia.

The first of these tasks is connected with what we have already said about sincerity. It consists in recollecting ourselves, in meeting our intimate self face to face, in allowing our feelings of personal responsibility to become more and more intense and active.

This sense of responsibility is the real source of moral life. It does not matter if it is rather confused and even obscure to the eyes of our reason in the beginning. It is still the prime mover in our moral life. It is not this sense of responsibility, of course, that tells us clearly what we are to do, but it does keep us alert and awake to moral values. It does impel us to look for what we have to do in order to realize our human vocation. In allowing ourselves to grow drowsy, we fall into mediocrity. And when this sense of responsibility disappears, we are alone and faced by a world of monsters.

That is why nothing is more important to our moral progress than keeping this sense of responsibility alive. It can always lose its way and become corrupt. In certain cases it can become scrupulous and neurotic, like everything else that really counts in our human make-up. This is a reason for keeping watch over ourselves, in order to keep our minds healthy. But it can never become a reason for running in the other direction, for trying to avoid the difficulties it involves. Man recognizes himself as man, says Saint-Exupéry, by the fact that he is responsible. What is he responsible for? For himself first of all, for his moral growth, for his human development. The everyday language that we use is a testimony to that. When we say that someone is irresponsible, we mean that he has lost, completely or in part, the exercise of one of the most essential prerogatives of human life. This responsibility is a burden, the heaviest burden of human existence. No one can deny that. But that is precisely what distinguishes man from animal. We recognize our vocation by the very fact that it weighs upon us.[8]

Thus it becomes necessary to develop within ourselves a taste for what is good—in fact, a taste for what is better. In other words, we must nourish a really sublime ideal of life.

At the outset this all seems rather poorly defined, far removed from any concrete action, a very indefinite proposal. This general orientation, provided we keep it active and alive, is no less essential for the formation of the atmosphere that is necessary for the moral development of man.

Everyone who has ever reflected upon the moral life with any real depth insists upon the necessity of this factor.

Le Senne calls it *aim* as opposed to *intention*. Whereas the *intention* pursues some clear and precise and well-defined goal, the *aim* is more obscure, more hidden from clear consciousness. But it still sets the deepest strata of human personality in motion. "Its source is in the depths that the ego has never been able to analyze and which are bound to remain the mystery of its most intimate self." It is in the *aim* that our fundamental preferences and the grounds for our decisive choices are to be found. It gives us a certain orientation without our ever knowing it. Mysteriously it commands our intentions, our decisions. We can be unfaithful to it, but it still fixes the dominant thought of our life.

That is why it is so important for us to keep in contact with the moral values: truth, honesty, justice, sincerity, purity, love. Nor can we leave out the One who synthesizes and personifies all the other values: God. Ideas lead to acts, the acts they represent. We have to entertain within our minds the ideas of the acts we hope to put into action.[9] But these ideas are not really put into action unless they leave the realm of the abstract behind and enrich themselves with the "affective" elements that will make them really dynamic. We can never arrive at this goal without meditation and reflection[10] and sustained attention.[11]

This is certainly one of the most important elements of the moral life. This we know from the way Christ speaks of it in the Gospels. His teaching is not restricted to drawing up a catalogue of acts that must be performed and acts that must be avoided. His one concern is to develop within our hearts a taste for poverty, renunciation, justice, purity, patience, the spirit of truth and charity.

There can be no moral life at all without aiming at perfection. "Be ye perfect as your heavenly Father is perfect" (Mt. 5:48). In the same order of ideas we must note the necessity, in the moral life, of both general intentions and particular resolutions. There is no doubt that a frequent re-evaluation of self, a new and earnest consecration of self to moral values, does much to assure the growth of good in the human personality.

If this self-orientation towards a high ideal is realized, there is a good chance that a second factor essential to the moral life will develop as well—what we call purity of intention.

The real value of a life does not depend only upon the acts that are performed, but much more upon the spirit in which they are performed. Two men might be, materially speaking, equally temperate; but their act of temperance can have an entirely different human value if the first man abstains or drinks moderately because he is concerned with his health or impelled by avarice and the second man is concerned only with keeping himself more fit for his work, more prepared to assist his neighbor. And perhaps a third man might do the same thing out of a desire for spiritual perfection, or out of charity towards his fellow man whom he will be able to help more substantially if he can succeed in cutting down his own needs.

The moral value of an act is to be found essentially and basically in the intention of the person who performs the act. We have all known for a long time—and modern depth psychology has taught us much more on the subject—that motives which are more or less unconscious and impure can easily succeed in mingling their own cunning effects together with the motivation that we see clearly in our consciousness. They can manoeuver our motives. They excite them and hide them and intensify them and reduce them to nothing, all without our really knowing it. This means that we have an uncompromising task: to make our conscience more and more lucid and pure, to free it more and more from the base motivation that so often disfigures those of our actions that seem to be the loftiest in appearance and the most heroic in their goals. One of the most significant signs of progress in the moral life is this search for enlightenment in the face of the secret motivation of our own activity and the honest attempt to act with a constantly increasing degree of purity and light.

It is still necessary for us to examine the objective content of our acts and to learn as well as possible what we must avoid in our lives and what we must bring into them as the ideal answer to our human vocation. What must we do? And what must we not do?

The choice depends upon our personal judgment, enlightened by divine revelation, the Church, and the moralists.

In brief, we must reject every act that does not contribute to the development of the wholeness of the human person. And, on the other hand, we must perform every act that has a part to play, here and now, in the development of our concrete personality. It takes everything into account, not only ourselves (individual morality), but also all those with whom we live in the same family (family morality), the same profession (professional morality), the same society (social morality), the same universe (international morality). To everyone who enters into relationship with us we owe respect, truth, justice, love, and brotherly assistance. We owe them active and real concern for their welfare. By the spiritual radiation of our personality as well as by the active gift of our services we must give them a taste for becoming sincere beings themselves, loyal, pure, unselfish, devoted.

Finally, our moral life demands a strong will. Without this will, we would tend to run away from the sense of responsibility instead of going to meet it. We would tend to be taken in by the useful and short-range values, material and secondary values (science, technology, the arts), instead of fixing our eyes bravely upon the first, absolute, moral values. Without a courageous will, we shall never devote ourselves to the necessary but disagreeable task of refining upon the hazy world of motivation which directs us without our even knowing it. Finally, when it is time to act, when we have to avoid something that has a strong attraction for us, or perform some task at the point of a sword, we will be vague and undecided and shifting unless we have prepared for it by cultivating decision and courage and will power.

Moral life is a whole just as man is a whole. We have to keep watch over all its many elements and implement all its many mechanisms.[12]

The religious life of man is closely bound up with the condition of his moral life.

The Moral Life and the Other Activities of Man

The moral life must not be separated from the other human activities. It is immanent in them; it is their form and soul. Its mission is to inform,[13] to inspire, to animate, to rectify and purify all our scientific and technological activities.[14]

All these other acts are, of themselves, morally neutral. Studying, working, business, sports, art, politics—none of these is either good or evil. Its moral value depends entirely upon the manner, the conditions, the aim, the intention. Studying out of pure ambition or a thirst for glory, or devoting so much time to science that wife and children and God are neglected is a moral fault in the pursuit of science. Being a partisan in politics, or working for personal interests rather than the public good is a moral fault in the political sphere. Writing a novel or painting or making a film that is based, whatever its principal theme may be, on a false or cheap or degraded outlook upon life is a moral failing in the exercise of the arts.

We must live morally in everything, everywhere, always. We can do this spontaneously, "instinctively," just as soon as we have purified the source from which all our activity springs, just as soon as we have enlightened our interior eye, corrected our basic intentions; in a word, when we have worked to make ourselves into men of lofty conscience.

IV. Communion

The activities we are about to consider make up a plane of human activity that has been only little explored. Still, they are activities that we all perform, and not infrequently. But most of the time we perform them superficially, with poorly informed consciousness. Western civilization and the Cartesian formation of intelligence have, unfortunately, given these activities only scant consideration, stifling them and almost reducing them to nothing. But in themselves they are the highest, the richest, the only activities that carry within themselves the promise of eternity for man.

We cannot hope to understand anything about religion unless we grasp the nature and importance of these activities. They deserve a careful study because they are important, not only for religion and moral life, but for many other important aspects of human relations as well.

A. *Discovering the Spirit*

In order to analyze these communion activities more easily, it will be most useful to examine some texts from profane authors who have succeeded particularly well in grasping the essence and prime importance that these activities deserve in our life.

First Text: Saint-Exupéry, *Pilote de guerre* (*War Pilot*), p. 28.

"I am shocked by a discovery that no one will admit: the life of the spirit is intermittent. Only the life of the intelligence is permanent, or nearly so. There is very little variation in my faculties of analysis. But the spirit does not consider objects; it considers the meaning that binds them together. It sees through the countenance of things. And this spirit passes from full, perfect vision to absolute blindness. A man may love his estate, but the time will come when he can see nothing in it but a collection of incongruous opposites.

"He may love his wife, but the hour will come when he can see nothing but care and contradiction and restraint in love. He may like a piece of music, but the hour will come when he no longer wants to hear it. The hour will come, as it has now, when I no longer know what to make of my country. A country is not the sum total of districts and customs and material elements that my intelligence can always grasp. It is a being, and the hour will come when I am blind to being."

Second Text: Alexis Carrel, *Prayer* (Tr. by Wright; New York: Morehouse-Gorham Co., 1948), pp. 13f.

"To us men of the West, reasons seem very superior to intuition. We much prefer intelligence to feeling. Science shines out, while religion is flickering. We follow Descartes and forsake Pascal.

"Also we seek first of all to develop intelligence in ourselves. As to the non-intellectual activities of the spirit, such as the moral sense, the sense of beauty, and above all the sense of the holy, they are almost completely neglected. The atrophy of these fundamental activities makes of the modern man a being spiritually blind. Such an infirmity does not permit him to be an element of good for the constitution of society. It is to the low standard of the individual that we must attribute the collapse of our civilization. The fact is, the spiritual shows itself just as indispensable to the success of life as the intellectual and the material. It is therefore urgent to revive in ourselves mental activities which, much more than intelligence, give strength to the personality. The most ignored among them is the sense of the holy or the religious sense."

Third Text: Alexis Carrel, *Reflections on Life* (Tr. by Antonia White; New York: Hawthorn Books, Inc., 1953), pp. 51 f.

"Most people are incapable of close contact with themselves, with each other, or, indeed, with anything at all. They are the victims of their education and their habits. Their only intellectual formation has been acquired by cramming for examinations. In the artificial life of the factory and the office, they have never looked reality in the face. They ignore the beauty of the virgin snow, the noonday hush on the still cornfields, the anguish of the sick in lonely farmhouses. They are incapable of observing exactly what happens in and about them. Yet the reality we need so desperately to know is not made up of notions picked from books and newspapers but the immediate data of observation and experience."

Fourth Text: Alexis Carrel, *op. cit.,* p. 55

"The exclusively intellectual formation of the young violates an essential law of the development of the mind. The human spirit displays nonrational as well as rational activities. Activities not specifically rational, such as the moral, esthetic and mystical senses, play a most important part in the development of personality. We have made the mistake of neglecting the affective formation of the child."

Fifth Text: Simone Weil, *Waiting for God* (Tr. by Craufurd; New York: Putnam, 1951), pp. 111 ff.

The keyword of life for Simone Weil is *waiting, attention.* These two activities are, for her, very close to each other; in fact, they are almost the same thing. Attention is the most hidden of hidden things, whether it is a question of study, literary creation, moral life, love of neighbor, love of God. This is what she means by attention.

"Attention is an effort, the greatest of all efforts perhaps, but it is a negative effort. . . . Attention consists of suspending our thought, leaving it detached, empty, and ready to be penetrated by the object; it means holding in our minds, within reach of this thought, but on a lower level and not in contact with it, the diverse knowledge we have acquired which we are forced to make use of. Our thought should be in relation to all particular and already formulated thoughts, as a man on a mountain who, as he looks forward, sees also below him, without actually looking at them, a great many forests and plains. Above all our thought should be empty, waiting, not seeking anything, but ready to receive in its naked truth the object that is to penetrate it."

Farther on, speaking of love of neighbor, she makes this attention spring from a different source, our way of looking at someone: "This way of looking is first of all attentive. The soul empties itself of all its own contents in order to receive into itself the being it is looking at, just as he is, in all his truth."

B. *The Spirit and its Functions*

The authors just quoted all bear witness to the importance of a function which they consider fundamental in human life and which they regret seeing neglected and even ignored so much of the time. This function is that of the human spirit. They oppose the spirit to intelligence (Saint-Exupéry), to rational activity (Alexis Carrel), to active attention and particular thoughts (Simone Weil).

In order to understand what this spirit is, we must remember that human mental activity cannot be reduced, in its activity, to one single mode. The faculty that we generally call intelligence includes a whole gamut of distinct and different activities.

First of all, I can use my intelligence to analyze being and to distinguish its component parts and essential properties; for instance, in the study of chemistry or psychology or even philosophy. Then, my intelligence is called reason. That is the name under which it comes into play with the scientific and philosophic activities described above. The principal role of reason is to divide reality into sections. It divides, it makes an inventory, it counts, it measures, it weighs, it compares, it classifies, it abstracts, it gives names, it demonstrates, it discourses. Reason is the speculative, discursive, analytic, scientific, philosophical, Cartesian function of intelligence.

I can also use my intelligence to draw up plans for a building, an organization, an institution, a country, a world. The activities just mentioned under the general name of technical activities all belong to the realm of practical reason.

But there is another plane of activities in which human intelligence acts in a more delicate and rapid and subtle and mysterious manner. Examples of this activity are appreciating the moral values of sincerity or loyalty, the beauty of a painting or a cathedral, the mystery of a soul, the reality of God, the divinity of Christ.

All these activities are proper to the spirit.

The spirit is one of the modes of activity which are proper to the intellect. But it infinitely surpasses the progress of speculative reason in readiness, in suddenness, in depth, in simplicity, in eagerness.

The only way to understand what the spirit really means is to analyze its activities in some of its most important roles.

1. THE VARIOUS ROLES OF THE SPIRIT

One of the most fundamental roles of the spirit is the grasping of existent being in its concrete, general, global, and existential reality. Our first meeting with the world we live in is a simple perception on the part of our spirit. It is this simple perception that makes us admit the real presence of other beings and puts us into contact with them. This perception is more or less confused, more or less rich, more or less conscious. Before I can analyze a painting, I have to become aware of its reality as a whole. Before I can form an opinion of a child's character, I have to recognize the child as something real and living and present.

The activity of the spirit precedes that of reason. Reason cannot undertake its methodical and laborious work without basing itself upon the "immediate data of consciousness."

In the second place, the role of the spirit is bound up with perceiving the bonds, the relationships, that exist between things. It is this spirit that tells me, for instance, that this particular armchair should be placed in this particular corner of the office or living room in order to form a harmonious arrangement of the whole room.

It is the spirit once again which, all of a sudden, joins the various data of observation, makes a quick analysis of them, and leaps to a conclusion that was never suspected before, or uncovers a hidden natural law that was being searched for in vain up till then. The spirit is the instrument of scientific discovery and artistic creation.

And finally it is the spirit—we shall see this once again in the study of faith—that is efficacious in perceiving signs and leading us swiftly to the reality which is represented by the signs.

It would be wrong not to add that it is also the spirit that lets us attain what is spiritual and invisible, the fundamental reality of beings, our own intimate mystery, the soul of other men, the reality of God, beauty, good, the truths that count.

"Look! All of a sudden you have become someone," writes Claudel, speaking of the discovery of God. What he is describing is an illumination of the spirit.

There is a fourth activity proper to the spirit. It is the one we paid particular attention to in the texts quoted above. This activity consists in perceiving—or rather in receiving, in welcoming into ourselves—the hidden, mysterious, secret, non-material, and eternal value of a being or a composite of beings. Reason lays hold of being while it is still rough-hewn. It dissects and analyzes. It is like a tax assessor making an inventory of someone's personal property or real estate; like a chemist who would see in man a compound of water, fat, albumin, limestone, sugar, and iron; like a biologist who would define man as a composite of various tissues and liquids; like a philosopher who would count the various elements in man: body, soul, the different faculties.

The spirit, on the other hand, grasps the meaning of things, that quality in things which talks to me when I perceive them, that which enters into conversation with me, their value, not their value considered as utility or merchandise or consumer goods or mechanical power, but the power of radiation and life and development that they exercise upon me by the simple fact that they exist. Saint-Exupéry calls it seeing through the countenance of things, that is, understanding the expression, that about a thing which touches and charms me and stirs up the emotions in the depths of my being. I need only think, for example, of the wave of feeling that spreads through my inmost being when I approach a man I thought was unknown to me and discover that he is one of my best friends. One moment ago his face had nothing to say to me; now it has suddenly turned into meaning for me, expressing everything that is in the man's heart.

Saint-Exupéry also calls it simply *being*. He does not mean merely the act of existing, being there, nor the sum total of the things that go to make up this being. What he means is, rather, that which is deepest in a being, most intimate and hidden, most telling and stimulating, most active and encouraging for me, whether it is some countryside with which I am familiar, the hearth that shelters me, the country in which I was born, the person whom I love.

This spirit is not satisfied with seeing. It must love, unite; it must join things together with all its vital energy in order to set up a place to stay, in order to participate in their deepest reality and have some share in the mystery of their concrete existence.

The role of the spirit is singularly active. It creates bonds between itself and other beings; it nourishes these bonds with all its creative power; it makes them stronger and stronger, deeper, more intimate.

2. COMMUNION

The last two roles of the spirit which have just been analyzed are the most far-reaching and freest and most vital activities of the human person. For if anyone reflects on the nature and destiny of man, he will easily discover that the final end of man is to be united with other beings, to have a share in everything spiritually, to be wholly present to everything and to possess everything interiorly by means of a communion which works upon the most intimate depths of his fundamental personality in order to transfigure it.

This communion is, on the one hand, a spiritual grasping,

an opening of self, a receiving into self of the value and meaning and countenance of beings, and at the same time, a mighty surge within the depths of being, a gift of self, an intimate adherence to the beings who are to be participated.

That is why this activity of communion belongs to the intelligence (spirit) and to the will (love) at one and the same time. It would be better perhaps to speak of its source as being beyond the faculties in the mysterious depths that form the fundamental personal self. It is this fundamental self that acts here, trying to touch, to taste, to grasp, to receive into itself, to experience the intimate, profound, mysterious, telling, stimulating reality of beings, and to abide with them, to set up its lodging there, to take its pleasure among them, to give itself over to them without reserve.

What happens is this. We come to have—in degrees which vary according to the depth of the act of communion and according to the various manners in which we are bound to these beings—an impression of unanimity, harmony, mutual agreement, a feeling of response and secret expectation, a complement for our own being, a feeling of possession that is not at all self-centered or passionate, but rather a belonging that is selfless and self-sacrificing, free, elevating, glowing.[15]

3. Different Names for Communion

These communion activities have not escaped the attention of philosophers and theologians or of spiritual writers and mystics.

These men have used the most different terms to describe the activities and to point out the human faculty or the fundamental source to which a man must go in search of them.

This variety should not surprise us. In this matter, we are in the heart of man, the mysterious center which is the secret sanctuary of his personality, and here the common names lose their force because everything that we are trying to find a name for is proper and unique to each individual. What actually happens in the communion activity is this: our fundamental personality recollects itself; it takes other beings into its interior and bathes them in the light of its unique mystery; then it plunges in turn into the depths of their own being.

These secret depths of being have not been studied scientifically at all outside the studies on spirituality, which are interested solely in the relations of the soul with God, especially in the elevated stages which belong properly to the mystical state. In such studies, these activities are given the name of contemplation.

Spiritual authors say that the mystical union is effected in the higher part of the soul, in obedience to a special supernatural impulse on the part of God.

This mysterious part of the soul is often called the *peak of the soul,* the *inmost soul,* the *heights of the soul,* the *intimate depths of the soul,* the *holy of holies.* Or it is called the *pinnacle of the soul;* that is, the summit of the soul, the center of the soul, so to speak, in which all its other powers are grouped. Still others call it the *deep-seated motivation,* the *foundation of the soul,* the *force that is elemental in the soul.*

These activities of communion have not only held the attention of religious and mystical souls. They have also intrigued poets and artists, wise men and philosophers, in short, everyone who lives in the depths and has passed beyond the utilitarian and temporal aspect of things in order to touch upon whatever essential and eternal is hidden in the world.

Plato already said that we have to go after truth *with our whole soul.*

St. Thomas distinguishes two types of knowledge, not only when he is speaking about God, but no matter what mode of being he is discussing. The first is knowledge by *notion and definition,* that is, the knowledge of reason. The second is knowledge by *affinity, connaturality, union,* that is, the knowledge that the spirit achieves in communion activities.

Pascal is famous for his distinction between the *spirit of fineness* and the *spirit of geometry.* The spirit of fineness is the capacity for grasping, in its singularity, the fundamental reality of beings, and of men in particular, the reality that is distinct from the simple bodies themselves which, in physics and chemistry and mathematics, are studied by the spirit of geometry.

Pascal also speaks of the heart which "has reasons that reason does not know of." For him the heart is not, in the words of Guardini "some nondescript irrational way of feeling. It is a spiritual experience and it results in a form of knowledge in the most exacting sense of the word. It is as if there were a sort of logic of the heart, motives and realities impregnated with value."[16]

Closer to our own time, Bergson speaks of intuition. This can be understood in different ways.[17] Bergson himself understands it this way: "Intuition enables us to fall in with the becoming of being. It enables us to grasp the real from within. Intuition is the complement of reason. It helps us feel the pulsebeat in the soul of things."[18]

"Intuition," he goes on, "is a supra-intellectual, complementary faculty which opens up a new perspective on the spirit and on life and introduces us to the real depths of being itself."

Bergson opposes intuition to conceptual and rational knowledge. Edward Le Roy has devoted an entire work to *intuitive thought*. He opposes it to discursive knowledge and describes it as an effort to "re-discover, beyond the common point of view and symbols, the profound and original datum of reality, in its qualitative purity, in its total wealth, in its rising flood."[19]

Maurice Blondel never tires of making the distinction between *real* knowledge, which puts us into living contact with other beings, and *notional* knowledge, which supplies us with concepts.

Claudel has a famous parable about *animus* and *anima*. *Animus* is reason, reasoning, scientific, clear, "vain and pedantic," or at least inclined to be that way. *Anima* is immediate knowledge, mystical, poetic, real but obscure. Because it keeps perpetual silence, it passes for an "ignoramus and a dunce" who "has never been to school." But when *anima* is alone, it sings a song that *animus* cannot possibly understand. "There is no way to find the notes or the words or the key; it is a strange and marvelous song."[20]

We have already called attention to Saint-Exupéry's distinction between spirit and intelligence. By intelligence he clearly understands reason, that is, intelligence in its abstractive and discursive role. Carrel uses a terminology which is only slightly different. He speaks of *irrational activities*. This term *irrational* should obviously not be taken in the sense of "infra-rational" or purely emotional, nor in the sense of "unreasonable," but rather in the sense of "supra-rational," that is, as describing an activity that calls the very summit of the soul into play.

No matter what terminology these writers use, there is still one thing that strikes the attention: the tremendous importance they all attach to this function of the intelligence, or, to be more exact, the fundamental depths of personality, the aptitude of every man for uniting himself, for participating, for opening his spirit, for communicating with everything that is, even with him who is *par excellence*—with God. The closeness of the relationship between the soul and God in this fundamental depth of soul is so unspeakably great, as Tauler puts it, that we have neither the presumption nor the power to discuss it at any great length.

C. *Objects of Communion*

Men can enter into communion with everything that really exists, whether in the world below man, *nature,* or the world of man, his *fellow mortals,* or the world above man, *God.*

His act of communion will certainly take on a variety of nuances according to the variety of the objects at which he aims. But in its essence it will always remain the same. It will always be the immediate presence of what is most spiritual and free in his personality before what is most secret and mysterious in reality outside.

1. NATURE AND ART

Saint-Exupéry once made a forced landing in the desert. His plane was destroyed but he and his copilot were uninjured. After a fruitless search for some trace of a human being, they decided to walk in one straight direction as long as their strength lasted. They were on the point of collapse when they met a Bedouin who gave them some water. This is how Saint-Exupéry describes the situation: "Water, you have neither taste nor color nor smell. You cannot be defined. We taste you without knowing what you are. You are not necessary for life; you *are* life. You fill us with a pleasure that our senses cannot express. With your help the powers we had despaired of return to our control. It is you who restore the dried up springs within our heart. You are the greatest wealth in the world and you are the most delicate, so pure and clear in the bosom of the earth. . . . You do not have to be mixed with anything. . . . You are the natural enemy of all impurities. . . . You are the deity veiled. . . . But the happiness you spread throughout us all is infinitely simple."

It is not only the organic sense of relief at recovering from dehydration that Saint-Exupéry is singing about here; it is something deeper. This burning thirst that set his body on fire was an occasion for him to penetrate more intimately into the mystery of water, into its innate worth, into the creative power which it spreads not only upon our senses and our bodies, but even upon our most spiritual powers, upon our whole personality. "You fill us with a pleasure that our senses cannot express," he says. "The happiness you spread throughout us all is infinitely simple."

Claudel puts a similar thought into the mouth of Violaine when she gives this answer to her sister Mara: "I can hear things existing with me."

Mere poetry, the wise man will say. But not if he is really wise. The mere technician, perhaps, might say so, or the laboratory assistant who never goes beyond his test tubes.

Art, on its part, succeeds in casting us under its magic spell only because it is a radiating hearth of the most varied activities of communion.

There is the communion of the artist, first of all, together with the object he is presenting. It is not simply a general non-descript perception, common to everyone else, that he is projecting on the canvas or marble; it is his living and personal communion with reality. The work has no power to move us, writes Maurice Zundel, unless the artist has abandoned himself to the embrace of beauty, unless the vibration of this contact is still alive in the model he produces.[21]

By the magic spell it casts upon us, the work of art predisposes us for communion; it recollects and deepens our whole being; it makes us interior; it sets free our fundamental faculties of reception and intuition and attention.

To really appreciate a work of art, we have to come into intimate contact with the artist's own vision, look at his product through his own eyes, and feel his own reactions to the real. Then, by meditating upon the artist and his work, we become prepared to grasp the world about us more fervently, presented to the heart of the reality of being, even drawn more or less confusedly into the presence of Supreme Beauty itself. For every work of art, says Zundel, is a reflection of that beauty.[22]

2. HUMAN BEINGS

Francis, the extraordinary young man whose life and writings have been preserved for us by Auguste Valensin, could not see another young man, the author tells us, without immediately placing him in his proper position in the order of being and experiencing a sudden metaphysical thrill from the thought that "Here is a man who has to accomplish a tragic destiny. Amazing! It is an infinity that I am considering here, a being who bears eternity within himself."[23]

Francis had a feeling for humanity. Think of the difference between a doctor who sees nothing in the sick man but a business proposition, a patient, a case, even a new field of experience, and a doctor who receives the sick man as a man, a spiritual creature with his own life, his personality, his conscience, his responsibilities, his secret drama, his interior dialogue, his eternal destiny. This second doctor gives the impression of having consideration for the sick man, respecting him, taking charge of him in order to restore him not only to health but to a new taste for life, a more courageous and loyal and just kind of life. Moreover, he does this not only by the moralizing advice he gives, but much more by his whole attitude, his conduct, the radiation of his personality, the whole tone of his spirit.

Having a feeling for humanity, being in communion with humanity, means penetrating spiritually into the very heart of a human personality. It means catching sight of the ontological value of a spiritual being, free, immortal, responsible, redeemed by Christ, called to an eternal destiny, even if its psychological value is still no more than embryonic, as in the case of a child, or little developed, as is frequently the case, or even sunk into an abyss, as in the case of a man who is morally unable or perhaps a criminal. It means being conscious of what is unique in him by the very fact that he exists. It means feeling bound to this man in one common destiny. It means making this bond grow in strength and in intensity. It means identifying self with this man in a certain sense, being ready, at a moment's notice, to do everything possible to arouse and stimulate and increase this man's interest in existing and his desire to aim at a higher goal. Think of Christ before the woman taken in adultery. Instead of crushing her spirit, he restores her in her own sight. He gives her new confidence and a relish for the courageous struggle that can win back the dignity she has lost.

Every real love is a communion with the being that is loved. Whether it is the love of a husband or wife, of a mother or father, of a son or brother or friend, or whether it is social love, always —when it is really on a human and spiritual plane and not merely sense or carnal love—it is an interior grasping of the

person loved, an immediate perception of his worth, an identification with what makes up his concrete personality in all its
singularity. A child looks at his mother differently from the way
a stranger looks at her. He sees her better; he grasps her reality
as mother, the value of love and support and protection and
security that she represents for him, and the bonds that join them
both together. It is true that he does not have a clear and distinct
and analytic knowledge of all this. He experiences, he feels, he
lives these bonds, this presence, this person. That is what we
mean by communion.

The purer love is, that is, the less self-centered it becomes,
the more it gives way to an altruistic love, self-sacrificing and
forgetful of self, a love in which it is the *other* who is really
loved and admired and contemplated, wanted for his own sake
—then the more profound the communion becomes. Loving
someone, says Abel Bonnard, does not only mean having a
burning desire to possess him. It also means being concerned for
his happiness. There is no more sacred and tender moment in
the whole experience of love than that in which the veiled self-
interest that first moved us towards the loved one is held in
check by the real interest we have in him, when we no longer
even think of taking him for our own because we have become
enraptured at merely looking at him, when the need to possess
disappears in the pure emotional experience of just seeing him
alive.

Today we often use the word *community* in opposition to
society. The order of a society is fixed by juridical rules that
leave the members completely outside each other. A society cannot become a community until its members enter into a true
communion with each other and go beyond the exterior rules
of society in order to fashion new relations illuminated by a true
spirit of love, in which they begin to feel that they are existing
as one unit. Every society should be a community. But many of
them cannot ever become communities because of the egoism
and indifference and lack of inspiration that are characteristic
of so many of their members.

Even the family, which has a more urgent call than any other human society to develop into a perfect community, often turns into a dull and mediocre atmosphere whose members live far away from each other spiritually and are only held together by habit and certain material bonds. Then some occasion of great joy comes upon them—their son does well in an examination; or some great sorrow overtakes them: an accident or a death—and a moment of really intense communion follows upon the thousand other moments of shriveled communion, in fact upon the almost total lack of any feeling of communion which preceded it. The bonds are linked together once again, all the old intimacy returns, the members can see into each others' souls again: once again they have become *one.*

The same thing can be experienced in the national community. In certain countries this feeling of community is very lively; in others it is more reserved. But in every country there are moments—some great danger, some great disaster, some great national triumph—in which the feeling of community rises to a new burst of life.

When this happens, individual human groups cease to be juridic and administrative entities, pure societies governed by laws. They become living communities where every member can feel the life of every other member beating loud within his own breast.

3. God

Finally, there is one communion higher than all the others, the communion that unites man to God. This communion will form the subject of the following chapter, for it is the essential element of religion.

D. *Science and Communion*

In order to shed greater light upon this communion and to set up a stronger safeguard against our Cartesian tendencies to be concerned with nothing but rational knowledge and to reduce everything to this one form of knowledge, it would be useful to make a more complete comparison between scientific activity and communion. Then we will be in a position to give each form of activity its proper consideration in life.

1. INTERMITTENCE AND PERMANENCE

"The life of the spirit is intermittent," writes Saint-Exupéry. "Only the life of the intelligence is permanent, or nearly so."

What does that mean? It means that, at any moment, except in a case of illness or some really serious preoccupation, I can study chemistry or geometry or history or psychology. But I am not always in the proper condition to appreciate Beethoven or Racine and I do not always feel really drawn towards my friends or the members of my family.

Why? Because my fundamental personality, the part of me that is called into play in every activity of communion, is easily veiled, easily bound, easily enmeshed, easily deafened and blinded by everything that affects my being. It is much more difficult to stir the faculties of intuition into action when we are experiencing some great physical pain—as, for example, a tooth-ache or some especially vivid uneasiness, as, for example, the anguish suffered by someone dear to us (this anguish is in sharp focus then, and nothing else "matters" any more); or when our faculties of analysis are intensely occupied, as, for example, in preparing for an examination or a thesis, or when we are all taken up with organizing or producing something. Scientific activities are also impaired by all these exterior influences upon personality, but to a much lesser degree.

2. QUALITY AND QUANTITY

Communion activities can be found in different degrees, on different planes; but it is a difference in depth, in intensity, in interior quality. I can appreciate the Ninth Symphony today more than I did yesterday. There is nothing new about the symphony today; that is not the difference. Because I have heard it several times, it has become more familiar for me. It has a richer meaning for me. There are "bonds" between it and me. I "recognize" it; I am "born again" with it. I participate in its rising development.

Science, on the other hand, continually grows in extension, in quantity. I can know more or less about geography or physics. My knowledge of the inner workings of the human body, or of the world of matter, or the development of literature, can always be enriched by the addition of new elements.

3. RECIPROCAL UTILITY

Scientific knowledge can be a real help in increasing the depth and intensity of activities of communion. The analysis of a concerto or a painting or a work of literature, a more detailed knowledge of the fauna and flora and mineral make-up of some corner of the earth, a more and more profound study of the world of matter—all these scientific acquisitions can help me communicate more fully with the concerto, the painting, the poem, the countryside, the world at large. That is why Zundel writes that "Bergson's intuition is so rich because of all the scientific knowledge that great thinker succeeded in assimilating."[24]

There is one condition that must be fulfilled before scientific knowledge can have this desired effect. After the work of analysis, dissection, classification and comparison, I have to return to a total and intuitive grasp of the work or object under analysis. I have to recollect myself, listen "with my whole soul," look at it with more than my eyes, and let all the analysis and scientific explanation blur into a sort of backdrop for the inner eye of my spirit.

On the other hand, experience teaches us that the great thinkers and inventors are generally endowed with a mighty potentiality for communion with things. It is not only with their cold reason that they come ino contact with the real, but with their whole being. That is why they succeed in penetrating deeper into its secrets. Their contemporaries might be clever technicians, good at taking memos or making lists or keeping records; but these men are lovers of reality. That is no doubt why spontaneous intuition surges up within them and why the writings of all really great thinkers are carried along by a breath of lyricism and poetry.

4. INTERIOR PREPARATION

Scientific or philosophical study does not demand a long interior preparation. I can sit down at my desk and within a few moments I can be completely lost in the examination of some lecture notes or a geometrical theorem.

But communion calls for much more elaborate spiritual preliminaries. In fact, we have to call the most intimate part of our personalities into play. It would be more exact to say that we have to put ourselves into a state of complete receptivity; for this is a question of taking in the world, some work of art, some person, or even God himself, with open arms. There is no possible substitute for this state of attention, recollection, renunciation, availability and openness towards the object with which we hope to set up communication. Every real communion always demands that we lose sight of self—lose sight even of the impression we are receiving—that there be only humble submission on our part so that we neither hear nor see anything but the thing, the work, the person with whom we want to enter into a spiritual sense of communion. This is what a young lady said about her visits to an art exhibition. "I had both the habit and the firm desire of profoundly 'receiving' every new thing in order to draw a maximum of profit from it. In order to do that, I would empty myself of every trace of intellectual thought and, in the midst of this voluntary suspension of my judgment, I would set up contact only with the fundamental being of the object itself."[25]

5. ABSTRACTION AND EXPERIENCE

Scientific and philosophical activity lead us to an ever clearer and more distinct knowledge of the world, man, and God; but this knowledge is parcelled out, cold, abstract, thought knowledge. There is no doubt, for example, that psychology gives us a more precise knowledge of man, his essential components, his faculties, the scope of his intelligence, his liberty, his instincts. And this knowledge—for it bears repetition—is certainly not to be passed off as negligible.

In communion, the knowledge remains confused, obscure, global. It is not even always conscious of itself. But it is concrete, immediate, experimental, lived. The object is perceived in its real presence, in its individual existence, in its innate value, in its power and radiance. In this case, knowledge results in the wedding of mind and object, a profound union of my personality with the true reality of the object I perceive, and not merely with the idea of the object as it is produced by my intelligence. We need think only of the type of knowledge—confused but marvelously rich—that results from hearing a symphony or a tragedy, from looking at a landscape or a work of art, at a child who is playing or sleeping, or in a mother's eyes as she looks at her baby, in a friend's eyes when he meets his friend, or at the love in a young bride's face when she smiles at her husband.

6. Spiritual Emotion

Emotion has its place, a great place, in communion. It sustains and nourishes and surrounds the outward surge of the spirit towards the wholeness and the inmost center of the being with which it is communicating. The outward surge of communion is at once both knowledge and love.

We must not imagine that the emotion we are speaking of here is only of the sense order. What is moved in me is the very roots of my being, my spiritual personality. As long as this feature is lacking, the communion activity must remain superficial. Sentimental or carnal intoxication is not the best medium for two human persons to communicate with each other. The best medium is for their love to be given its proper depth and be purified from everything that is self-seeking in it. Then they can be joined together in the respect, admiration and selfless bestowal of everything that is most spiritual within them.

7. INCOMMUNICABILITY AND COMMUNICABILITY

It is easy to understand that the sciences have no great difficulty in formulating the results of their findings. It is an essential part of their activity. They are constantly engaged in making up words, formulae, labels to describe their discoveries.

We can realize, then, that the knowledge at which they arrive is more or less easily communicated to other minds. A scientist is capable of teaching his students all about chemistry, physics, biology, historical grammar.

Communion is, on the contrary, beyond the limits of expression by formula. It cannot be put into words. The concrete experience of an individual thing—love, friendship, the esthetic emotion that I experience in looking at a masterpiece of art— is something inexpressible and incommunicable.

The real—in its inmost value—is in no way "discursifiable," as Edward Le Roy puts it. That is, it cannot be expressed in any form of concepts or propositions or reasoning. We can only live it, love it, and make it loved, according as it is called True, Beautiful, Good.[26]

I can attempt to recall my communion experience by putting a great many words together or by frequently repeating the same word. I can also try to share my experience with someone else by describing the circumstances under which it takes place, the interior conditions which have to be fulfilled before the spirit and heart can come into play within a person. But my living contact with other things is basically personal, unique. Art— and especially music, poetry, oratory—is no doubt the best way to help others approach our own personal way of seeing things, to make others participate in our own way of communion.

This is how Edward Le Roy defines the fundamental purpose of art. It is to awake within us the meaning of things, to make a habit or even a sort of instinct of them, to make some progress in fathoming them, to furnish the means of living in their innermost familiarity.[27]

8. BEING AND HAVING

Philosophy and the sciences, as we have seen, do contribute greatly to the enriching of the human being, and their pursuit is always accompanied by great joy. But the riches they give are concerned only with reason. The fundamental personality of man is not necessarily set in motion. There are thinkers, philosophers, even theologians whose personality is as dry and withered as the desert. And there are other thinkers and philosophers and theologians who have not only succeeded in remaining human beings, but have actually become more human as the result of their studies. The second group are those who have passed beyond philosophy and the sciences and have entered bravely and completely into the innermost reality of things. Activities of communion actually effect a qualitative advance in the human person, not unlike the advance produced, from another point of view, by the cultivation of moral activity. In pursuing them a man does not *acquire* anything more, not even one idea that he can express by means of a formula; but he *becomes* more—spiritually he "becomes the other with whom he communicates": he participates in his being, he enriches himself.

We have also said that scientific knowledge can be of assistance to communion by giving it a much greater "density." Still, it is possible to enter into communion with persons and things without becoming a scholar. It can even happen that a too one-sided concern for scientific knowledge of reality makes a man less and less fit for communion.

In the hierarchy of values scientific and technical activities are inferior to moral activities and communion. Modern man, the product of Western civilization, has reversed that order; he has given the primacy of importance to science and technology. That is the essential cause for the crisis of contemporary civilization: a poor proportion among human activities, the primacy given over to what is really only secondary, the stifling of communion, a way of life that separates and compartmentalizes human activities instead of exercising them all in a healthy wholeness and letting each man live with all his soul in everything he does.

V. Religion

The Essence of Religion

Religion is essentially a communion, the highest communion that is accessible to man. It consists in the communion between man and the Being who exists *par excellence,* God. It is a symbiosis between man and God.

Religion means the effort of the human being, the effort of his most fundamental personality, to become intimately present to the supreme reality of God, to reach, to touch, to taste this reality, to come to rest on the bosom of the Infinite, to be united to him, heart to heart, to find shelter beneath his creative radiance, to offer self to him in affirmation, recognition, admiration, praise, adoration, love, and to find in this offering and this union the accomplishment, the happiness, and the fulness towards which the creature aspires, even if only confusedly, by the fundamental and unforced dynamism of his spirit.

It is true that religion does not always live up to this description when we consider the manner in which it is frequently made up and practiced. Religion, just like all the essential and vital activities of man, is frequently disfigured by the imperfections, the lack of reflection, and the moral weakness of man. This will be discussed more thoroughly in the fourth chapter.

Religious communion can be broken down into a great number of different feelings, actions and activities because of the the basic complexity of the human being, who is a component of body and soul and distinct faculties, and because of his existence which unfolds rather chaotically over a long period of time. But these feelings and activities have no meaning unless they are rays that spring up from one single hearth, that is, from the infinitely simple act of my person communicating with the Being of God.

It is always possible to make a more or less scientific study of religious communion. This would give rise to a body of doctrines about God, man, and the bonds that join the two together. These doctrines owe their origin either to the reflection of man upon the natural impulse that makes his being surge upwards towards its origin and goal (natural theology) or to his study of the supernatural relations which God has established between himself and man by a perfectly free gift of divine love (supernatural theology). But religion itself is not a doctrine, a teaching, a science; it is the living meeting of a human being with the living Being of God; it is the act by which the utmost heights of the human spirit penetrate deep into the reality of God. It is not a concept of God or of his attributes that is the object of religious communion; it is God in his very being.

If we seem to be insisting upon this point, it is because we know only too well that for many men religion appears to be nothing but a compact mass of dogmas, formulae, and acts of worship. Dogmas have their role, as we have just said; and the act of worship has its place, as we shall describe it later. But all this remains entirely without meaning as long as we do not understand that religion is first of all and essentially a communion. My person is present before the very person of God and it is the most intimate and total presence possible, a living participation of my being in the being of God.

Religion and Prayer

Religion and prayer are one. That is, they are one if we have the proper idea of each of them. In the thought and life of modern man, they both suffer the same deplorable disfigurations.

"Prayer," as Carrel so well describes it, "seems to be essentially a tension of the spirit towards the immaterial substratum of the world. In general, it consists in a complaint, a cry of anguish, a demand for succour. Sometimes it becomes a serene contemplation of the immanent and transcendent principle of all things. One can define it equally as an uplifting of the soul to God. As an act of love and adoration towards Him from Whom comes the wonder which is life. In fact, prayer represents the effort of man to communicate with an invisible being, creator of all that exists, supreme wisdom, strength and beauty, father and saviour of each one of us. Far from consisting in a simple recitation of formulas, true prayer represents a mystic state when the consciousness is absorbed in God. This state is not of an intellectual nature. Also it remains as inaccessible, as incomprehensible to the philosophers and to the learned. Just as with the sense of beauty and of love, it demands no book knowledge. The simple are conscious of God as naturally as of the warmth of the sun, or the perfume of a flower. But this God, so approachable by him who knows how to love, is hidden from him who knows only how to understand. Thought and word are at fault when it is a matter of describing this state. That is why prayer finds its highest expression in a soaring of love through the obscure night of the intelligence."[28]

In this wonderful account Carrel applies to prayer almost all the characteristics which we have analyzed in communion in general.

Prayer—or religion—can be found in the most different forms. But no matter whether it is mental or vocal or even corporal, whether it is individual or community activity, it is not really prayer unless it is an effort to communicate with God. In order to pray, says Carrel, it is essential at least to try to turn our thoughts towards God.

Prayer is an activity of the whole human person.

"We pray just as we love, with our whole being."

That is why it is essentially the spirit, the upper reaches of the soul, that are operative in prayer. Prayer has to be mental;

that is, there must be an interior attention before God in every form of prayer. Otherwise it is no longer prayer.

But there have to be words in prayer too (vocal prayer), because words are the ordinary and most important manner in which a man expresses his mind and communicates his soul to his fellow man. If we consider prayer only from God's point of view, words might not seem necessary; for God can read the soul. But as far as man is concerned, words are normal and spontaneous. Man feels an undeniable need to express himself, to make his interior self known by means of words. Words are the only thing he has with which to arouse, to sustain, to intensify the impulse of his soul.

The body comes into play by the folding or raising of the hands, by genuflections, by prostrations, by the casting down of the eyes. All these actions mean that the man at prayer renounces every worldly activity. They mean that he is voluntarily immobilizing all the members of his body that could be used to go or come, to study or work. He seals off his hands, his legs, his eyes, in order to recollect himself with humility, in order to be with God alone.

Prayer, then, is an activity of the whole man. "We pray by our actions, too," says Carrel. That is, we pray by the performance of everything that we have called scientific or technical activity. St. Aloysius used to say that faithfulness to duty was the same thing as prayer, whenever this faithfulness is consciously aimed at God. And the best way to communicate with God is certainly the complete accomplishment of his will. That is, we must perform every good thing that is imposed upon us as if it were something expressly willed by him and leading us to him.

Finally, since man has been called to live in community with other men, it is only natural that his prayer would take on a social and communal form which in turn expresses itself in collective and determined activity—liturgy—and especially in sacrifice. This last is essentially an effort on the part of man or of humanity as a whole, to offer itself to God, to find its way into God, to communicate with his reality.

Natural Religion and Supernatural Religion

Religion is essentially an attempt at communion with God. But there are varying depths of communion possible.

Left to the mere powers of our own nature, our communion with God, even if it attained the highest realization possible in this life, would still remain veiled. We could never enter into contact with God face to face. It would be only mediate communion, for we could not communicate with God without the intermediary, the mediation, of the created world. This world would become a sign, a sparkling symbol of God. But God himself would not be known except by his reflection in his creatures, never directly, never as he is in himself.

Between God and mankind there exists no common measure. We are on different levels, different planes, different degrees of being. We are separated by the distance there is between the Existent by himself, God, and the created existent, mankind. Even if man by his very nature aspired to see God face to face in an act of total communion, he would never be able to reach that height by the unaided power of his created faculties.

God himself has to help mankind bridge the abyss. God has to lift man up to his own plane, his own level. He has to communicate to him something of his own nature, his own life. He has to find a place within his heart and his spirit so that he can give man a new power of vision and love that are like his own. Then mankind can know him even as he knows himself and love him even as he loves himself. After that, it is a short way to the intimacy of God's secret heart.

All this, and we shall describe it more exactly in the following chapters, is the essential object of Christian revelation and religion. This whole process both initiates and at the same time realizes a communion between man and God that is not limited to the unaided powers of our human nature (natural religion).

It is a deeper and more total communion, on a plane that surpasses the whole scope of nature (supernatural religion). It belongs to a plane of activity that is properly God's.

Religion, Science, Technology

We pray by our actions too, says Carrel. As a matter of fact, we pray, as we have seen, with our whole body—from the very first moment that we really understand the meaning of prayer. Prayer—or religion—is our whole personality rising towards God, offering itself to him, putting itself under the influence of his creative and life-giving radiance, participating in his infinite reality with everything that makes us up and everything we do, no matter what it is.

The upward surge that carries us towards God should not leave out a single one of our activities. Religion, properly understood, respects and utilizes and transfigures all the natural activities of man.

It would be a serious misunderstanding of religion to believe that it has even the least bit of scorn for scientific research, technological development, municipal or international politics, for any of the many realities that go by the name of culture and civilization. Religion does, of course, demand that we do not transform science or technology into an idol. They are not the whole of man. But, while religion regards God as the primary center of attraction, it also respects these secondary activities as being things proper to man, and thus, by their physical content and their final aim, things of God.

We said above that religion utilizes every human activity. Religion is nourished by human activities; it makes them into its substance; it integrates them into its motion towards God. A man is not a pure spirit when he prays. He still has work to do upon earth. He does have an eternal destiny, but in the meantime he has a calling to science or technology or culture. Seen in this light, work, labor, is the order that sounded in man's ears from the dawn of his history.

[73]

All this labor must be present to my spirit in its rise towards God. Although their immediate object is worldly, my studies and all the other work I do must become sacred by being incorporated into my rise towards the Infinite.

Finally, we also said that religion transfigures all our activities. It gives them an entirely new dignity, an interior splendor they would never have without religion. My actions have value not only because of their material content. They also derive a value—in fact, they derive their principal value—from the intention, the spirit, the soul that animates them.

From the purely technological point of view, two foundry workers might succeed in making an equally perfect axle-tree. But there will be a great difference between the workman who gives himself to his work only for the sake of the salary he will be paid and the workman who admires the piece of work his hands have produced, who says, "There is beauty in an axle-tree well made," and who offers it to the Lord, saying, "This is my offering to you." The whole person enters into the work here, and not only the working man, the hands and the intelligence. His whole being radiates upon the work he has accomplished, and, together with it, finds the final impulse of its motion in an elevation towards God. This workman illuminates his own personality with a reflection of the divine and confers an infinite dignity and an everlasting value upon the product of his hands.

The material results of our activity will pass away. The words written upon this page will one day perish. But the light they will give to some reader, the impulse towards God that they will leave upon his life—these, please God, will remain. For the writer with his pen there will only be one reality left, the spiritual imprint left upon his own soul by the intention that animated his activity in behalf of his friends and God, deep in the heart of his work. The only imperishable things are the spiritual traces that our actions imprint upon our personalities. And even these spiritual traces, even our personalities themselves have not been promised everlasting life except through the bonds that religion constantly weaves between us and the Everlasting.[29]

Religion and Morality

It goes without saying that religion is a duty and that under this aspect it enters the field of morality. Man is a created being who has received all that he is from God. Endowed with the intelligence to appreciate these facts, he can and must make some return of giving, consciously and deliberately, that is, by a religious impulse.

But, basically and essentially, religion is something separate from morality. By morality a man tries to overcome, to develop, to perfect self. By religion he wants to give himself to God and to have some share in the very reality of God. Morality embraces all the aspects of the conscious life of man: work, study, politics, art, social activity, love, religion. It regulates the content, determines the circumstances, and purifies the intention of all his many activities, including communion.

Religion is an activity of man, the highest certainly, and destined to envelop all the others within its light, within its vital impulse. But its proper object is rather to unite us to the reality of God.

Religion and morality are both activities which give evidence of the deep interior life of the human person. They lean upon each other in the mutual mission that they both have of "creating," finishing, developing the human person.

A person can be moral in many aspects of his life (for example, in his profession and in his married life) without, on that account, being a religious man or a believer. Everyone can understand that. But in that case, his moral life would be deprived of its basic support and its ultimate orientation, which is God. It will never be steeped in a living communion with the existing and personal Infinite. That is why the so-called "lay moralities" are so basically deprived of warmth, and those who profess to teach them are so stiff and dry—for all their good will.

On the other hand, a man can be religious and a believer, and at the same time be guilty of even serious moral stains. "The Christian is not a man who does not fall," writes Father Samson;

"he is a man that gets back up." That is where the real support of religion is appreciated. On the one hand, he realizes that only God can touch him in the secret sanctuary of his liberty, purify him of the evil he has done, and restore some measure of relish for a life that is more ascetic, more watchful, purer, freer. And on the other hand, he realizes that, if he wants to enter into a constantly greater intimacy with God and thereby pass from a superficial practice of religion to a more interior and more real and more living experience of religion, then he has to make an effort to live a morally better life, to purify his life, to make his heart and his spirit more obedient, more receptive, more open to the visits of God.

Religion, the Queen of Human Activity

All this makes it easier to understand why religion is the summit, the synthesis, the queen of human activity.

Religion is our personality going back to its source and its goal, returning into the depths of God in order to share in his being. It is really the crowning act of the human person. There is none other to surpass or even equal it in excellence. Scientific and technical activities are oriented towards the care of the creaturely in our existence. Morality is, above all else, a work of rectifying and purifying man himself. Communion with the world below man and even with human persons has finite realities as its goal. But religion gives me to God and God to me. It makes me present before God with my whole being. It makes me exist in God and with God. No other human act could surpass this.

The act of religion must not be isolated. Its radiance must spread over all the activities of the human person. It must inspire them, place them in their proper perspective, put them in their rightful place, penetrate them with its warmth and life. The really religious man tends to live in the presence of God in everything he does. Moreover, when he leaves his occupations aside to devote himself more intensively to prayer, his whole life is there with him. All his actions, even the most material ones, the most lowly ones, come with him to be united to God, to offer themselves to God's creative radiation. A queen who really deserves the name constantly lives in her subjects' hearts and keeps them all alive with the warmth of her own heart.

Finally, it is the duty of the queen to draw her subjects towards their ultimate development and make them sharers in her own glory. That is the role that religion plays with regard to all our secondary activities. We have described all this before, how religion gathers together all our activities, orients them toward God, aims them all at their final end and helps them to realize that goal as their supreme achievement. Every activity of the human person has to end in God. Otherwise it remains hanging, out of balance, spoiling for a fall. Religion can reap eternity from it.

Phases and Degrees of Religion

Religion consists essentially in an act of communion between our personality and the reality of God. There are two main phases in this communion.

The first of them is enacted here on earth. It is only a preparation for the perfect communion that will take place hereafter. It is a time of strife and combat. God, of course, gives us help. He sends his lights and his grace, but we have a hard battle to fight to make our interior self clearer and more transparent, to call our fundamental personality into play and allow God to penetrate down into the heart of our life and all its activities.

Everywhere we have to overcome the illusion of the immediate and the quantitative and the material in order to let the spiritual and eternal grow more and more predominant within us. All the while respecting science and technology, we have to free ourselves constantly from the soft spell of their seduction and monopoly and let ourselves be drawn—and them together with ourselves—towards God.

It is no wonder that religion is subject to so many fluctuations and can be found in so many different states and degrees in the human heart—and in so many disfigured forms.

Authentic religion is always a conscious presence of human personality to the reality of God. But this presence can be more or less short or prolonged, superficial or profound, intermittent or constant.

Some men seriously try to orient their lives towards God. The time comes when, after long groping and periods of great dryness, his presence becomes close and familiar for them. They live in a habitual semi-consciousness of God. Their "dialogue with God" is, so to speak, uninterrupted. It is no longer directly conscious, but God is present to them side by side, we might say, just as the harmony and warmth of our apartment is present to our consciousness even though we are not explicitly thinking about it.

In the case of mystics, this contact with God reaches an exceptional depth and intensity. They all describe their experience the same way: an immediate grasping of God, a grasping that is dim for the reason, but immensely rich in feeling and capable of producing great fulness of life, an inexpressible superabundance of "being," in the soul of the favored saint. The physical phenomena that accompany these states are completely secondary and accidental. They only serve to underline the weakness of the human organism in these superhuman meetings of the creature with God. They are only a proof of how powerless we are to withstand such a height of spiritual strain without breaking.

The essence of mystical life is communion with God, communion granted by God's own free activity, communion of a fulness so perfect that the unaided efforts of humanity could never hope to attain it.

This is not yet the beatific vision. The beatific vision is reserved for the hereafter. It is the final and perfect phase of religion. Heaven is complete and perfect communion with God, perceived in a complete transparency, loved to the full depths of his inmost self. "We shall see God as he is," each of us according to the promptness of spirit and power of love that we have created within ourselves with the help of his grace, during the time that we walk as pilgrims upon this earth.

Religion, the Full Development of Personality

Everyone who has ever lived religion and experienced the results for a length of time has always spoken of its happy influence upon the development of the human personality.

"Prayer is a blossoming of the whole personality," says Carrel. "When prayer is habitual and really fervent, its influence becomes very clear. It is slightly comparable to that of an internal secretion gland, as for example the thyroid gland or the adrenal gland. It consists in a kind of mental and organic transformation. This transformation operates in a progressive way. One might say that in the depths of consciousness a flame is kindled. Man sees himself as he is. He discovers his egoism, his cupidity, his errors of judgment, his pride. He bends himself to the accomplishment of moral duty. He endeavors to acquire intellectual humility. Thus there opens before him the Kingdom of Grace. . . ."[30]

Emile Boutroux was also aware of the depths of its activity: "Religion knows how to exercise an interior and substantial activity upon man. It is not only his external acts that it wants to influence, his habits, his morals, but his very being, in the inmost depths of his feeling, his thought, his desire, his will."[31]

Above all, they exalt its unifying and pacifying power. Religion reunites the being of man together with his manifold activities, all in the inmost center of his spirit where he communicates with God. It is constantly engaged in producing a more complete and more perfect internal cohesion, a "unity of spirit" which we all long for in the secret of our hearts.

Finally, religion opens up a real brotherhood for us. Far from being self-centered—as certain people have presumed to describe it, basing themselves only on some of its degraded forms—religion opens the human person to other persons. It increases our power of communion with the whole world, and especially with other human beings, in whom it allows us to see brothers, destined to love together with ourselves, in communion with God.

In order to produce this maturity, this flowering of the personality, religion has to be lived for a number of years. Most men grow discouraged too quickly.

Religion also has to be oriented towards an increasingly higher ideal of purity. Religion is not God for me; it is me for God. It is the most selfless relationship possible between my personality and God.

We do not like the term *possession of God* so often used to express the essence of religion and especially of religion in its final stage, heaven. This word has too many self-centered overtones. It conjures up the picture of "having," of "appropriating," of a God who only exists for man's service.

Everyone can use the words he likes best, of course, providing he makes his meaning clear. But we are especially fond of the word *communion*. This word conjures up—as we have already explained—the idea of sharing in the deepest reality of another being, in the absolute sense of that being, with a total self-presence and self-surrender to that being. In communion we contemplate, we admire, we take our pleasure in the "other." All of this we do in utter selflessness, in the most perfect self-abandon, with a profound interior attention for the "other," his beauty, his being. By this activity, spiritually, we "become" that "other." We leave our own petty boundaries behind and expand to new horizons. We adjust ourselves to the measure of the world, to the measure of humanity—and, in religious communion, to the measure of him who is beyond all measure, God.

It is in giving that we receive.

It is in forgetting self that we find self. "He who loses his soul, finds it" (Matt. 10:39).

That is the secret of every act of communion. Above all it is the secret of the highest among them, religion.

CHAPTER III

The Christian Mystery and the Christian Religion

Introduction

RELIGION is an act of communion, the highest communion possible to man.

It consists in an effort on the part of the human person to unite itself with God, to give him glory, to share in the richness of his being, to discover in this union the perfect accomplishment of his most secret desires.

Religion is the simple and supreme act which unifies and crowns every other form of human activity, giving it a definite goal and object.

Religious awareness, that is, the consciousness that there really is a sovereign reality in the world and that our personal drama is closely and essentially bound up with this reality, is something spontaneous and natural in man. This awareness can be very obscure and very confused. It can be an experience that is lived only marginally and unconsciously. It can be stunted by the activity and tumult of everyday life. It can even be denied in good faith by a clear consciousness and speculative reason. But nonetheless it still exists. Whenever a man allows his fundamental self to act with perfect frankness and freedom, he always discovers God by a spontaneous and subtle impulse of his spirit, an impulse which is, basically, beyond analysis. Deep within him, in a degree that corresponds to the earnestness of his search, he feels the thrill of the sacred.

This pure, basic religious consciousness faces three ordeals, each of which can prove fatal: the ordeal of expressing the experience, the ordeal of socializing it, the danger of disfiguring it.

The Ordeal of Expression

By a sort of natural bent, man is inclined to express everything he experiences, to himself and to others. Of necessity he casts about for an idea, a concept, of this higher order of being whose existence he has just learned from experience.

Inevitably his concept is incapable of adequately expressing the being he has had contact with. His concept is what we call anthropomorphic. It is in human stature. Even when he attributes to God the very best of everything he discovers in the world and in his own being, man still creates a God according to man's image and likeness.

The very words he uses to express his concept of God help to reduce the reality with which he has come into contact, God, to human proportions. His words are nothing but a little bit of wind, a little bit of noise. They are never anything more than poor and inefficient signs, always liable to be misunderstood, even when he is only expressing human realities. They are all the more inadequate when he wants to use them as vehicles for his expression of the absolute being of God.

To compensate for their inadequacy and to exteriorize their experience of God, men have had recourse to other means of expression which nature has put at their disposal, various gestures and positions of the body: raised or folded hands, genuflections, prostrations, sacrifices. That is how, from a spontaneous source deep within man, religious rites, liturgies, came into being. All these ceremonies have deep roots within human nature itself. But even in the midst of all this effort and activity, men are still aware of their fundamental inadequacy, their basic inability to express in fitting terms the reality that they experience so vividly in the religious consciousness of their hearts.

The Ordeal of Socialization

Deep and basic needs within human nature force man to live

in society. He cannot be born or reared without the society of the family. Nor can he make any human progress without becoming a member of larger societies, which go from the tribal society to that of the modern city.

The result is that every human activity tends to socialize and institutionalize, that is, to create special organs, more or less autonomous and more or less distinct from other institutions and other social divisions.

Religion is no exception to this natural tendency. It was only natural for it to develop everywhere into a more or less well-organized social institution and to achieve a certain measure of independence from the family and the state. Sometimes it is little more than a department of the state. At other times it strives to preserve or regain a very high degree of autonomy. It can even happen that it threatens to dominate the state and absorb its functions. But at any event, religion always has its own heads and ministers, its body of doctrines, its institutions, its laws, its social ceremonies.

There are many advantages for religion in this social structure. There is strength and continuity and greater protection, and the ability to develop and communicate its teachings with greater effect.

But religion is also faced with certain very definite dangers which menace everything that is social and collective in nature: routine, formalism, monotony, constraint, political exploitation.

The Danger of Disfiguration

What has just been said concerning the individual expression and the socialization of religious consciousness might give us some presentiment of the perils that religion would have to face in the course of human history.

The opponents of religion have every advantage when they want to discredit it in the eyes of the world. They only have to describe the absurdities, the perversities, even the monstrosities in which religious instinct has involved humanity from time to time: magic and superstition, idolatry, the creation of a whole pantheon of gods all afflicted with the most revolting defects and vices, licentious ceremonies and orgies, human sacrifices, to mention only a few.

But these men forget that it is precisely the higher values that mankind is likely to disfigure the most, and that the most abominable form of corruption is that which attacks the most noble institutions. We shall return later, at greater length, to this sad phenomenon of disfigured values. We shall discover that it does not even spare the one religion that God himself has revealed to man, the Christian religion.

Once we have discovered and understood this fundamental axiom of the corruption of human values and institutions, we can no longer accuse religion itself. Only the weakness of human intelligence and will is to blame. But we can become more attentive to the task of rediscovering various elements of religious value which are hidden even under the most shocking forms of disfiguration.

Variety of Religions

A study of the threefold ordeal which religious consciousness necessarily has to undergo in the evolution of humanity also helps us to understand how there can be so many different kinds of religion.

If Almighty God himself had not freely and obligingly taken the initiative and revealed how and by what means man is to unite himself to his maker, then these many different religions would all be legitimate forms of worship.

It is not difficult to understand how religious consciousness can be expressed differently, according to the individual temperament of each succeeding age and each individual nation and even each individual person. Without the natural phenomenon of socialization, there would be as many religions as there are people. And when the law of socialization comes into play, it is only understandable that the majority of these religions become closely attached to the tribe or city and turn into national religions.

And furthermore, if God had not revealed the manner in which he wants mankind to approach him, we would have to admit that all religions are true, and that, without being a traitor to objective truth, a man might change his religion every time he changes his nationality.

We cannot, of course, deny the fact that all religions, even with their disfigurations, do preserve some elements of perfectly respectable religious value. It is these basic elements that make up what we call natural religion:

1. The recognition of a Power that surpasses man.
2. A consciousness of dependence regarding this Power.
3. A complexus of rules of conduct which are imposed upon man under the direction of this Power.
4. A system of rites and practices which are intended to convey and promote the relationship which exists between man and this higher Power.

Revealed Religion

Still, it is not hard to see why God wanted to instruct mankind himself in religious matters and teach them the true relationship that he wants to establish between creation and the Creator.

This is the teaching of the Christian religion. It claims to be the only religion authentically revealed by God. It recognizes the real religious values in the other religions, but it still sets itself up as the one solitary custodian of the whole of religious truth and the only satisfactory means of salvation.

To be more specific, it claims that God, by a purely free act of his divine love, has entered into human history and communicated with man in a way far beyond the exigencies of human nature. This divine communion was inaugurated at the very dawn of humanity and kept alive despite the explicit refusal of mankind. It was entrusted to the chosen people, the Hebrews, and its full realization here below occurred when the Son of God himself came to earth, becoming man in order to teach and redeem men and guide them towards their eternal destiny. This supernatural gift of God to humanity is realized and perpetuated now by the Church, in humble dependence upon the glorious risen Christ.

That, in outline form, is what we might call the Christian revelation, the *Christian mystery*.

In a later chapter we shall see how a person can learn to recognize this Christian mystery and acquire certitude that it is not a human invention, but something actually offered by God, something to which he must give the full allegiance of his thought, his heart, and his mortal life.

But, first, it is necessary to understand exactly what this total allegiance of our whole being must embrace.

I. The Religion of Divine Transcendence

Christianity, as we have just seen, establishes a union between mankind and God that completely surpasses nature. But it does not, on that account, abolish any of the relationship that results from creation. In becoming the Father of mankind, God does not at all cease to be the Author, the Creator, the Lord of all mankind. For the religious soul, this results in a variety of different attitudes, none of which he can neglect in his relationship with God.

For us Christians, God is first of all *the great Reality*. God is not at all an abstraction, as so many people have been led to believe and say. He is invisible to the eyes of our flesh, but he is nonetheless accessible to our spirit, and he can be recognized as existing, in moments of attention or of grace, within the depths of our consciousness or in the clear mirror of creaturely existence. He appears to us as the most concrete reality that there is, the most existent Being that we can possibly know. He is *He who is,* pure Being, the Absolute. He is not this or that being; he is Being whose essence is to be. "For the vast majority of men," writes Guardini, "the body is more real than the soul, electricity is more real than thought, and all these things together —the world—are more real than God."

For us God is more real than the world. The world has only a reflected reality; it has only a created existence, participated, absolutely dependent. God, and God alone, really *is*. He *is* in himself; he is identical with his Being. This consciousness of the reality of God is one of the first characteristics of the Christian.

God is a *personal Being*. This means that he is not a blind or hidden or unconscious force, a sort of primeval energy which is either the original substratum of every other form of energy or else mixed together with it. He is rather a Being endowed with thought and love, conscious of his own existence and personality and everything else that is. He is conscious of my existence, too; in fact, more conscious of my existence than I am myself. For the Christian God is not some*thing;* he is Some*one.*

We can enter into personal relationship with him. In the most profound depths of our consciousness, when we recollect ourselves, we are in the presence of an intelligent voice, a Being who speaks to us and listens to us. Every attentive soul knows this fact well. There is a conversation carried on within her consciousness between herself and God. God is present to us as an imperious and kindly appeal to everything that is best within us. And we debate, we run away, we come back, we say yes, we say no, we are confusedly conscious that our whole existence is playing some role in this secret rendezvous. Is it God? Often we are afraid to lose him; often we are afraid to find him.

God is our *Creator* and the Creator of everything else that exists.

There is a relationship of total and fundamental dependency between the world and God. It is inherent in the very being of things. Man can, by his natural activity, succeed in modifying what already exists. But he can never *create* in the proper sense of the word. Only God can make what does not exist come into being. That is what is meant by the word *creation.*

It follows that God is completely distinct from his creatures and that he is infinitely superior to them. He is, as we say, *transcendent.* To understand this, we must go beyond all ideas of extension and space and the tendency to assign God a place "beyond the farthest star." It is by the fulness of his being that God is above the world. He *is* absolutely, in himself, whereas the world exists only relatively and because of God.

God is the "Distinct," the Holy, the Maximum, the Unique One, the Sovereign, the Master. As a result of this fundamental fact, respect, humility, adoration, and the consciousness of a total dependence and an inexpressible inadequacy can never for a moment cease to animate the soul of the Christian in its ascent towards God. Even in heaven the full communion of creature with Creator will retain some imprint of this consciousness that religion is the union of him who is not with him who is.

Even though he infinitely surpasses the created world, God is present in it. He exists in all his creatures; he is immanent in them by the very fact of creation. "In him we live and move and have our being," St. Paul tells the Athenians (Acts 17:28). And St. Bonaventure says that God is more intimately present to us than we are to ourselves.

He is present to every creature by his *power,* just as the workman is present to his work. But with this difference: human activity always leaves something in the depths of the being upon which it operates that man cannot reach, cannot give, and consequently where he is not present by his power. But God is present at the very root of being, not only on the surface.

God is also present to the created by his *knowledge,* in the sense that nothing, no matter how hidden it is, ever escapes his notice. This is not a speculative and abstract knowledge, but a concrete knowledge which penetrates the heart of things, uniting them to itself in their inmost recesses, in the final mystery of their being. Man can do no more than try to attain this center of things. But God exausts the mystery of every creature. All his creation is utterly transparent before him.

Finally, God is present to the world by his *essence.* This means that, like the workman or the artist, he has put something of himself into what he has created. All his creatures are reflections, imperfect and partial copies, relative sharers, images of the essence of God.

The true Christian grows more and more interiorly conscious of this omnipresence of his God. Religion is no more than an effort on the part of the human person to become more and more present, ready, open to the creative activity of God, to God's watching eye, which is fixed with divine love upon the inmost depths of our consciousness, our soul.

This active presence of God in the created world does not mean that the world is nothing more than a mechanical toy with God at the controls. That is the best that human activity could produce by way of creation. No; God has created beings endowed with their own activity, capable of acting as causes in their turn. They are called secondary causes in distinction to God, who is the primary cause. Once these causes have been created, they go into action according to their own proper laws. Some follow only the force of necessity (matter), others have instinct (animals), and still others follow the choice of their own wills, with a greater (angels) or lesser (men) degree of freedom. Miracles, or direct interventions in which God suspends, modifies, or supplements the activity of secondary causes, are rare in the history of the world. They are almost solely bound up with God's establishment upon earth of an order which surpasses the order of nature—the supernatural.

Outside of these miraculous interventions, the created world seems to be subject to a twofold causality whose effects are intermingled.

On the one hand, matter and instinct weigh heavily upon the world and its gradual development with all the weight of their determinism. A great area of creaturely existence is occupied by what we call *necessity*. Necessity is a source of order and beauty, but it does not exclude disorder and ugliness. On the other hand, it is equally obvious that in the very bosom of this force of necessity there exists a directive principle, a finality, a general orientation, which has its goal in man—that is, in the appearance of a being endowed, in the image of God, with thought and free will, capable of knowing God and aiming its activity towards God, capable of uniting itself with God and leading all of creation to him by a fully conscious and deliberate, free act. This order that is visibly superimposed upon the world of necessity can be due only to the intervention of a cause which is superintelligent and all-powerful, that is, to God. We call it the *natural providence of God*.

The Christian never denies the power of necessity in the world. He realizes that the laws which govern the universe of matter and the world of vegetative and sensitive life produce great marvels as well as terrifying disasters. He knows that they can make these forms of life suffer or even obliterate them. In giving in voluntarily to his natural necessity, he overcomes it and makes it subject to the direction of his own freedom. He makes it contribute to his own spiritual victory and to the absolute gift which he makes of his entire being to God. At the same time, he recognizes, admires, and glorifies the divine activity that is manifest in the very heart of evolution. And, finally, he believes that, even if the brute forces of the world stamp out his life, God will still manage to achieve the providential work of salvation for himself and for every other human being who is in communion with God. That is one of the most significant marks of the Christian spirit.

The Christian, then, is a tireless seeker after God. He understands that the spiritual meeting with God is an incessant and never-ending conquest of his heart and his intelligence. For the Christian, too, is well aware of the attraction of sense reality and the facination of earthly fare. He is tempted, as every man is tempted, to put all his trust in finite values and to offer up his life to "substitute gods," to power, money, pleasure, art, to a thousand other "synthetic" deities. Without ceasing he must struggle against the idolatry that always threatens to spring up within him. Every moment of his life he must become newly aware of the fact that he is a pilgrim of the one true God.

At the same time, he knows that his idea of God has to be constantly purified to keep from betraying the divine reality and reducing it to human stature.

He is wary of words, even the word *God*. He knows only too well that every human word, "which begins and has an end," tends to limit and make static whatever reality it is trying to express, and that it is especially and inevitably inadequate when it is describing the infinite. But he has to express as well as he can the truth that he can never express as it is in itself. Accordingly he chooses words which seem to him to go furthest in awakening an image of the reality in which he believes: God, the Existent, Pure Act, Pure Being, the Perfect One, the Lord, Light, Life, the Infinite. He never stops augmenting the intensity of these expressions and he goes as far beyond their limits as he can in order to place his spirit in the presence of God's unique reality.

He is equally wary of his idea of God. For he well knows that it, too, is always inadequate and that it is an indication of the reality towards which his mind inclines rather than a representation of the reality. His knowledge of God is not false, but it is poor and relative to a greater degree than the rest of our knowledge. That is why, after having taken what creation has to offer of beauty and good as a springboard from which to rise to God, he is not willing to stop at any of the mere representations of God that his spirit develops along the way. He knows that God is not to be found in them. God is infinitely more.[1]

He also understands that the arguments that prove the existence of God are nothing but ways of access to prepare the vital meeting with the divine reality, and that this meeting when it comes, this intimate union of our being with the being of God, must be worked out in an incomprehensible and ineffable operation of his spirit. The proofs are nothing more than attempts to transcribe into clear terms and distinct propositions the mysterious process by which man on earth finds himself in the presence of Someone greater than himself. We would not try to prove the existence of God if we had not already encountered him.[2]

God is beyond every name, every thought, every logic. That is why he is never really given to us except in the one act in which our spirit and our heart communicate with his reality: the act of religion, the act of prayer.

Thus, the Christian knows that to find God he has to provide himself with the interior dispositions that permit the Lord to visit him. He must recollect himself, become humble, renounce himself, efface himself, lose sight of himself. He must be ready to welcome and submit, ready to give everything and lose everything. He must already be in a state of adoration and offering. These are indispensable prerequisites for God to reveal himself to us and to become, in our lives, more and more the Great Presence who shelters our existence.

II. The Religion of the Living God

Religion is essentially a communion of our person with the Being of God. Christianity is nothing more. The only thing that distinguishes it from all the purely natural religions is that it has a revelation content and that it sets up between man and God an intimacy, a closeness, a familiarity, a communion that surpasses the powers of human nature and, on that account, is known as supernatural.

In Christianity God has revealed himself as possessing an intensity, an intimacy, a depth of life that our intelligence, left to its own feeble powers, could never know with any real certitude, even if it managed to surmise its existence.

This intimacy of life was taught by Christ, not in a theoretical and speculative way, but through the great scope of activity that he came to accomplish upon earth in order to communicate these truths to us. He spoke to us of the Father, with whom he is One. He presented himself as the Son *par excellence*. He promised us the coming of the Spirit.

At the same time, he invited us to live together with him the life of a son, "my Father and your Father," in the Spirit of love.

Jesus is not a professor giving a catechism instruction or a course in theology. He is a living Person, intimately related with the other living Persons in the bosom of God. He comes to lead human persons to a living communion with the Father, with Himself, with the Spirit.

For us, the essential feature of the mystery of this Trinity is that we are now in the presence of the highest form of life, the most total intimacy, the most complete beatitude.

After that, we have a perfect right to focus our reason on the mystery of this life, in order to arrive at a clearer understanding and more appropriate expression of what Father, Son, and Holy Spirit really are, and what the mutual relationships are that exist between them.

The theologians have done this. In order to arrive at a clear translation of the revealed realities, they have, with a greater or lesser degree of success, made use of human concepts and human words. Finally, the Church approved their formula: a trinity of Persons in the unity of one divine nature.

To give us a still clearer explanation of the closeness of the three Persons, theologians have made use of all kinds of comparisons, analogies, and philosophical concepts. In our own day, the profound study of human personality is shedding greater light than ever upon the problem.

We have discovered, for example, that a human person cannot find his proper self-fulfillment except in love, in communion with other persons, and thus in a bond, a relation that he freely creates and by which he gives himself as perfectly as possible to other human persons. It is in giving himself that he finds himself. It is in stripping himself that he enriches himself. It is in uniting himself with someone else that he produces the most perfect intimacy and union.

Let our human spirit continue from this point, let it prolong and intensify this sublime adventure as well as it possibly can, and it will begin to catch a glimpse of the mystery of mysteries. It will understand—insofar as a finite spirit can understand—

that each divine Person is grounded upon the gift of divine nature that he gives to the other divine Persons and that thus he realizes (stripping himself on the one hand and receiving anew on the other) the most perfect union and relationship and communion. In the Trinity we are in the presence of "personality" in everything that is indescribable and perfect about it, and at the same time we contemplate the most profound intimacy and the most absolute unity.

It goes without saying that these explanations will never eliminate the element of mystery with which the inmost life of the three Persons is surrounded. But they can give our reason some orientation and impel our mind our heart, our whole person towards the fulness of love and giving and intimacy and beatitude that is comprised by God in the Blessed Trinity. They help us, insofar as they can, to enter into communion with the radiating hearth of all life.

That is the whole issue at stake. Jesus Christ did not come only for the purpose of revealing the mystery of his life and unity with the Father and the Spirit. He came to draw us into that life and unity. He came to call us to a share in that intimacy, and give us the means to reach it. This is where the real essence, the distinctive characteristic, of Christianity is to be found.

In order to enter into contact with the inmost life of God, man has to be raised above his natural powers. This spiritual transformation, which touches the ultimate depths of his personality, we call sanctifying grace.

Sanctifying grace is the result of a divine operation which is distinct from the activity of creation. In it God simultaneously offers himself to us in his hidden life and makes us capable of accepting his gift and drawing our life from it. God, we might say, acts in us and is present in us—for God, it is all one same thing—in two ways: by his creative power and by his supernaturalizing or elevating power.

By the first means, God gives us everything that makes up

our human essence: body, soul, faculties. By the second, he gives himself; he opens to us the intimacy of his own hidden life.

By the first, he makes us exist. By the second, he makes us sharers in his own life.

By the first, God is present as Author, Creator. By the second, he is present as Father, Brother, Friend.

By the first, he is present in everything that is. By the second, he is present only in beings who are endowed with spirit.

His presence as creating is incessant and it continues in the whole of creation. His presence as elevating the natural can be found only in the man who, once he has received God in baptism, does not reject him by personal sin.

His presence as creating is, for man, the foundation of natural religion. His presence as elevating nature is the foundation of supernatural religion, the Christian religion.

It is this presence of the Three Divine Persons within us, this loving and transforming and unifying presence, that must be the first object of our attention—more than the grace itself, more than the transformation of our being, which is at once both the effect of this Presence and a preparation to share in it. Our religion is a personal act, one person to Another. We must never forget that. It is a gift, a loving knowledge, a communion.

There are two phases to this communion: here and hereafter.

During the first stage, life on earth, our supernatural powers of communion are partially blocked and we can exercize them only obscurely, in faith. We actually do have within us everything we need to enter into immediate communion with the Divine Persons, something like the child who during the last months before birth possesses faculties which are all ready to go into action. But there is this difference. Even though we are not completely conscious of the divine life within us, we still have some knowledge of it by faith and we can live our life according to this faith. From that moment on, our whole religious consciousness orients the upward surge of our mind and our heart towards the Divine Persons. It is towards the Father, through the Son, in the Spirit of Love, that the religious impulse of our person is actuated. From that moment on, we become part and parcel of the vital impulse of the Trinity. And we are aware of it, though only in a dark manner, through faith.

In heaven, finally, we shall be born into the divine life. Our power of vision and love will be completely loosed from the shackles of earth and free to enter into their fullest activity. Heaven is grace in blossom, bearing fruit. In heaven we shall be fully conscious of God's gift, of his loving and elevating presence within us. We shall be in complete communion with the inmost life of the Three Divine Persons. We shall live the life of a son in a completely transparent way, with Jesus, in the unity of the Spirit.

This life of sonship does, as we have already said, begin upon earth, in a real but veiled manner, in germ.

The Christian is a man who has an unshakeable faith in his divine calling. Each day he penetrates deeper into the mystery of the love that is his from God and the great dignity of his adoptive sonship. He considers his life with God as the greatest of all his riches and he is prepared to sacrifice everything rather than part the bonds that unite him to the Trinity.

He makes every effort to live as actively and actually as possible in the atmosphere of his divine calling and to fulfill the challenge of divine sonship in everything he does. He goes on, here below, encompassed by certitude. He knows that God is his support. He knows that it is God's love that loves him. He knows that God lives within him.

For him, faith is not a purely mental acceptance of abstract and colorless theses. It is the living adherence of his whole personality to the Father and the Son and the Holy Spirit.

For him, hope is not waiting for a vague and undefined heaven and graces which are conceived of as impersonal and automatic aids. It is humbly opening the whole of his being to the life-giving and transforming activity of the Trinity. It is a growing and ardent desire to meet the Trinity face to face.

As for charity, already here below it is communion with the Three Divine Persons, a presence face to face with their Presence, the unreserved gift of self to their own boundless gift of Self.

III. The Religion of Christ

The Christian religion is not the religion of Christ in the same way that Buddhism is the religion of Buddha. Buddha certainly succeeded in launching into the world the great spiritual current which bears his name and which is inspired by his example. But he did not set himself up as its object any more than Mohammed set himself up as the object of Mohammedanism.

Christ, on the contrary, did set himself up as the object of the religion that he founded. He is indeed sent by the Father, and he acknowledges that he has all things from the Father; but still he makes himself the equal of God. "My Father and I are one. Whatever the Father does, the Son also does. You believe in God; believe in me also." The demands he makes are absolute. He lays claim to a love that must surpass every other love, even the closest of human relationships. "He who loves father or mother . . . more than me is not worthy of me." Referring to himself, he affirms things that would be utterly without meaning in the mouth of anyone else but him. "I am the way, the truth, and the life. I am the light of the world. I am the resurrection and the life."

Modern rationalism has done everything it could to reduce Christ to merely human stature. In general, it likes to recognize in him a great religious leader who wanted to recall men's minds to the primacy of moral and spiritual values. Perhaps he is even the greatest of the "great initiated." But he is on the same plane as all the others: he is only a man.

Christ's conduct, his actions, his words all protest violently against these attempts to reduce him to mere humanity.[3]

Jesus did not set himself up merely as a prophet or a great religious preacher. He set himself up as a Person to whom we must adhere, to whom we must entrust and completely abandon ourselves, without condition, without reserve. He set himself up as a being to whom we must be subordinate, subject, to whom we must pledge the whole of our personality, all our mind by faith, all our heart by love. He offered himself as the one reality that could achieve the development, the accomplishment, the supreme realization, the "perfect joy" towards which our whole personality aspires. The adherence to which Christ laid claim is the adherence which only the Absolute, only God can claim.

That is what it means to be a Christian: to believe in Christ just as he presented himself, to accept, without any change or loss, the whole mystery of Christ.

That is what Christ is, a mystery. He is one of those ultimate realities whose depth and fulness eludes our common sense of measurement and from the outset baffles the powers of reason. He is immense, eternal, inaccessible, transcendent, and he enters personally into human history. He is more than a man in whom "dwells the fulness of divinity." He is God himself. He possesses the divine existence, the unique being of God. He is a God no longer entirely veiled. He is subject to all weaknesses of human life excepting sin. He suffers and dies. He is a man with divinity always shining through.

Even for the man who believes, this mystery of Christ and the place he occupies in the Christian order of salvation—the place, consequently, that he should occupy in our heart—are revealed only gradually.

For a good many Christians, Christ is God, of course. That is a truth that they have learned from their religious instruction and they admit it on the same evidence as they admit the existence of God, the infallibility of the pope, and the Immaculate Conception. But this truth remains locked up within their reason, theoretical. They never draw any practical lessons from it for their own religious lives. And their religious lives remain centered about a God who is Creator and Master, distant, vaguely feared, little loved.

They go to Mass and sometimes to Communion and from time to time they pray. But all these activities are no more than obligations in their eyes, and they would omit them if it were possible to do so without sin. The idea that these activities are supposed to be an intimate meeting of their personality with Almighty God hardly dawns upon them. Christ remains external to them, a stranger, distant, like a moral ideal that can never quite be reached, a sterling example that can be followed only from a distance.

In order for Christ to reveal himself in his fulness, we must never cease looking for him, keeping alive all our spiritual forces of reception and love. "It is not enough," Guardini says, "to hold as true the proposition that Christ is the Savior. We have to center our whole life, seriously and vigorously, upon Christ and upon knowing him—as seriously, as actively as a man who is trying to get ahead in his profession, as an intellectual who is sparing no effort to solve his problem. We must work as diligently as an artist does to complete the masterpiece of his career, or the lover to win the heart of the one he loves above all others.

"Moreover," continues Guardini, "we have to realize that this is not merely a goal, a task with which we are concerned, but a Person, a living Being, Someone who wants us to know him, Someone who wants our two loves to be joined into one, Someone who comes to meet us and wants us to go out to meet him. That is the kind of trust with which we should think of him; not only with our reason but with all the longing of our heart. That is how we should wait for him, not without a trace of sadness, concentrating on him, leaning our ear towards him, calling him, always prepared to welcome him."

That is how to be a Christian, searching for Christ, trying to know Christ just as he really is.

"How long does this waiting last?" asks Guardini. "No one can say. God may give you what you are asking overnight. Or he may make you wait twenty years. But what is twenty years compared to the grace he has to give? Someday he will come.

Someday, in the silence of your profound recollection, you will know the answer. It is Christ. Not through a book nor through someone else's words. No; all by yourself—and through Christ alone."

Once this contact is established, Christ is no longer a remote personality lost behind twenty centuries of history. He is a Person, actually alive, directly interested in me; and I must accept him into my heart just as he appears in the Gospels: as Master, Friend, Bridegroom, Brother, Truth, Way, Life. All these words were once dead and colorless, purely conventional, perhaps even insipid. But now they have become sparkling, incandescent, alive.

Christ, then, is truly the Savior, not only because he has redeemed me on the cross, but because, resurrected and glorious, he is actually offering his sacrifice for me in heaven and on the altar, and actually, at this very moment, exercising his creating and transforming power upon my soul. He is saving me at the very moment that I write these lines. "He is in me more than I am in myself," writes Claudel. That is an echo of St. Paul: "It is no longer I who live, but Christ lives in me."

Christ is Mediator, Priest. These are no mere empty expressions. His office was very definitely that of forming a bridge between God and man. From the side of God, he is the living and visible expression of God among men, the real incarnate presence, the witness, the messenger, the gift, the truth, the life. From the side of man and the world of man, he is the cornerstone of our faith, the synthesis, the "recapitulation," the pontiff, the offering *par excellence,* the way of return, the head, the king.

Once this contact is established, we go on living much the same as before. We have our profession, our work. We love, we raise a family, we bring up our children. But our whole life is transfigured from within. Everything is bordered with a fringe of light. Life is full of meaning and earnestness. Everything has a goal. We feel secure and at peace with everything and everyone.

This is not to say that the presence of Christ within us always retains the intensity of the first moment of illumination. But we do realize that we can give ourselves over absolutely to him, that we will never go astray in adopting his teaching, and that in following him we know what we are about.

Men, even the most intelligent, the most devoted, the most selfless, the most concerned with our welfare, are never a complete and total support. But there did exist one man—and he is known to history—whose life and words and activity and death I know, a man to whom I can surrender myself with absolute trust and work out my whole destiny.

"You have to have something certain. You have to," says a character in Malraux. We have—Christ. "If anyone should ask," says Guardini, "what is certain, so certain that we could base our whole life and death upon it, so certain that we could anchor everything in it—we should answer simply: 'The love of Christ.' "

IV. The Religion of the Incarnation

The word *incarnation* has many meanings today. We speak of the "incarnation of man" and what we mean is that, while constituting one single and individual substance, the human person is composed of spirit and matter, body and soul, that he is spiritualized flesh and incarnate spirit, and that in the conduct of his life he must take into account the living paradox that he represents unless he wants to fall into the most dangerous errors and aberrations. If you try to make an angel out of man, you end up with an animal, writes Pascal. Our calling is to take men of ourselves.

On the other hand, since the whole of creation is a manifestation of God, the expression of his divine idea, a reflection of his essence, and since God is intimately present in the world, as we have explained above, it would not be inexact to state, provided we understand what we mean to say, that the created world is an incarnation of God. Sertillanges calls creation "God in blossom," and he is a theologian, not a pantheist.

[101]

But these are both natural and improper meanings of the word *incarnation*.

When we say that Christianity is the religion of the incarnation, we use the word to signify a divine action of the strictly supernatural order. The Incarnation that constitutes one of the essential foundations of Christianity is the descent, the penetration, the incorporation of the living God, the triune God, into the created universe and especially into humanity, in order to bind mankind together, to put them in order, to make them one, to give them new existence in himself, to make them live from his own spirit, each of them according to his own nature.

The first stage in this descent of God into the created world is the Person of Christ. The first incarnation, the key incarnation, the main incarnation is the Incarnation of Christ when the "Word was made flesh and dwelt among us."

We have explained in the preceding chapter how God, in coming into our midst in the form of human flesh, wanted to be one of us, appear to us visibly, make his own concrete entry into the course of history. The Eternal willed to live in time, the Invisible in the visible, the Immutable in a world of constant change.

Moreover, in so doing he has given the human race a new and outstanding dignity: there is now a human being of whom we can say that he is really God.

Finally, this Man-God is not only a man among other men. He is the chief, the head, the peak, the key, the "recapitulation" of humanity and of all created things. The world and humanity make up a great and noble structure which is built upon Christ and consummated through Christ in God. Whether we realize it or not, whether we want it or not, whether we admit it or not, Christ is something, in every man and in every created nature. "In him all things hold together" (Col. 1:17).

The second stage of the incarnation of the living God and his spiritual treasures is the Church. The Church is the prolongation of Christ. It is "Christ distributed and communicated," as

Bossuet says. It is divine life, creating—by the will of Christ, in dependence upon his lasting activity—a social body, visible, on earth, hierarchical, organized, possessed of a goal and its own proper structure and its own proper methods of activity.

The family, the state, and all the other human societies have their origin in the nature of man or in his free will. But the Church is born directly from the living God, from the will of Christ. It is divine life, the supernatural life of Christ, the "mystic" life of grace, becoming incarnate, taking a body, becoming a social unit, tangible, visible. But its interior animation springs from Christ and through him from the Father and the Holy Spirit. It is a social incarnation of the living God, just as Christ is an individual incarnation.

In the Church, God has adapted himself to the social nature of man, to his community sense, the natural, material, bodily, temporal solidarity which binds men together and makes them indispensable to each other.

The function of the Church is exactly that of Christ himself, for the Church is the tool with which he operates in human history. Its mission is to reveal the Living God to men; to graft them upon Christ so that they will receive from him the very life of God; to guide them so that in all things they will live animated by love like true sons of God; and, finally, to gather everything, men, the works of man, and the whole world in which men live, into one vast panoramic return of adoration and praise and communion with the Father.[4]

In order to accomplish this office of inspiring man with the spiritual and Godlike, the Church has been furnished with sacred signs, the sacraments. They, too, are a combination of matter—human words, human gestures, the material world of water, oil, bread, and wine—and the work of grace. Principal among them is the Eucharist, which contains, under the appearances of bread and wine, the real presence of the living Christ. It makes up the primary sources of divine life here on earth and forms the center of the worship by which humanity, redeemed and elevated to the supernatural, makes its return to the Father. The Mass is, on earth, the one act in which this mutual giving is expressed and realized in the most perfect manner. It is the communion of man with God.

The third stage of the incarnation of the living God is man. If the Son of God has become man and if he continues his active presence in the Church, it is in order to reach man. It is in order to make him live interiorly through grace and to make him a sharer in the inmost life and sacred beatitude of the Holy Trinity.

Unlike the humanity of Christ, the humanity of man retains its own personality. It is not God in the strict sense of the word, as Christ is. But it is Godlike. It is associated, through Christ, with the life of the Father, the Son, and the Holy Ghost. It is in this sense that we call grace an incarnation of the living God in man.

Finally, the fourth stage of the incarnation of the living God is the whole of creation. By this we understand not only matter but also man himself considered in his created nature and all his earthly activities, everything that we call human or temporal values: work, science, professions, technology, art, love, family, country, culture, civilization.

All these things are not only good in themselves, but, in the will of God, they are all mysteriously bound to Christ and their vocation is to serve as instruments of his grace.

Because of man's sin, all these values have been falsified; they have fallen from their proper sphere. They have become dangerous. Their principal danger lies in the fact that man is inclined to give them a sort of idolatrous worship as if they were absolute instead of making them instruments of love and grace and praise. This is what gives rise to the tragic conflict that involves the life of every man who comes into this world.

Still, these earthly values have not become essentially evil. They, too, have been redeemed and reintegrated, together with man, into the order of grace.

There is a certain indeterminacy about creation. Everything in it can turn into a source of spiritual progress or an occasion of eternal perdition. Inasmuch as man has been saved by Christ and directed by his teachings, it is his duty to work out the redemption of earthly values, to subjugate them to himself effectively, to make them contribute to his growth in Christ, and thus to restore all things in Christ. That is the most noble use to which he can possibly put his creative freedom.

This is the imposing spirit of life in which the Christian sees himself caught up. Man is not an atom lost in the cosmos of a world that is ruled by absurdity. He is part of a whole that has been bound together by Christ and joined through Christ to God. His position is marked out by God. He is in the over-all picture. All he has to do is accept his place and fill his role in God's great plan.

Deeply aware of the fact that he belongs to Christ, the Christian is also conscious of the fact that he belongs to the Church, the mystical body. This consciousness is expressed by his interest in the Church's life, her purity and progress, her struggles and sufferings, by his active and organic cooperation in extending the Church, by the attention he gives her teachings and the orders and directives of her hierarchical heads, by his unchanging respect and his ready obedience, by his constant concern to adapt the Church more and more effectively to the changing world, and, finally and principally, by his serious and sincere participation in the Church's prayer, in her sacramental life, her praise, her worship, and above all the principal act of her worship, the Mass.

Finally, far from pouting at the world as so many people accuse him of doing, the Christian has a really sacred respect for creation, for work, for all the human values.

It is true that he is very conscious of their limitations. He does not make gods of them. But he does see something divine in them, something of God, something that leads to God. His faith teaches him that all of creation is fundamentally good, that in every creature, the most material as well as the most spiritual, there is a reflection of the Creator, that it is a being drawn into unity with the Incarnate Word, a sign, a voice, a message from God. His religion, his communion with God includes the entire created universe and draws it powerfully into his own interior ascent towards God. "All you works of God, bless the Lord."

He has this same religious consciousness in every aspect of his properly human activity, not only when he sees himself as a creator together with God the Creator, but also because he has come to understand that in every one of his activities, whether they are the product of his intelligence, his heart, or his hands, he touches upon a world in which God has become incarnate, and enters into contact with realities that are joined to Christ.

Everything he does is divine, not only because of the supernatural intention with which he does it, but by the very material content of his activity. The intention is certainly important, because it could pervert the whole activity, throw it out of equilibrium. That would be sacrilegious. The intention must be purified and frequently renewed and supernaturalized. Whether I am working with a pen, a pick, or a paintbrush, I do not have to inject an element of the divine into my work: it is already there. I only have to discover it and respect it by living as intensively as I can in my discovery. In order to turn towards God by means of the world and my work, I only have to model myself as closely as I can upon the elements of the divine that I discover there.

St. Paul has a magnificent description of what it means to be a Christian upon earth. "Everything is yours; you are Christ's; and Christ is God's."

V. The Religion of Moral and Spiritual Perfection

One of the most striking things about the Gospel is the importance which Christ attaches to the interior, moral, spiritual formation of man. He is not concerned with any theoretical doctrines, any abstract principles, and especially any subtle casuistry in an effort to define sharp boundaries of good and evil, venial and mortal. He issues a constant call to spiritual perfection and purity of heart, to interior liberty, to open simplicity and trusting directness in the whole of our personality.

The morality of Christ tends less to define the object of our actions than to impart light and purity to the source from which they emanate. As long as man is not revitalized within, nothing is accomplished. He remains a threat. But if he develops the spirit of poverty, there is no longer any need to preach against theft, to discuss the moral implications of violations of justice, or to define venial and serious matter.

Besides—and this has not been given the notice it deserves—the morality of Christ is a real morality of communion. The kingly commandment is to love God and man. But Christ realizes that this love is impossible until we have succeeded in unblocking our communion faculties, our spirit and heart. That is why his moral instruction is essentially a series of vital appeals to humility, simplicity, detachment, and purity.

A random gleaning from the Gospels will convince us of this truth.

From the Sermon on the Mount it is already apparent that Christ has no love of earthly grandeur or external preferments. Power, wealth, and strength are not the things he praises. Quite the contrary. Self-conceit, pride, hardheartedness, the desire for power and domination, sensuality, deceit, the spirit of injustice and quarreling and revenge and scorn and violence and self-aggrandizement, everything that traps the spirit in darkness, everything that shuts men up within themselves and makes them inaccessible to their fellow-men—these are what he condemns, without appeal.

Those who receive the promise of joy for their souls—*beati*—are quite different. They are the men who have not made gods for themselves out of the goods of this world. They are the pure hearts, those whose soul is transparent and open and free, as free as it can be, from all undue reliance upon self. They are the meek, the peacemakers, those who have not let themselves grow hard or bitter at the sight of injustice, those whose soul has overcome the natural instincts of self-defense and agressiveness and the poison influence of reprisal and hate.

All these will see God; starting right now they will recognize his presence and enter into communion with him.

The whole Gospel continues in this tone. When it tells us to leave aside all our useless anxieties and all our exaggerated concern with the problems of daily life, that is so that we will remain open to the Kingdom. When all women are invited in the person of Martha to overcome their uneasiness, to reduce the burden of their household cares and responsibilities, that is so they will have time to give to the peaceful contemplation of the Master. When Jesus says that if our eye is simple and sound, our whole body will be in the light, he is speaking of the purity of our interior eye, which is to make our whole personality bright and spread its light in every direction. When we leave everything to follow him, we are sure to find an imperishable treasure, to discover the one thing that is necessary. It is not enough to pray; we have to pray with humility, like the publican. God cannot find his way into the heart of a Pharisee so full of self and so conscious of his merits.

Christ was just as insistent upon the virtues of childhood. "Unless you turn and become like little children, you will not enter into the kingdom of heaven" (Mt. 18:4).

This has to be understood correctly. Christianity does not advocate a sort of infantilism or sentimentalism. It is not a superficial, poetic preoccupation with the grace and innocence of childhood. And still less does it advocate fear of life or retreat from the obligations of everyday living.

What Christ means is this: We must be constantly and seriously on guard to root out of our lives whatever developments of our adult experience might prove harmful to our spiritual recollection; we must protect within our hearts the powers of communion that are so lively in childhood.

Mistrust is the one thing that makes grown-ups closed and introverted people, poorly fitted for spiritual activities. Mistrust—the unwholesome fear of being deceived, the dread of being known for what we are, dissimulation, artifice, ruse, "dust in the eyes," the big front, refusal to face reality, bitterness and revolt against the human estate, an interest that centers exclusively upon the immediately practical, the craving for possessions, an obsession with self, the need for self-assertion and self-importance, a tendency to abstraction and logical construction, to ideologies and systems, a preference for words and conventions and classification to the detriment of direct contact with existent being.

Christ's whole purpose is to sustain and restore this freshness of approach to the complete reality of everything that is and especially to God, to protect or rediscover for us the way that leads to the wealth of the kingdom, life with God. This is his purpose when he appeals to us so earnestly to preserve the virtues of childhood.

The qualities that are especially characteristic of childhood are trust, abandon, faith, simplicity, frankness, the spirit of truth and selflessness, conscious and readily admitted weakness, indifference towards money and social rank, a preference for goodness rather than beauty and knowledge and power, and above all a great degree of promptness in creating living bonds between things.

This same strain is tirelessly repeated by our Lord, in different circumstances and ways. We must learn to have a receptive soul, a transparent heart, an open countenance: then we shall see God. Then we shall enter into the kingdom and communicate with the Being of God. Then we shall also possess the earth, not like dictators and conquerors, but like St. Francis of Assisi, in an interior surge of spirit, in perfect freedom, permeated with wonder and praise. It is important to realize that this meeting and this possession need not be put off till the hereafter. It is true that our communion with God and with the world will not be perfect until we are in heaven. But its beginnings are here below. "I can see God," said an old Belgian guide on his sickbed. Everyone who perseveres humbly along the path marked out by Christ will one day come to know the meaning of these words.

Christ's basic moral orientation makes the Gospel a closed book for those who see the whole of human life, not in a spiritual communion with the world and God, but in scientific and technical and artistic activities. For them Christianity is a complete reversal of values. It is, indeed; but it reverses them in order to put them back in their proper place and to call attention to values that outweigh all the rest: moral activities and communion.

Unfortunately, as long as a person does not begin to experience these truths, he remains an unbeliever. Religion, for its part, properly understood, does not look down upon science and technology. It recognizes their value; it helps them find their place in life; it makes them an integral part of its vital experience of rising toward God. But science and technology have an open disregard for spiritual and religious values, because these are inaccessible to the scientific method. God cannot be discovered in the same way that germs are examined and atoms smashed. He reveals himself to the humble, waiting spirit.

As for those who think that man's goal is within man himself, in his human progress, in his earthly possession of the world —the protagonists of atheistic humanism—these theorizers fly into a rage against the Gospel's invitation to purity, detachment, humility, self-denial. It is a refuge for the weak and lazy, they say, a compensation for men who desert the world and its life, a way out, thronged with the poor and the persecuted, the oppressed, and the discouraged.

There are even some Christians who are somewhat wary of the "passive" virtues. Instead, they want to see the "active" virtues, an enterprising spirit of initiative and conquest, action, strength, courage. It goes without saying that these "active" virtues do make up a part of the Christian soul. But only a total ignorance of the Gospels could make anyone relegate the virtues of recollection to the background of the Christian life and insinuate that they are easy to come by, something for children and women. The virtues of childhood are learned only with great effort by an adult. Christ did not leave us any illusions. The way he outlines is a narrow one. It is a complete reversal of the standards of value that our contemporaries judge things by; we must put it to work in our spirit and heart.

This is an essential aspect of Christianity. In fact, we shall understand nothing about Christianity if we do not hear these first words of Christ, calling us to interior perfection, if we do not make our own the spirit of the Beatitudes.

VI. The Religion of Responsibility and Sin

The modern world no longer believes in sin. "I have abolished sin," Renan wrote ironically. But Christianity implies a lively awareness of moral disorder, the decay that it produces in man, and the crime that it is against God.

Christianity believes in sin because it believes in the natural and the supernatural nobility of man. It considers man as a free being, responsible for the direction he gives his life, and as a holy being bound up in a close relationship with God. It invites him to work at clarifying and refining his consciousness of God. We have to keep awake, attentive to the coming of God's graces, ready to grasp every occasion of good, to fill the role of careful stewards, completely taken up with the business at hand, faithful in big and little things alike, realizing that we are to give an accounting for what we have received. There is only one answer for those who have frittered away their lives without concern, like the foolish virgins in the parable. The Lord will tell them, "I do not know you."

For the Christian, sin is not only a blunder, a mistake, a

piece of folly, a failing against the harmony of the world, a breach of polite conduct. It is an offense against a personal, infinite Being, God. It is an affair between self and God.

In giving us a consciousness of God and his sovereignty, in establishing a relationship of unhoped-for intimacy between God and ourselves, Christianity could not help intensifying the consciousness of sin, making it bear upon our relationship with God like a severing of relations between human persons. This paints sin in its proper light: superhuman, infinite.

The consciousness of sin, the consciousness of the universality and gravity of sin, plays a primary role in the person of Christ.

In himself, Christ is entirely free of moral evil. He is insistent upon the fact. He invites others to repent, to do penance, to guard against temptation. His own soul is beyond danger. In the desert, face to face with his tempter, he is infinitely free. In his own person he is so far removed from the very notion of sin that we can see in his perfect liberty one of the most obvious signs that he has come from God, that he is God.

Not only that, but it also explains his intense and poignant awareness of sin in man. He was familiar with our disordered nature. He knew it with a human intelligence and a human heart, enlightened directly by God.

No doubt it was this deep awareness of moral disorder in man that accounts for the gravity, the seriousness, the melancholy that we constantly notice in the Gospel account of his life. That is what gives us the key to his agony in Gethsemane with all his repugnance and sadness and sweating blood, as well as to the mysterious cry which escaped his lips on the cross, "My God, my God, why hast thou forsaken me?" Christ has been "made sin" for our sakes, he who never committed a sin; and at this moment of final agony, he experienced in his own heart the tragic loneliness of all mankind under the burden of its faithlessness.

Christ wants to discover this same awareness of sin in his disciples. It is true that he shows himself accommodating to sinners. Those who come to him repentant are sent away absolved, restored to their first innocence. But there is always the insistent command: "Go and sin no more."

Christ warns us that we have to watch and pray not to enter into temptation, to be delivered from evil. He urges us with the utmost insistence to avoid every occasion of sin, to root out everything that can turn into a source of faults, even if it is something indispensable for our natural life. He wants us to do penance. Otherwise we run the risk of being lost for all eternity. He has never concealed the fact that our eternity lies solely in our own hands.

We do not see Christ trying to minimize human culpability. He does stress the existence of fallen spiritual powers—the devils —who are trying to lead man to sin. But no one will ever be tempted beyond his own strength. Christ wants us to build our spiritual structure on the consciousness of freedom and responsibility.

It is interesting to note that outside of Christianity and Judaism, which was the preparation for Christianity, men were not interested in developing their consciousness of guilt. They were more concerned with escaping from it.

The Greeks and the Romans had a tragic concept of man's failings but attributed them to fate and the jealousy of the gods. Even if man was not actually completely irresponsible, there were always the gods to take the responsibility for his downfall.

As for the modern world, it thinks it has discovered conclusive grounds, in science, for eliminating sin. For intellectuals of a materialistic bent, there is no sin, just as there is no liberty. There are only troublesome hereditary factors, pathological states, faulty functioning of the endocrine glands.

Far be it from us to deny the importance of certain recent discoveries. They have been of the greatest assistance in clarifying our appreciation of the influence of physiological factors on the human psychic structure and free will. But to conclude from this that free will does not exist involves the denial of a whole gamut of experiences that are both constant and immediately verifiable.

When we take an honest look into the whole complex of our life, we are well aware of the fact that there are things we cannot approve and things that we could change if we made a firm and intelligent resolve to change them.

The Church, just like Christ, believes in the responsibility and culpability of man. She has always condemned the trends of thought that kept a very vivid consciousness of man's disordered condition but tended to lose sight of his responsibility. She is well aware of the heavy yoke that weighs upon man as the result of his first fall. She is well aware of the extent of man's fall and the hellish plot of the tempter that is so subtly woven into the natural melee of pride and passion and psychic shortcomings and modern ideas. She insists upon the absolute necessity of a Redeemer if we are to be saved. And, finally, she tells us that we must not presume to judge and that only God can form an adequate picture of the conduct of each individual man. Still she insists upon the personal responsibility of all men, in general, for the conduct of their individual lives. That is how she safeguards the nobility of man and maintains a constant element of progress in human society.

The fear of sin is an essential feature of the Christian spirit. This fear can become scrupulous and morbid in the case of certain people who have natural neurotic tendencies. But it would make little sense and, besides that, it would certainly not be Christian to dwell exclusively upon sin and isolate all the other aspects of Christianity. Really religious souls have always shown a very high degree of insight into the evil that is in themselves and in the world. They never believed that human progress consisted in taking a light attitude toward things, running away from responsibility, deadening conscience, hiding the real truth from themselves. They tried to develop a true picture of themselves. They pray for the light of the Holy Spirit to help them. They become more and more accurately aware of their impurity in relation to the purity of God. They refuse to live their lives "beyond good and evil." They look upon the good and evil in the same serious light as they do any other important matter in life with which the whole of their human destiny is bound up, and which must be solved correctly as the choice between eternal life and eternal reprobation.

VII. The Religion of Redemption

We cannot isolate the consciousness of sin from the other elements which go to make up the Christian spirit. Otherwise it would turn into a prison for the human psyche. It would leave man in a predicament from which there was no escape. It would expose him to discouragement and despair.

Christianity has a triumphal answer to this tragic problem—Christ the Redeemer, salvation, redemption.

"God so loved the world that he gave his only-begotten Son, that those who believe in him might not perish, but might have life everlasting" (Jn. 3:16).

This is Christ, Jesus, in the very heart of his divine mission. "And thou shalt call his name Jesus; for he shall save his people from their sins" (Mt. 1:21).

Christ's whole teaching is a message of salvation, freedom, and deliverance. He came for the sake of sinners. He came to save what was lost. The great majority of his directions have one single purpose—to deliver us from evil. He calls us to fight without growing weary against all the powers from within and from without that are bent upon clouding our spirit, engulfing us in the neglect of the true values, in pride, inordinate love of the flesh, deceit, injustice, and hardheartedness, making us slaves of sin. If we are faithful to his orders, we will remain in the light. We will know the truth and, learning to understand the truth more and more completely, we shall be made free.

But there is more than teaching and more than commandments in Christ. There is a redemptive act. Christ was set up as Head and Chief Priest of all mankind by the will of his Father. By freely consenting to sacrifice himself, he was able to offer the reparation that our sin demanded and at the same time work upon the very roots of human beings, remaking man into a new creature, making it possible for him to have communion with God.

All this, once again, is found only in Christianity. Christ is the bearer of a strange mystery. He reveals himself as God beyond all shadow of doubt and denial; but his mission, instead of proceeding here on earth with power and brilliance, is met with constant opposition which finally ends in triumph. After the meager success of his apostolic ministry, the earthly life of Christ comes to a sudden close in the tragedy of Calvary. There can be only one answer to this paradox. The essential mission of Christ was in his cross, in his redemptive act. "It was necessary for Christ to suffer and die" in order to save us and to bring us with him in his glorious return to the Father.

The other founders of religions had no such destiny. Buddha's life was surrounded by a more than royal glory. Mohammed subdued vast territories at the head of his victorious armies. Christ ended his life the object of insult and derision. The others were only prophets; Christ is a redeemer, *the* Redeemer. He alone, by his life, by his suffering, by his death and by his glorious resurrection, was able and willing to redeem mankind and reintegrate it in God.

The words "and by his glorious resurrection" were added above because the redemptive activity of Christ did not consist only in his passion. It was the work of his whole life. The redemption is the Word coming to share our flesh. It is his existence on earth. It is his suffering and death. It is his resurrection and his glorious existence in heaven.

It is incorrect to think of the redemption as an act that has been accomplished once and for all some two thousand years ago. Christ our Redeemer is living and active now within ourselves. He is above all time. He is at work every moment in each one of us, to purify and free us and to reunite us to himself, to root and incorporate us into himself, to create a new

heart and a new being, to live within us himself in his holy
and spiritual reality, to animate us with his spirit, to permeate
the whole of our fragile personality, to overshadow us with the
glory and triumph of his own personality.

It is true, of course, that our own personality is not done
away with, and the forces of evil continue to rage. We remain
a battlefield. But we can always consent to Christ's activity,
renewing life within our hearts. Our faith and our will aided
by God's grace can always start again, always make a new
beginning. There is no such thing as loneliness, a closed heaven.
There is no impasse. Christ is there as the way that leads back,
present to our heart of hearts. All we have to do is follow him
and we will come to the Father.

Being a Christian means having a strong faith in this state of
things. And even more than that, it means living with an unshakeable trust. The Christian is not a man who denies that he
has been unfaithful, who finds excuses and tries to justify himself in his own eyes, who clouds his judgment and tries to hide
from his real responsibility. But neither is the Christian a man
who grows discouraged and tends to despair. A new start is
always possible, even when a person's life has been filled with
sin.

Being a Christian means admitting that Christ actually restores the soul that entrusts itself to him. It is just as important to
insist upon the reality of this imputability as it is to stress the
reality of the renewal of life in Christ. Christ is not satisfied with
veiling our faults; he purifies us down to the very roots of our
being. He re-creates us; he restores us to our first freshness. This
is what gives the Christian a feeling of intimate belonging, complete deliverance, a new beginning in life, prepared to receive
God's new favors. The Christian's faults no longer exist except
to increase his humility and his prudence and to sing the praises
of God's newly discovered love.

The Christian realizes that he is personally and actively
involved in the work of his own salvation and the redemption

of the world. Christ has done his part in reopening the way to intimacy with God. The Christian has to do his part. He has to belong, consent, deliver himself over completely to the activity of Christ.

The struggle goes on. The forces of evil continue. This is the spiritual combat. But man is not alone. Christ elevates him above nature and the determinisms of nature. He becomes associated with the creative freedom of God. The spirit of Christ comes to bring new life into his innermost self.

In this increased union with Christ and with God, man gradually frees himself from sin and becomes better disposed toward good. He does nothing without God. He does nothing without himself. Our salvation is the joint work of divine and human freedom. We have to work it out in the intimate communion of our person with the person of Christ.

VIII. The Religion of the Cross

Christianity is not philosophy trying to explain the problem of suffering. It is religion trying to integrate suffering into its impetus towards God. Christ did not preach an esthetic appreciation of the cross; he took it on his shoulders and he invited us to do the same.

For the Christian, suffering is a fact which, together with death, is closely bound up with another fact, sin. Sin, suffering, and death all go together to complete one gloomy picture.

In the eyes of the ancients this trilogy was a hellish ring, and it would still be a hellish ring if it were not for Christ. Christ transformed and transfigured it. He lived the effects of sin and suffering and death in his own person and showed us a glorious way out. More conscious of sin than any other man, without being a sinner himself, he voluntarily gave himself up to suffering and death. That was his way of return to the Father. It is by his passion and cross that Christ re-entered into his glory. And since no one can go to the Father except through him, there is no other way for us to re-enter into communion with God except the path of suffering and death.

The important place occupied by the cross in the Christian way of life has always been a violent objection for men who live on the fringe of Christianity and subscribe to its teaching only superficially. Suffering remains a stumbling block for most of our contemporaries. It is the reason that they most frequently give for not belonging to the Church.

There is a mystery there. The efforts of mere reason will never completely do away with it.[5] Insisting, by way of preamble, upon the elimination of everything we do not understand is a very poor way of arriving at an understanding of the truth. Our human intelligence affords only a limited grasp of things. We never have more than a partial and fleeting knowledge of life and the world. Nothing is ever in a fixed state where we can grasp its wholeness and completeness. Everything is in flux, everything is in motion, everything is developing. That is no doubt why so many of the partial aspects of reality that we come into contact with seem contradictory and irreconcilable with reason. Even matter, in the light of modern physics is "paradoxical" in its basic make-up. It leaves the expert puzzled in the face of two "irreducible" components whose harmonious coexistence he simply cannot explain.

All the more reason, then, when we are dealing with man and his destiny, with God and Christ, why we should hold fast to everything certain that we can gather and accept the fact that there are always going to be opposing principles that will not be completely clear to our human mind until the end of our journey, in the vision of God.

The understanding of the cross is one of the most basic tests by which the true Christian can be recognized. The true Christian does not pretend to have the final solution to the problem. But he has recognized Christ and fixed his eyes on Christ with an absolute trust. His whole life is surrounded with the lights that he finds in this message.

The first thing he realizes is that suffering is the result of sin. If suffering is a universal phenomenon, then it is because from the dawn of history man has turned away from God. That was the beginning, the springboard. The first sin was full of consequences for all man's descendants and even for the world of matter. For spirit and matter are intimately joined together with the most mysterious bonds.

We can arrive at a certain degree of understanding of this primeval disaster if we consider the disproportionate amount of suffering that one single man can cause in this world if he is in a position of leadership and if, instead of allowing himself to be led by the spirit, he acts under the influence of his earthly instinct and ambitions.

There is only one conclusion for the Christian. The only real way to reduce the suffering in the world is to replace the kingdom of deceit and selfishness and jealousy and hate with the reign of truth and purity and justice and charity. We must follow in the footsteps of Christ and go about doing good. Like Christ, we must be a power for goodness, even for the earthly life of men.

The truth of the matter is, of course, that Christ was not primarily concerned with reducing suffering. It would be a big mistake to envision Christ as a philanthropist, a noble heart trying to find solace for human pain, a social reformer taking the part of the downtrodden.

Christ *was* moved at the sight of human pain and he commanded the respect and love of all men, especially little men. But as far as suffering is concerned, he was much more interested in taking it upon himself, making it the tool of our redemption and transforming it, together with the curse of death, into our long road back to the Father.

It is not hard to see why the cross should be the essential element of Christianity, why the sacrifice of Christ is the crowning point of his life, "his hour," and why the Mass, which is the symbolic continuation of this sacrifice really present, is the summit of all worship, *the* Christian act.

Nor is it hard to see that the really religious soul is never scandalized at the suffering it meets in life. There is nothing of the bitter reflection or murmuring which are evidence of a faith that is not yet sure of the mystery of Christ. The religious soul keeps humble silence when it can do no more. Patiently it waits for the day when love will let it make its offering, when the light will dawn within its spirit.

The holiest men rejoice at their crosses and even ask for more. The world sees this and calls it masochism, the cult of suffering for suffering's sake. Nothing could be further from the truth. When a St. John of the Cross asks Christ's permission to suffer and to be despised for his sake, he knows very well what he is doing. He has understood sin and the cross, Christ and the Christian mystery.

After all, every man has one goal and one goal only, and that is to arrive at a state of total communion with God, to share in his life and his intimate beatitude, to be completely one with him.

Really loving, really being united to someone always means leaving self, renouncing self, forgetting self, effacing self, going outside of self, dying in what we love. Our selfishness holds us fast, fixed, bound within ourselves, to a certain extent. And to that certain extent we do not love. This is true of every authentic form of love. And it is especially true when we are speaking of the greatest of all loves, the love that is supposed to lead us to union with God.

If there had been no sin, this self-renunciation could have taken place with real joy. Our freedom would have surged forward spontaneously towards its goal and object, God. But as it is, the evil forces that turn us away from him and lead us back to ourselves must be resisted constantly. The only way to do that is by sacrifice. Every act of detachment, from ourselves or our goods or our works or even our self-detachment, is an act of suffering in this world. And every act of suffering produces a degree of purification in our personality. We root out something of self in order to make room for him who is our object and our all.

We all know that in order for us finally to escape from self-scrutiny and pass over into God there has to be a rooting-out process, a self-effacement, a decisive and absolute renunciation. This renunciation is death. Death is the final, total, radical sacrifice which, in the world of sin in which we live, is supposed to be a reparation for all our faults, all the idolatries we have committed in turning to the world and self. Death is supposed to dispossess us of everything, to take us suddenly far beyond our depth, to lead us over into God. Death has an air of nothingness about it. When it comes, we really have to give in to the idea of no longer existing, of "losing our soul," that is, our personality, but always with the calm assurance that we shall find it back immediately, purged, transfigured, in communion with God.

That is the Christian meaning of suffering and death. The Christian necessarily makes both of them into a religious act, a sacred reality, a sacrifice that draws its supreme value from the death of Christ, leading us into the love of the living God.

IX. The Religion of Charity

In the whole of the Gospel there is no more urgent command than to love. God, first of all—with our whole heart, with our whole soul, with our whole mind, with our whole strength. The whole human person is urged to commit himself, to give himself, to unite himself, to devote himself to God. And the second call is "like to the first." "Thou shalt love thy neighbor as thyself." There is no greater commandment.

In this commandment, more than any other element of Christianity, we can see that God meant to set up a perfect communion between himself and us. And not only between himself and us, but between us and other men as well. In our drive towards God we must embrace all men without exception. The union we are to have with our neighbor is similar to the union we have with ourselves; we love our neighbor as ourselves. Besides that, it is compared to our union with Christ: whatever we do to the least of his brethren—a cup of water to the thirsty, a home for the homeless, a visit to the sick—we are doing for him. And, finally, this union is compared to the union that joins Father and Son in the Holy Trinity: we are to be one just as Christ is one with his Father.

Love, unity, charity—that is the whole of Christianity. That is Christ in the heart of his mission: reuniting, re-forming, sweeping the world along in an intense current of love to restore it to its wholeness in the Father.

His insistence on union up to the very moment of his death, and his prayer to the Father that all may be one, show how he feared he would be misunderstood and we would remain unmoved by his appeal. He knew what a treacherous mass of selfishness and resentment, hate and revenge, injustice and enmity and opposition was at work in the heart of man.

In asking man to be poor in spirit, to be pure, to be gentle, to bear with injury, he was not only trying to open man to God. He was preparing man's entry and lasting communion with other men, no matter who they might be, without exception. Our commandment bids us love not only those who are sympathetic, good, virtuous, members of our family or race; we have to love all men, everyone, even enemies and criminals and wicked men. We have to be a neighbor to everyone. We have to approach everyone, like the Good Samaritan.

Until we have come this far, we remain on the level of instinct life. We cannot rise to that of charity. We cannot begin to understand what man is in the eyes of Christ, the infinitely precious value of the human person, the nobility that is his in the possession of a spiritual and free and immortal soul, the infinite potentialities of his divine calling, the gift of the living God, the restoration effected in his heart by love, crucified and redeeming.

Every human creature is a workshop of grace. God is constantly working in him by his creative and elevating love. And Christ is active in him unceasingly by his redemptive power.

That is the fundamental mystery which we have to recognize in every man. The next step is to associate ourselves with every man, actively, with all our heart.

Charity is like a delegation of creative and redemptive causality in us. We have to love everything in every man who crosses our path except the disfigurations of sin. We have to help develop everything in him: body, heart, mind and soul. We have to make him conscious of his human and divine dignity and help him form an image of the Son of God within himself. "Love is a network of bonds that makes things develop," says Saint-Exupéry. That is perhaps the best way of putting it. Charity is a creative communion with all men. Its purpose is to make them conscious of their true human stature and to deliver them from everything that limits the power of divine activity within their person.

There is probably nothing better suited to make us understand the essence of charity and its creative and restoring mission than the law of pardon.

There are few things that Christ spoke of in more urgent or more pressing terms. The Father will pardon us in the same measure as we pardon other men. We have to forgive seventy times seven times, as our Lord told St. Peter. We will be treated with the utmost severity if, like the unmerciful servant, we do not forgive our brother from our heart.

Christ knows exactly what happens when someone wounds or offends us: ill-feeling, resentment, anger, fear, suspicion, humiliation, revenge, the burning desire to humiliate the offender in turn, to get even, to injure, to prove our strength, to restore our honor in our own eyes. All these feelings surge up within us like a pack of furies.

Christ tells us we have to forgive. All this tumult that is poisoning your soul, he says, everything that is shutting you up within yourself and making you hard and mean must be got rid of first. You have to find your way back to humility and gentleness and charity. You need to have a free heart again. You want

to be on guard against what looks like real nobility in some of
the motives that well up in your mind, such as the need for
re-establishing order and justice or wanting to see the cause of
right and reason triumph. Try to win back your brother. He
is the only one who is important in your eyes, no matter what
he has done to you. You ought to go beyond justice, go beyond
reason, and rise to the order of charity. You ought to unite yourself to the all-embracing love of God, without fear for yourself,
completely free in everything that matters. You ought to start to
purify the man who has injured you of all the evil feelings he
harbors against you. You ought to set up the old bonds of union
again, the very moment they have grown slack or parted. "Overcome evil with good," says St. Paul.

Naturally, it is necessary to cut off some member from the
Christian communion from time to time. But only after every
means of conciliation has been tried. And even then the whole
purpose will be to break his bad will and lead him to better
dispositions. We use severity "for upbuilding, not for destruc-
tion" (II Cor. 13:10).

This lofty and vivid consciousness of communion which we
must inculcate in our hearts with respect to every fellow man
is naturally going to flow over into service in his behalf, whether
it is a question of individual and spontaneous service or general,
social, organized activity. The Christian ought to be in the
vanguard of social progress not only in the spirit of justice but
also in virtue of charity, which is his law and which is supposed
to make him eager to go beyond justice and create a more
brotherly world out of love.

One of the biggest services he can accomplish for his fellow
men is to work for them as well as he can. Christ laid great stress
on this in his discourse on the Last Judgment when he promised
heaven as a reward to those who feed, clothe, shelter, visit, and
care for the person of their fellow men. The examples that
Christ enumerates are the main professional capacities in which
one man can come to the aid of another.

"Whoever works," writes Letoussey, "does something to help somebody, whether his work is to feed others or clothe them or instruct them or raise their way of living in any manner. And he can consider himself as a servant and a benefactor of the Man-God. One day the farmer will hear the words: 'You have fed me.' And the builder: 'You have sheltered me.' It will be Christ speaking. And what he says will not be a sentimental fiction; he will mean it; because, in taking our flesh, he has made all humanity divine, and 'we are all members of his body, made from his flesh and his bones,' as St. Paul says" (Eph. 5:30).

That is why the farmer ought to work the earth with a sacred joy, thinking of those whom he will feed, and the builder ought to lay each block with love, thinking of those whom he will shelter. That is what every craftsman ought to do, so that his trade will turn into something bigger and better than a livelihood. That is what every man who works ought to do, to give a divine value to his life, to give his work all its real meaning and all its eternal beauty.[6]

Above and beyond the realm of temporal services there is a higher service that makes demands upon charity. It consists in making our fellow men acquainted with God himself, his Christ, his love. It is the apostolate. Christ spoke of casting fire upon earth; he wants it to burn. We have to pass along the message, "teach all nations," "be ready always with an answer for everyone who asks a reason for the hope that is in you" (I Pet. 3:15). Above all, we have to "give testimony," to be "the light of the world," the "salt of the earth," by the lustre of our faith and by our calm and tranquil courage whenever we meet with open hate for the sake of his Name.

The demands of charity seem to be so lofty that we are almost seized with panic when we first hear them. We want to say that they are impossible. We can never follow them.

And they would be impossible if we cut ourselves off from God in our works of charity and relied upon nothing but our own strength. But that would no longer be charity. Charity is the love of God coming down to live in our own heart as the principle of life. Charity comes from God; it is sharing, communion with his creative and elevating love. In order for charity to come to life and grow within us, we have to abide in Christ's love. In fact, the most certain proof of love of God in our heart is love of neighbor. "If anyone says, 'I love God,' and hates his neighbor, that man is a liar," says St. John (I Jn. 4:20).

The whole first epistle of St. John is devoted to this theme. It is striking evidence of the fact that God's plan for the world is to restore the living bonds among his creatures and gather them all back into his love.

X. The Religion of Unity and Community

The preceding chapters contain many references to the unity that exists between the world, man, and Christ. Christianity is dominated by the idea of unity and community. That is one of its most essential aspects.

Almost every page of the New Testament shows the important place occupied by the idea of unity. It comes up under a great many images: the Kingdom of God, the vine and the branches, the body and the limbs. The many exhortations of Christ taken up by St. Paul and St. John are one long, urgent call to unity. All the sacred treasures put at man's disposal—the Faith, baptism, the Eucharist, the Church, Christ himself—are at the same time symbols of unity and instruments for its ultimate achievement, signs and principles of unity.

But there are many kinds of unity. In the created world, there is a natural unity in the sense that all existent things, despite their manifold differences, nonetheless have many things in common. They are related in many ways; they are principles of reciprocal influence; they depend upon each other. They make up a whole, whose secret can be grasped in a certain close approximation by human intelligence, which is always trying to penetrate deeper. Science and philosophy are expressly concerned with discovering and expressing the unity that man is confusedly aware of in the universe.

Christianity recognizes this unity; but the unity that it has been authorized to reveal and effect is of a higher order. It is supernatural. It has its origin, its foundation, its center in Christ. It is a mystic union, but that does not make it vague, ethereal, or inconsistent. Quite the contrary. We must learn to look upon it as something more real and more effective than the natural unity of the universe.

In saying that it is mystic, we mean that it is mysterious, inaccessible to the sense knowledge and even to intellectual research. It is supra-rational, known by revelation, the object of faith, supernatural.

It is wrong to picture this unity as something purely symbolic or purely moral. It is perfectly real; but it is beyond the realm of our reason, just as ultra-violet light is beyond the visual capacity of our eyes.

This unity in Christ extends to the whole created universe. God wanted to "re-establish all things in Christ, both those in the heavens and those on the earth" (Eph. 1:10). "All things have been created through and unto him, and he is before all creatures, and in him all things hold together. . . . For it has pleased God the Father . . . that in him he should reconcile to himself all things, whether on the earth or in the heavens" (Col. 1:16-20). In speaking of the Incarnation, we said that everything is mysteriously bound up with Christ. He dominates all time, and his power moulds the universe.

Among men, this unifying power of Christ is active in an outstanding capacity. It is men who are called to enter into the Kingdom, to become branches of the vine, to become one single body in Christ, to join each other as "members of one another" (Rom. 12:6), to share the same Faith, the same baptism, the same Eucharist, the same Spirit, the same Lord, the same God and Father of all, to share, finally, in the fulness of sacred goods that are put at man's disposal by Christ in his Church.

Every sincere man, even if he is living separated from the Catholic Church, even if he does not know Christ, is touched by the vital influx of Christ and enlightened by his grace. Thus all men are members of Christ and the Church, but in an imperfect way. Only those men are fully members of the Christian community who live in the true Faith, share the same Eucharist, obey the authorities who get their power from Christ, and do their best to subject their whole life to the pattern of Christ and make charity shine out in all their acts.

This idea of unity and community in Christ ought to be one of the constant inspirations of the Christian conscience. It does not disregard the natural unity and solidarity which bind men to the world and to each other. But still it goes beyond them, enlarging and transfiguring.

The Christian realizes that there are relationships of a new order between him and the world, supernatural relationships. He can always abuse creatures and, despite their natural innocence, make them suffer when he sins. Creation is then subject to emptiness, to nothingness, not of its own accord, but through the perverse will of man who so subjects it. Man can also make nature serve the works of grace. He can deliver it from its bondage and corruption and make it share in his own spiritual freedom. The Christian realizes that his conduct has mysterious reverberations upon the cosmos.

But it is even more the consciousness of the supernatural solidarity uniting him to other men that animates the Christian consciousness.

We have already said, in speaking of charity, that all men must somehow grow close and interior and intimate to us. For we are all one single body in Christ, and we are all members of one another. Furthermore, this must not remain a purely abstract or dogmatic consideration. It has to turn into a reality that is lived every day of our lives.

It is not only Christ and Almighty God who are to be the object of our conscious communion. There is also the Virgin Mary, who has given us Christ and who lives from him and in him more than any other creature does. There are the saints, who have now entered into the fulness of his radiation and his joy. Nothing is more Christian than the veneration of Mary and the saints, provided it does not turn into sheer materialistic beggary, provided we see it as a fine network of interplaying relationships which make our needy and restless spirits communicate with their glorious, delivered souls.

It is likewise no more than normal that we should aid those who have departed and who still have to make good their faults before they can be admitted into a total and conclusive communion with God.

As for those who are still with us on earth, they ought to be present to our mind in our prayer, in our efforts to do good, in our suffering, in our labor, in our charity. Being a Christian means developing a progressively greater power for deep and universal interiorization. It means constantly making ourselves more able and ready to welcome all of humanity to our heart really and sincerely, and especially every person who comes into contact with us in any way. They all have a right to share our prayer, our victories, our interior progress, our tears, our hidden charity.

And they, in turn, have something to give to us. Their interior presence makes us much more actively conscious of our personal responsibility. It influences us to pray better, to suffer better, to act better, to love better. Besides that, their very presence is a source of strength for us, an assurance; because their prayer completes our prayer, their holiness makes up for our faults, their efforts fit in perfectly with our own. In the unity which binds us together everything is common and everyone shares in the good of everyone else. "Every soul that rises," says Leseur, "raises the world along with it."

XI. The Religion of Final Realization

Nothing is ever really finished in this world; everything is moving, transforming, developing. This is an aspect of life with which the modern world is quite familiar. The men of today have, more than ever before, a consciousness of evolution and history. Many thinkers are predicting almost infinite progress for humanity in the temporal order. Some thinkers even hope to see the establishment on earth of a golden age created by human genius and capable of completely satisfying all human aspirations—aspirations, that is, on the same scale as the world in which men live.

Christianity gives men the duty of working for the conquest of the material world and the most perfect possible management of the human community. But it has nothing to say about the temporal future of mankind. It remains silent, even skeptical, about the hope for an indefinite material and moral progress. One thing is certain. Christianity plunges deep into the fundamental make-up of man in order to fix his attention, his hope, his life, his all, upon a goal that is beyond his present life, in a world where his person will discover its conclusive and absolute realization, together with other men, saved as he has been saved, in perfect communion with Almighty God.

Christianity is essentially eschatological. It is aimed at the final appearance of each man before his God after his mortal life is over. It is aimed at the glorious second coming of the Lord, who will return to raise men up, to give each man the reward that he has justly merited by the secret decisions of his heart, to let the elect share the life of God in perfect transparency and total consciousness.

Christ's preaching keeps bringing us back to the thought of death, judgment, Kingdom, punishment and reward without end. Christ wants us to live from this moment on in heaven through hope. He wants our hearts to be there already, there where our true joys are to be found.

In all of this there is no disdain for the goods of earth. There is only a constant and sustained effort to stress the fragile and transitory and provisory character of the world we live in and the work we do there. Earth has nothing conclusive to offer except when earthly living is consciously aimed at the hereafter. We have no lasting home here, only in eternity.

No matter what the angry prophets of the "here below" have to say, the Christian conscience is fixed in the "hereafter." That is one of its characteristic traits.

It is this same quality that makes the Christian look upon his earthly sojourn with a degree of real earnestness. This is, he realizes, the test that will decide his destiny for all eternity, his and that of his companions in life. Constant vigilance is the only password; we know neither the day nor the hour, and Christ will come as a thief in the night, to judge, to give each man his due: eternal communion and eternal happiness or eternal separation and eternal fire.

Still, it is this selfsame consciousness of the passing transiency of life and this selfsame steady waiting for a final realization in God that lends the truly Christian soul an air of serenity and unshakeable constancy. Christ has given us a flash of insight into our present life and we see that it is shot through with suffering and persecution and catastrophe. It is only too true that up till now all of creation is groaning and laboring in the pangs of childbirth. Being a Christian means being ready for the difficult situations that will surely come. It means knowing what to hang on to. It means being watchful and detached, but always without anxiety, without alarm, without distress. For nothing can separate us from the love of Christ, not death, nor life, nor things present, nor any other creature. . . . Christian conscience has a twofold hallmark: the shock of battle and the calm assurance of ultimate triumph.

The Christian lives in wait for the perfect joy and recompense that he will have in Christ. There is a lot of petty quibbling about this joy and recompense. It would be less selfish, they say, not to expect anything as a reward. It is more noble, they find, to live for nothing, looking towards nothing.

Christ judged the matter differently. For him, man is part of a system that comes into open contact with the infinite and the eternal. He hungers and thirsts for God. He feels a constant urge to realize himself in glorifying God.

The development of man and the glory of God are correlative terms expressing the utmost perfection in meeting and communion.

And this communion is not a self-centered return toward self. Man and God are no longer anything but mutual gifts, like the gifts that are mutually given and received in the perfect altruism of the Blessed Trinity. In heaven there is nothing left but love. Everything will be a gift—love. Everything will be joy, for everyone: in everyone and in everything and in God.

CHAPTER IV

The Disfiguration of Christian Religion

THE ESSENTIAL ASPECTS of the Christian mystery have just been explained, together with the main characteristics which gradually develop in the soul that is open to receive this mystery in spirit and in truth. We have made every effort to present both aspects in their full purity and wholeness and authenticity, the gift that God makes of himself to man on the one hand, and the return gift that man must learn to make of himself on the other hand.

But when we examine religion as it is conceived and lived in the everyday life of men, we cannot help being struck by the imperfection and poverty of the concepts of religion that pass current in the world and by the utter mediocrity of religious ideals as they are actually lived. Even in civilizations and cultures that are advanced and well-educated, it is surprising to see how many men have only imperfect ideas, or even outright caricatures, on the subject of religion. And there are even more men whose life is only a weak external expression of their religious ideals, entirely unworthy of what religion really is and means.

This phenomenon of disfiguration is not restricted to religion. It affects every sphere of human values, especially the higher ones, and it is a serious threat. Religion suffers more than the other values, because too many men do not even try to go beyond the disfigurations that veil religion on the surface. They take for authentic what is really only an adulteration. Consequently they scornfully reject the hidden pearl because all they see is the ugly shell that hides it. Any convert can demonstrate this fact. When a convert finally discovers religious truth in its real purity, he is always disturbed and somewhat embarrassed at having wasted so much time stumbling against the absurd prejudices that hid the essence of religion from him, prejudices which he accepted without the slightest examination. The magnitude of the problem cannot be overemphasized. It is basic, fundamental.

I. The Disfiguration of Values

The Drama of Values

The idea of value has always had its place in the human mind. By way of proof we need only think of the many uses of the word *value* in everyday language.[1]

Moreover, this idea of value is a predominant one in human life and conduct. Men make value judgments; they build a hierarchy of values; they live and die for values. "The name *man* means evaluator," said Nietzsche. Without the faculty of evaluating, the kernel of existence would be hollow. The idea of values brings us to the very heart of the human mystery.

That is no doubt why the philosophers have always wandered about in the field of value concepts. It has been left for our own era to make value the central theme of philosophical thought.[2]

Concerning all the realities of this world, I am not only interested in discovering whether they exist but I also want to know what relationships they have with me, what power they have to help me, to elevate me, to make me happy.

Value is a thing's capacity for advancing my being, my life, my person. Value is the creative radiation of a thing. It has something objective about it. In fact, we can go further. The value of a thing is always in proportion to its nature, its essence, its being. The degree of value in a thing is always correlative to its degree of being.

Still, the attitude of the subject, man, does play a very important role in the world of values.

Since man is a composite being, made up of body, sense life, and mind, there are different kinds of values for him: material goods, power, truth, good, sincerity, love, religion. It is obvious that some of these touch more upon the surface strata of our being, whereas others work directly upon the fundamental aspirations of our person. That is the hierarchy of values. Moral values, such as sincerity, are superior to intellectual values, such as scientific or philosophical knowledge. And intellectual values are superior to material and bodily values, such as money and power and the pleasure of the senses. The highest value of all is charity.[3]

There is, then, an objective hierarchy of values. But it is evident that man is not always attuned to this objective hierarchy.

There are many values to which he is entirely cold. They leave him indifferent, unmoved. Value demands a breakdown of indifference. It is a gigantic task to make men conscious of the true values and the hierarchy of values.[4]

Values do not shed their creative radiance upon us except insofar as we make ourselves open to their radiance. They demand an effort on our part, an effort that is progressively more costly as the values are progressively more essential to our proper human development. We have an expression for it: if something is "worth while," "worth the trouble," then it has become a value for us. The expression is meaningful: a value demands an act of evaluation. It has no value for us until we have evaluated it. This makes the idea of value an active and dynamic one, so that the role of the subject, the human person, takes on a great importance. It is essential if what is a value in itself is to become a value for us.

A value can never really become a value for me until I learn to understand it, until I recognize it, until I share in it and agree with it and open my mind and heart to its creative radiation. It has no meaning for me except through an interior act which depends upon my free activity to set up living bonds between the value and my person.

This is what ties the biggest knot in the drama of values. The loftier and more precious a value is, and the more it deserves to be received by mankind, the more insistent is the call it makes to be learned, to be understood and received. It calls for the manly effort of adaptation and consent which was described above; but this effort is rare and, when it is put forth, it is of short duration.

That is why the highest values, those which bear upon the central problems of our existence, the moral and spiritual values, are either completely neglected and abandoned or at least lived only poorly. And since men usually think the same way they live, it follows that they generally picture the highest values in a way that is imperfect, disfigured, and corrupt.

Examples of Disfigured Values

This natural tendency towards losing its original purity is common to every form of human value. Everything that has the primary objective of developing our person runs the risk of being altered and disfigured in and by human persons. There are many possible examples, even among the values whose great importance no one could ever think of denying.

1. *Sincerity*. Certain people confuse sincerity with boldness, insult, cynicism. These are the extreme forms of degradation. Others see it only as an exercise in introspection, designed to let them explore their social and liminal and character egos. This is a secondary and surface form of sincerity.

Sincerity cannot arrive at its true purity nor exercise its real spiritualizing power except in a growing interior awareness within the roots of our being, where we slowly become conscious of our fundamental needs in life and learn to respect what we discover there. The more transparent this meeting with self, the more authentic our sincerity. And the purer the idea we develop of sincerity. Values can be known only by living experience. Analysis from without and reasoned meditation on the subject are not enough.

2. *Love*. When the word *love* is pronounced before a group of people, each person understands the word in a different way.

The dissolute old roué can think only of the love of pleasure and selfishness and flesh. An engaged couple will quite likely think only of the very obvious and visible love that makes up their present happiness. Old friends, the married couple who have lived a long life together, think of the deep spiritual communion that the years have brought into being between them.

A mystic or any man who takes his religious life seriously will think of the love of God or the love of Christians, capable of animating and transforming every licit form of love on earth.

Everyone has his own idea of love, from the most debased to the most lofty. And this idea of love is in exact proportion to the level on which he lives love or sees love lived by others.

3. *Justice*. One of the highest moral values is justice.

For some people it is a purely univocal expression, a purely selfish concept. When they speak of justice, they mean nothing but the justice that other people owe them. They themselves never even think of the burden of justice that they, too, must carry in the world. Theirs is an instinctive and debased notion of justice.

Other people cannot go beyond the balance concept of justice: you do this to me and I do that to you. For them justice is vengeance, reprisal, self-protection, defense of society. This is a very limited idea of justice.

The only justice that really deserves the name is the kind that is concerned even with the person who has committed a fault, the kind that treats him with the respect that is due every human being and does its best to restore all the human virtues and values within his soul.

Reasons for Disfigured Values

The primary reason for these degraded ideas is one of the moral order. It is the law of least resistance, inertia, laziness, lukewarmness. Man is constantly subject to a law of gravity that tends to make him discouraged with himself, to hide the essential values from him, to make him reject what is worth while without a serious examination or at least to make only a cursory inspection of it.

Speak of wealth, comfort, power, prestige, pleasure; speak of any material value, anything appealing to the flesh, and man is all ears. But speak about becoming a true and sincere, loyal, pure, just, charitable, religious man, and he remains deaf. In fact, he even drags these values down into a lower order and does his best to prostitute their real meaning, to make them serve his material goals. Just think of what men have done to justice and at times even to charity. Or else they are filled with resentment at hearing about higher values to which they feel no particular attraction and which only make them uneasy, deep in their hearts.

Another reason is the tendency to verbalism. We are more taken up with words than with the reality they express. Not infrequently we refuse even to look at something just because its name has a hostile and unfriendly sound.

There are a great many examples.

The word *collaborating* meant, originally, nothing more than generous group work. Since the war we do not dare use the word, because too many people can understand it only in the sense of collaboration with the enemy. These people do not make the necessary effort to give it back its old meaning, its neutral, nonloaded meaning of working together with someone else. It is the work done or the purpose that would make it good or bad, not the idea of collaboration itself.

Another example. In his earlier works Lecomte du Noüy used only the word *anti-chance* to designate the intelligent principle which, in his theory, directs the evolution of the created world towards its final culmination: the appearance of man upon earth. In his later works he used both *anti-chance* and *God*. For him both are one. But one of his readers was annoyed at the use of the word *God*. In his opinion, the word should have been scratched out of the dictionaries. A sad example of verbalism. The man had forgotten that words are only conventions, signs, and that the only thing that is important for a serious mind is the thing that the words mean.

Another tendency which helps explain the disfiguration of values is what we might call primarism.

This consists in being more sure and more affirmative about a thing the more ignorant we are of it, and in taking little if any care to examine or enlarge our knowledge of it. Doctors are often shocked at seeing the cheerful assurance with which laymen pass judgment on diagnosis and prognosis when their whole competence in the matter has been gleaned from one reading of a medical dictionary. Theologians are no less disturbed at reading the *ex cathedra* judgment formulated by men of science operating in the religious field. In their specialized studies these learned men show themselves to be circumspect and moderate. The research behind their statements is the fruit of much careful study. But when it comes to religion, they give out with formal and categorical opinions without having bothered to come by the exact knowledge that is required. An example of this is du Noüy himself. When he was speaking about certain aspects of the Christian religion, he was satisfied with books written by non-Christians and, moreover, books with an extremely popular and superficial slant. This, of course, led the unwitting professor to monumental errors regarding one or the other doctrine professed by Christianity.[5]

One final reason is to be found in one of the defects from which the modern intelligence and the modern soul are suffering untold harm: the decline of the spirit of synthesis.

By isolating the domains of scientific research, man has achieved a scientific progress such as has never been realized before in the course of history. But he has not yet learned how to arrange his different values into one ordered picture. They have to be lived, experienced, each in its proper place, if they are to retain their real meaning.

Often they are different degrees of values as, for example, body, sense life, and mind in men. If one of these values is lost sight of or if a lower value takes the place of a higher value, the result is a serious and dangerous disturbance of the human whole. A fine example of this is human love, which can never be found in its fully human beauty and dimensions except when the human mind knows how to harmonize and subordinate all its lower elements.[6]

Besides this, values are generally complementary, like liberty and authority. They seem to be exclusive. But in reality their simultaneous presence results in a very wholesome balance. Separate them and they are meaningless and destructive. Authority turns into tyranny and liberty turns into anarchy.

II. Disfigurations of the Christian Religion

The higher a value is, we said above, the more it is exposed to disfiguration. And the more shocking the corruption to which it is subject. *Corruptio optimi pessima.* The corruption of what is best gives rise to what is worse.

Since religion is the most intimate, the most spiritual, the deepest and most fundamental of all human values and activities, it follows naturally that in the life and thought of man it is subject to the most humiliating degradations.

It has known every kind of degradation, even the most monstrous, such as human sacrifice, even the most scandalous and disgusting, such as the immoral practices of some ancient fertility cults.

We are not interested in these disfigurations here, nor with those which we could find in non-Christian religions. Neither shall we stop to examine the Christian dissidents—Orthodoxy and Protestantism—which, despite the elements of what are often very important values that they have preserved, nonetheless present a regrettable aberration from authentic Christianity.

We shall limit our treatment here to the disfigurations which blight the Catholic religion in the thought and behavior of Catholics themselves.

In this we can do a real service to the sincerity of the unbeliever, helping him to get beyond the disfigurations which hide the real face of Catholicism from his eyes. And at the same time we might put the believer on guard against himself, against off-center and run-of-the-mind and blunted ideas of what religion really means, against an insufficient Christian life, a life that gets tired of itself too quickly.

Superstition

Both in scientific and popular usage, the term *superstition* is used to cover a great number of the most different beliefs and practices. At the head of the list are idolatry, sorcery and magic, followed by another large group usually called "vain observances." This includes charms and good luck pieces, mascots, black cats, not seating thirteen at a table, and similar ideas. Finally, superstition is applied to aberrations from the correct worship which is paid to the true God.

Only the last meaning of *superstition* is of interest to us here. The other types are too obviously opposed to the very notion of religion to merit our attention except in passing. But the last group of aberrations present a real deformity in religious activity.

Understood in this sense, superstition consists in religious practices, usually very stereotyped in character, which are thought to produce infallible effects, such as obtaining certain temporal goods (health, success, fortune) or being preserved from certain evils which threaten our temporal life.

One of the most typical forms of superstition goes by the name of chain-letter prayers. It consists simply in passing along a written prayer, which is generally quite beyond reproach in its wording and content, with instructions that the prayer is to be copied and passed along to a certain number of people. If the recipient of the prayer-letter complies with the instructions, he can expect the most extraordinary results; but woe to him if he refuses. There is no telling what evils may befall him.

This is a very characteristic example. It does make use of a religious act. But it is an act which tends to relegate God to the order of blind mechanical forces and assure man that he can automatically disengage the machinery of God's vengeance by means of a prayer which works just like a machine automatically. Right here religion ceases to be a personal relation between a spiritual creature, man, and a God who is endowed with intelligence and freedom, a God who knows what is best for us and who governs us according to the secret designs of his love. It evolves gradually into magic, in which the following elements are to be found: fixed and set ceremonial practices, supernatural or preternatural powers which come closer to cosmic forces than to a transcendent and personal divinity, the idea that man can treat these powers with a sort of haughty self-sufficiency and force them to do what he wants them to do by the mere power of some prayer formula he pronounces or some ceremonial he observes.

The origin of superstition is frequently to be found in fear. That is why there is always an increase of superstitions when great calamities overtake the world, such as wars or epidemics of contagious disease. Prayer turns into a sort of magic spell to stave off the universal danger.

It goes without saying, of course, that it is perfectly legitimate to pray for deliverance from perils and calamities, even only slight ones. The Church teaches us how to do this very thing in many of her official prayers. But we might ask if there is not some tendency towards superstition in those who pray only on occasions like this and neglect all thought of God the rest of the time. Their thinking on the subject runs something like this. They are not really sure that God does exist; but still it is possible. Consequently, when confronted by difficulties, it is only logical to go to him for help. They never really know what is happening. If, by chance, they should meet with misfortune,

they will at least not have to blame themselves for having neglected this first of all precautions. And as long as the future is
still hanging over them uncertain, they prefer to get rid of the
vague feeling of anxiety that a refusal to pray would give rise
to within their soul.

There is no doubt whatsoever about the fact that there is an
element of fear in religion. It is a respectful, reverential, filial
fear, the fear of "him who is not" in the face of "him who is."
This fear is in perfect harmony with our created state.

There is a second kind of fear in religion, that of offending
and losing God. This second fear also corresponds perfectly to
our human condition. Both fears turn into one perfectly integrated whole in the purest forms of religion. But, outside the
realm of religion, there is a rapid descent towards forms of fear
which are, by their very nature, more or less superstitious. Then
God is no longer a God of love. He turns into a haughty, venge-
ful, and vindictive divinity, not unlike the ancient gods. No
way of looking at God could possibly be more alien to the true
spirit of Christianity.

Superstition is also characterized by the fact that it is always
interested in achieving some good of the purely temporal order,
the healing of some disease, the success of some undertaking,
preservation from some misfortune. Never does a superstitious
practice ask God for "the good spirit," that is, the gift of interior
renovation and spiritual perfection as it is described in the
Gospel (Luke 11:13).

This is not to say that everyone who asks for temporal goods
must be considered as superstitious. Quite the contrary. Even the
most lowly requests have their place in the most authentic concept of religion. In prayer we offer the whole of our personality
to God's paternal good will, the power that creates us and makes
us sharers of his life. Our whole person means body and soul,
en route towards heaven, living for the time being upon earth.
And we have to offer it to God in its totality. But we must observe the proper hierarchy in our desires and place our spiritual

necessities before our temporal needs. And, throughout, we must maintain an attitude of humble waiting in complete subjection to the divine will.

It is not at all rare to see men who are only little initiated into the real soul of Catholicism denounce certain ceremonials and practices of the Church which actually have nothing to do with superstition. The principal objects of their misguided zeal are the sacraments, the sacramentals, and the veneration of the saints.

The sacraments are visible rites instituted by Christ accompanied by ceremonies which have been developed by the Church. Their purpose is of a purely spiritual order, to fuse us into Christ, to submit us to his powerful influence so that the very life of God takes root and grows within our souls. Their effectiveness comes from their source, the will of Christ himself, who freely decreed to make these visible signs the ordinary channels of his activity in human souls. It is he, Christ, in his sacred person, at once human and divine, resurrected and glorious, who produces the effect of the sacraments.

That is why they all possess an infallible efficacy from the side of Christ. It is impossible even to imagine any failing in his power. But their grace is never really produced, at least after the recipient has reached the age of reason, unless he has the interior dispositions that are necessary to receive the gifts of God. Here we are caught up in the full tide of the spiritual and supernatural, a thousand leagues from the common misconceptions of superstition.

The sacramentals give evidence of an even more universal penetration of the divine into creation.

In the spirit of the Church which instituted them, they have a very lofty spiritual meaning, even though they are at the same time a request for temporal favors. There is, for example, the blessing for tools. It is intended to surround these tools with the Church's own power of intercession, that is, the universal prayer of the whole community of the faithful, so that in his use of them the workman might accomplish his temporal mission with success, without danger to his body or his soul and, above all, so that the work he does with their help will contribute to his moral and spiritual elevation. There is certainly nothing superstitious about that. This is nothing but a typical example of the respectful attention the Christian religion shows in even the most commonplace of human realities.

The practice of blessing and using certain other objects, such as medals, might seem a little more suspect. It cannot be denied that in the hands of persons who have been poorly instructed these objects run some risk of turning into a sort of charm or amulet which produces infallible effects in securing temporal goods. In such a case, there can be no doubt that the practice is superstitious. But the spirit of the Church is quite different. In blessing these objects, she intends only to make them symbols of her power of intercession and reminders of every man's need to be joined to the prayer and social communion of the Christian Church. If certain graces are attached to them, they are always of a spiritual nature, and they are never guaranteed as something "mechanical." They depend entirely upon the prayer of the Church and the fervor that these blessed objects awaken in the persons who use them.

It takes a very superficial and false idea of the veneration of saints to make a critic reject it as completely superstitious. It is rather surprising, for example, to discover that so distinguished and generally well-informed and well-meaning an intellectual as Lecomte du Noüy can make the categoric statement that "the Catholic religion, born on the shores of the Mediterranean, where imagination is both strong and fertile, had to tolerate the veneration of saints—something essentially superstitious—simply because there was no way of getting around it."[7]

There is no doubt, of course, that the veneration of saints does lend itself to exaggeration and superstitious disfiguration, and that these tendencies must be checked. But, essentially, the practice is at once very human and very Christian. It is based upon the natural and supernatural solidarity that exists among men, on the bonds of love that unite them, on faith in their immortality and on their power, stemming from the divine power, to help us in our temporal and spiritual life, and finally on the respect and admiration that it is only proper to cultivate towards those who were the best among us and who are now sharers in the life and glory of God. Far from being essentially superstitious, the veneration of the saints is an evidence of the purest Christian spirit, a spirit which—and the point bears repetition—is based ultimately upon the collective community of all men with God, brotherhood in God.

Formalism

Our life is lived in a jungle of symbols. We are so used to them that most of us are not even aware of them, no more than we notice the air that we breathe, the blood that circulates through our body, or the beating of our heart.

Symbols are the only way men have of communicating with each other. Each individual man would remain eternally shut up within himself if men could not use sensible signs to transmit to each other their thoughts, their wills, their feelings.

International treaties, commercial contracts, labor contracts, property deeds, wills and testaments, bank checks—these are all symbols to express human thought and will in a concrete form. They make exchanges possible and set up mutual bonds without which social life would be impossible.

But it is in the realm of love that symbolism reigns supreme. Communion of human persons cannot be realized by a purely spiritual process. It needs a look, a smile, a gesture, a word. The greeting that acquaintances exchange on the street, the handshake of friends, the child's kisses and caresses for its mother, the marriage union between husband and wife, the words men use to express their respect, their sympathy, friendship, feeling— all of these symbols are indispensable to the basic human relations that arise among human persons. They make up what might be called the essential liturgy of love.

Man also resorts to symbols spontaneously in order to express his communion with God. It is not that God needs to know our inmost feelings towards him. But in the human person body and soul are so closely bound together that they make up one single being, one single "subject," one single person, and everything that is in the soul tends naturally to express itself through the body. That is what gives rise to all the vocal prayers, the chant, the folded hands, the genuflecting and kneeling, the offerings of material goods, the sacrifices. All of these sacred signs, individual or collective, have one single purpose: to express man's soul to God, to assure God of his attachment, his adoration, his love, his repentance, his appeals, his recognition, his allegiance, his desire for union.

Christianity makes no attempt to do away with all this. It is the religion of the spirit *par excellence;* but it is also the religion of the Incarnation. Even God introduced himself through the medium of sacred signs, in taking our flesh, in instituting the sacraments, in leaving the sacrifice of Calvary as our heritage, in the form of the sacrifice of the Mass.

The Church has been lavish in decking out the sacraments she received from her founder, adorning them with additional ceremonial rituals to bring out their meaning even more clearly. She has instituted or authorized other ceremonies which occur officially in her liturgy, like the sacramentals, or what are generally called approved customs, such as processions and novenas and pilgrimages.

There can be no opposition in this respect between the Church's ceremonial signs and the spirit of pure religion, as long as everyone is careful to keep all these ceremonies and rituals in the realm of the spirit, in living contact with interior prayer, in union with the soul. But this is just where we usually run into one of the limitations of our human estate. All too easily we fall into formalism. Even though the rites and ceremonies have only one real purpose, to establish contact with God and express our interior life, it is easy to go through them in a purely routine and mechanical way. Not only do we no longer see them according to their spirit; we do not even remember their real value and their basic meaning. We go through them only because they are traditional or prescribed under pain of sin. Sunday Mass, for example, means nothing more than this to a great number of Christians. Or perhaps we might practice them in a spirit that smacks of superstition more than religion.

This same failing preys upon all the ceremonies that are used in the sphere of purely human and profane relations. Originally, all the gestures or politeness and sympathy and love were developed spontaneously to express and sustain and intensify a real, spiritual union between persons. And if we reflect even for a moment, it is not difficult to discover the basic meaning of respect, loyalty, closeness, and belonging that lies beneath the surface.

The tendency towards degrading and materializing these basic meanings has worked much evil. In many cases, they have become gestures without meaning or worth, ceremonies without a soul, mechanical and conventional habits entirely void of spirit. What is to be done? They cannot be rejected on that account. When there is a question of religious ceremonies as well as profane ceremonies, they have to be preserved. There is no reason to believe that interior fervor stands to gain anything by doing away with, or wanting to do away with, exterior signs of devotion. Quite the contrary! Experience has taught us that, in most cases, the religion which sets out to confine itself merely to the regions of the spirit ends up by disappearing into nothingness.

The only way out of the difficulty is a persevering effort to maintain the life of the soul, to learn to understand the value of these sacred signs and prayers, and to restore them to their full measure of reality, truth and spirit.

One thing which is particularly scandalizing to unbelievers and the source of a certain amount of uneasiness even for some Catholics is the great importance attached to certain exterior ceremonies in religious life, for example, processions, pilgrimages, and the emotional responses of large crowds when statues of the Blessed Virgin or famous relics are carried by in procession.

In evaluating these ceremonies, it is absolutely essential to avoid two excesses, both of which are evidence of a certain narrowness of view.

The first of these consists in looking at the ceremonies as something essential to religion, when they are actually only its outermost fringe. It is precisely because they are external that they are the object of such prominent display. But the real value of a thing is not to be judged exclusively in terms of its size. In the real hierarchy of the means of Christianization and sanctification, the Church actually puts them in the last place, far removed from the Mass, the sacraments, prayer, and interior reform. They are only an invitation to come into closer contact with the living and essential sources of religion. And they are always optional.

It might be that they make no appeal at all to the religious temperament of more interior and less demonstrative persons. Then these have the right to make use of the liberty that the Church allows them not to take part in them. You cannot require every Christian to cry "Long live Christ the King" when the Blessed Sacrament is borne aloft in procession. It might seem more like a lack of proper respect to him, like something out of all proportion to the fervor he actually feels, a sort of half-lie. And the one who accuses him of lukewarmness or human respect might well be guilty of a very rash judgment.

But on the other hand, modern "intellectuals" have no right to show how small their intellects really are by qualifying all these exterior manifestations of piety as superstitious.

It is true that they run the risk of turning into acts of superstition, and everyone is free to decide whether, in a given case, the limits of decency have not been crowded or even exceeded. But basically all these manifestations of piety are the natural answer to the popular soul's deep-seated need for seeing and understanding and touching, and, in a work, incarnating its real

[151]

religious feelings. After all, there is no doubt that in the statue of the Blessed Virgin it is the person of the Blessed Virgin that is honored, and in the relic of the Cross it is the Savior himself who is reverenced and adored and glorified.

In this whole question there is great need for mutual tolerance and understanding. In the Father's house there is room, already here below, for many different temperaments. Each of us has to accept and love those who are different. And, furthermore, each of us has to keep watch over his own personal source of danger. The intellectual has to guard against a religion that turns into something thought rather than something lived. And the popular soul has to guard against an excess of materialism in following its religious impulses.

There is another danger closely allied to religious formalism: fanaticism. For certain unbelievers and certain mediocre Christians, every form of religion that is a little more intense than others is classed as fanaticism. Exaggerated devotion is really a narrow and misunderstood censure. There really is no such thing as exaggerated devotion. If we want to complain of something, we might complain of seeing our religious response to God remain so imperfect in the face of his absolute gifts. There are, of course, false and deformed and spurious forms of devotion— fanaticism is one of them.

Fanaticism is essentially a devotion without love, without interior life, excessively preoccupied with exterior gestures and a great many prayers. In this respect, it resembles formalism.

It places all its confidence in practices that are respectable enough but still only secondary and optional: medals, scapulars, novenas, pilgrimages, candles. It leaves the essential acts of religious worship, the Mass and the sacraments, completely in the background. In this respect, it tends towards superstition.

Very often it is a form of piety that is entirely separated from worldly activities. Instead of turning all of life into prayer and all of prayer into life, it shuts up each activity in its own little compartment. It has no idea of what a deep animation of all existence through the presence of God could mean. Besides that, it has little interest in moral perfection and it is blind to the whole gamut of social duties, especially justice and charity. And in this respect, it comes close to what we generally call Pharisaism.

Sentimentalism

Language is a tool that has to be handled with discretion. Otherwise it turns into a snarl of equivocations and causes the most regrettable misunderstandings. A prime example of these misunderstandings is the word *sentiment*.

Religion is often referred to as an activity which involves sentiment. And just that quickly it is relegated, in the eyes of intellectuals, to the realm of the infra-rational. They might be disdainfully tolerant of the interest it holds for sensitive and impressionable people. But it is utterly unthinkable that it should have any meaning for men who let themselves be moved only by clear ideas and the pure light of reason. Serious men can have no attraction for religion except in a phenomenological or psychological capacity, in the same way that they are interested in sorrow, pleasure, sympathy, resentment, and the whole gamut of human emotional activity. Their sole purpose is to analyze its causes, its biological substrata, its exterior phenomena, and to study its repercussions on the individual psychism or upon social life as a whole.

On the other hand, there are a good many theologians who are openly suspicious of the intentions of anyone who tries to classify religion in the category of sentiment or feeling. Together with the term *religious experience, sentiment* and *feeling* have been suspect for them ever since Protestantism and Modernism began progressively robbing religion of its objective content in order to reduce it to an affective ascent towards a problematical divinity.

There are distinctions that have to be made. Just like the word *love,* the word *feeling* can be applied to different levels of operation in the human person. It can be used to mean exclusively a movement of emotional sensitivity. In this case it refers to psycho-somatic reactions which are not essentially different from the emotional reactions of animals. Animals also experience fear and love on a sense level. But the word can also be applied to a movement of the mind, the soul, the basic personality of man, his "heart" in Pascal's sense of the word, his *"anima"* as Claudel would describe it. Then we are on the spiritual plane of human personality. Man is capable of a spiritual fear and a spiritual love and a sorrow that is felt in his soul.

As a matter of fact, because of the radical unity of the human composite, there is very often an interaction between sense and spirit, one of them generally eliciting at least a slight reaction from the other. Still, this is not always the case. There are purely spiritual states. Louis Veuillot was subtly aware of this when, informed of the untimely death of a friend, he expressed the very Christian thought: "There is joy in my soul, but it cannot pass over into my heart. And there is grief in my heart that cannot pass over into my soul."

Most of the time, though, it is no easy matter to determine the division between sense and spirit. This does not, of course, prevent them from being really distinct. Attempting to reduce them both to one is the work of a very short-sighted psychology that does not take into account the specificity of the phenomena it examines.

Moreover, because of the tendency for all human activity to lose its original purity, as we have noted before, spirit is constantly threatened with the danger of being confused with sense. This is true of the domain of human love and esthetics as well as the domain of religion.

This dilution of spirit life into sense life is an important aspect of the drama that holds the highest values of human life at stake. Instead of ascending higher and higher towards the pure regions of the spirit in virtue of their own innate idealism, they let themselves fall under the fatal spell of baser appeals and descend to the level of instinct, biology, and flesh. A ready example of this can be found in the fate shared by many of the most common values in the lives of men: liberty, love, authority, equality.

Who could possibly deny that religious experience involves sentiment and feeling? Provided, that is, that we understand the word correctly. If we meant to say that it excludes the role of the intellect entirely, that it is not only devoid of any rational justification, but even that it does not correspond to any objective reality, then the statement would certainly be wrong. In essence, as we have said before, religion is an impulse of the fundamental personality. It is a spiritual impulse, an impulse at once discursive and intuitive, an impulse of intelligence and mind which grasps the object, God, as a value, the life-giving and creating reality behind our personality. It is an impulse of will and love, uniting self with God and God with the inmost depths of self, sharing God.

Besides the intellect, then, the will—or, if you prefer, affectivity, sentiment, feeling—plays an important role. Provided, once again, that we use these words in a highly spiritual sense. It is the very summit of the soul that we are speaking about here, not the inferior psychic life of sense.[8]

We have already said that the drama of spiritual emotions often involves a shift of emphasis to sense values, sometimes even becoming completely absorbed with them. A really spiritualized religious life demands a great deal of renunciation, a high degree of purity in the interior life of the soul. Many men, looking for something they can feel, turn towards adulterated food instead. They help turn religion into an insipid and childish sentimentalism or an unwise appeal to man's lower sensibilities. There are many examples: the way some prayers and songs are worded, the way certain ceremonies are carried out, the form taken by some specimens of religious art in the field of music or painting or sculpture, the tone assumed by certain religious instructions and preaching.

Affectation and sentimentalism are the most harmful of all

the deformities of the authentic spirit of religion. In the eyes of many well-meaning men, they succeed in completely concealing the serious depths, the lordly demands, the urgent appeals to manliness, even to heroism. Christ was gentle and he invites us to follow his example, to be meek of heart. But there is no affectation and no sentimentalism in his personality, nor in the ideal that he sets up before us. Without gentleness it is impossible to have communion between persons. But this gentleness does not have to be sentimental. It has to be genuine, capable of grounding human personality in its own proper center of gravity and making men open and permeable to other beings. Everyone knows that this gentleness cannot be acquired except by a constantly renewed struggle against the natural instincts of egoism, self-defense, aggressiveness, domination, and possessiveness, which all tend to harden us and lock us up within ourselves.

There is a second equivocal term that is equally responsible for the oft-repeated accusation that religion makes men less manly. That word is *consolation*. And religion is very definitely consoling in that it gives meaning to effort, to work, to suffering, in that it has something more than life to promise, in that it makes all creation an open world, illuminated by hope. But there is also an imprudent and awkward way of describing religious consolations that makes them look more like lullabies or anesthetics. Nothing is more opposed to the spirit of the Gospel. The Kingdom of God is won only by those who do violence to themselves, who take up their cross and follow the narrow way. Joy has been promised, joy even in this world already, but only to those who are courageous enough to meet the proper conditions.

The occasional exhibitions of sentimentality which so debase the religion of Christ must never make us lose sight of what this religion has to offer in challenge, strength, basic spirituality. This is easy to see by simply referring to the authentic sources of the Christian religion, Scripture, the documents of the ecclesiastical teaching power, and the official acts of worship: Mass, Office, and the Sacraments. The predominant element in the language they all use is serious, balanced, humble petition.

Besides, it would be a big mistake to purify religion of every trace of sense, whether it is a question of exterior worship or interior devotion. The role of sense is there, but it has to be prudent, springing from a profoundly religious inspiration, aimed towards the spiritual. Otherwise, especially in matters of worship or preaching, it is too easy to be deceived by sentiment and feeling. Or when there is a question of interior devotion, there is too big a risk of looking for sense emotion, which is essentially self-centered, and forgetting that true religion is a manly and generous gift of self to God.

The other elements of religion, feeling and emotion, are only secondary. It is because so many persons put the whole emphasis on what is only secondary that they refuse to accept the desert stages of spiritual life, the purifications whose one purpose in the plan of God is to make us lose something of the natural religious fervor that is ours as the result of childhood or adolescence or the grace of a recent conversion, and to make us pass over from the tangible and physical to the spiritual. And many Christians only grow firmly rooted in lukewarmness, or even abandon the idea of religion entirely, under the pretext that God is no longer giving them any signs to follow. This is one of the most frequent and most regrettable consequences of confusing feeling and emotion with the interior attraction of the spirit.

Finally, a word of warning. It is well to be on guard when we read the writings of the saints, especially the prayers they composed. The language of religion and mysticism is the language of love. It cannot help being the language of love since love is the essential relationship that God wanted to establish between man and himself. But the language of love is equivocal. Its meaning changes according to the depth of the being from which it springs. The same expression that describes a purely spiritual state for the mystic might well be understood by the reader in a purely physical and even carnal sense. And if this

reader were to accuse the mystic of having fallen into a senti-
mentalized or even a sensual form of religion, he would be
making a big mistake, due entirely to his nearsightedness. Living
only on the sense level, he remains completely blind to the
spiritual. "The sensual man does not perceive the things that are
of the Spirit of God" (I Cor. 2:14).

Moralism

In the second chapter of this book we analyzed the relation
that exists between morality and religion. Morality consists essentially in building up the human person from within, in developing it harmoniously. Religion puts the human person into relationship with the love of God.

Morality and religion are distinct but closely connected activities. They are a powerful support for each other. Morality in
life—especially when it does not stop with simply correcting the
exterior acts, but actually penetrates deep into the soul and its
inmost dispositions—enlightens and moulds man's entire being.
It increases a man's potentialities for communion and prepares
the way for a really interior religious life. God cannot find his
way into a heart that is entirely dominated by pride, sensuality,
ambition, and the love of earthly things. As for the spirit of
religion, when it is lived in its real depth, it is usually the best
support for morality because it provides morality with a rock
foundation, a final objective, and an atmosphere of love. Christian morality is not something that is lived in a vacuum; it is
lived in warm personal contact with God. It is an act of humble
obeisance and total dependence, animated by real filial love.

Still, morality and the spirit of religion are not the same
thing. To reduce all our relations with God to a pure obligation
would mean falling into the first form of moralism.

Religion is, of course, a duty. That is why theologians classify it among the virtues that pertain to justice. The danger involved here lies in presenting it as nothing more than one obli-

gation among many others and concealing what it really and basically is, the joyful acceptance of the divine gift, faith, love, communion, complete adherence of our being to God's.

This point of view runs the risk of reducing religion to the minimum demanded to avoid grave sin. And that is the conception of religion that all too many of our Christian people have.

Following the same unfortunate tendency, morality itself naturally tends to become isolated from religion, that is, from faith and love. It turns into a purely rational imperative, with doing good and avoiding evil as its first concern. There is no longer any reference to Christ and God except as judges to punish human failings. It is a morality without a soul, without a single breath of air to give it life.

Cut off from its roots in religion, morality becomes secularized. It turns into a morality of permission and prohibition, venial and mortal, casuistry and cataloguing sins. The great commandment of Christ, "Be ye perfect," no longer makes its challenge heard or animates the soul with its inspiration. There is no longer any question of loving with all one's heart and all one's strength. All that matters is to do what is absolutely necessary to avoid punishment. It is a servile sort of morality: we still serve God, but with the soul of a slave.

The result of all this is a morality that is completely anthropocentric and individualistic. The primary objective is no longer God and his glory. It is self and security. As Kammerer writes, "If these Christians confess their sins, it is less in order to renounce evil and receive a divine remedy than it is to have a quiet conscience. Salvation ends up being a branch of technology, and an individualistic one at that. We only learn what we have to know *in order to save our souls*. Individualism, pure and simple. And finally it is completely self-centered, just like the words of the famous hymn, 'I have only one soul and must save it.' The only eschatology it aims at is a last-minute burst of speed to get on the right side of the line."[9]

Dogmatism

Since Christianity is presented as a revealed religion, many people get the idea that God has set himself up as a professor over all mankind and taught us a whole series of doctrinal propositions which make up religion.

Nothing could be farther from the truth. Far from being a sort of intellectual message or theoretical enunciation, the Christian religion is essentially an act, a free step towards us on God's part and, on our part, an active response to this gift. It is a union between God and man, making man the child of God. It is God showing himself, opening himself, giving himself. It is the Father sending the Son; it is the Son taking our flesh. It is Christ suffering and dying for us. It is Christ sending us the Holy Spirit, forming the Church, fortifying it with the sacraments in order to give us sanctifying grace. It is interior urgency. It is a challenge to us to live a life of active conformity to this supernatural vocation and meet these divine overtures with an answer that does not consist in words and ideas, but in a complete and total adherence whereby our person gives itself freely to Christ, hands itself over to God, and communicates in the blessed and beatifying fulness of the Three Divine Persons.

Such is the great and noble act of religion. It is one, but it is composed of many different episodes all working together to lead us into the hidden life of the Godhead.

Someone had to put us into contact with God's great act of love for us and make us aware of the obligations that it gives rise to. Christ did this in words that are very simple, very concrete, very much alive, themselves a sort of insight into the divine gift. "I am the way, the truth, and the life. If anyone loves me, my Father will love him. I will send you the Paraclete. I am the vine, you are the branches. You are Peter, and upon this rock I shall build my Church. Love one another. Blessed are the pure of heart, the poor, the meek."

It was only natural for man to be inclined towards the divine reality that was presented in such a way and to be interested in his own person, which was called to share the inmost life of God. Man feels the need to understand this wonderful undertaking more perfectly, to learn how to express it in clear and distinct terms, to defend it against those who deny it, to protect it against counterfeiters, to make it known throughout the whole world.

This need gave rise to the work of reason in religion. At first, the work was but little developed. The early Christians were more concerned with living the gift of God than with explaining it. But gradually, under the influence of many different causes, human intelligence began to play a bigger and bigger role in developing an idea of God, in arriving at a clear and coherent notion of the Father, the Son, and the Holy Spirit, three Persons in one God, in showing how Christ is only one person even though he possesses both a human and a divine nature.

This is the history of the science of revelation, theology. This is how we came by the great variety of concepts, terms, and formulae that try to express, as well as it can be expressed, the inexpressible reality of God and the mysterious elevation of human nature. Certain formulae the Church rejected. Others she approved. That is the origin of dogma.

Theology has analyzed man and the response he is supposed to make to God throughout his life. Theology has studied this free response down to its least detail and drawn up a list of virtues and vices. That is moral theology. Actually, there was a form of moral theology among the pagan philosophers before Christ. Aristotle had drawn up several excellent schematic arrangements of natural virtues and vices, and Christianity merely borrowed them, "baptizing" them with varying degrees of success.

This gigantic work of reason to explain revealed truth is condensed in the manuals or catechisms that are commonly used for teaching religion to lay people. It is hard to see how we could get along without the services of reason. Reflection, thought, concepts, words, and formulae are all indispensable to the man who wants to learn to know about religious realities, either to express them more adequately to himself or to communicate them to others.

This is another manifestation of the law of the "necessity of symbols" which we describe briefly above. And once again we come up against the same dangers that always go hand in hand with symbols. They tend to stop our progress, to attract our attention to themselves and actually to conceal the realities that they are really supposed to point out. They tend to make us think that religion is an intellectual system, a learned scaffolding of concepts and theses. They give us the idea that religion is nothing but abstract knowledge, familiarity with the catechism or book of instructions and that everything is done when we have learned to know, whereas in reality everything is just beginning. We still have to learn to live, to love, to unite our whole being with the reality of God.

There is a certain majesty about the formulae that speak to us of God. They contain God and they give us God by being a symbol of God and by conjuring up God's own reality within our spirit. There is some danger of our stopping with the mere words and lowering religion to the degree of pure verbalism, a mere battle of words. Those who first developed these formulae, for example, the one which states that the Holy Trinity is the mystery of one single God existing in three distinct Persons, together with the Church, which gives official approvation to the terms, all set out upon their mission from the living reality revealed by Christ, and they constantly had their eyes upon the Person of the Father, the Person of the Son, and the Person of the Holy Ghost. For them the formula was expressive, pregnant, full of meaning, full of truth and life.

But what happens to this same mystery of one God in three Persons for the child who picks up his catechism and sets out from the printed formula and not from the living reality in his quest for knowledge? Words, mere words. And many men, even when they have reached adult age, never get beyond this religious verbalism. They accept the formula, of course; but more likely than not it is only as a sort of official religious password that they have to know in order to be saved. The formula itself remains meaningless. It does not succeed in leading them to any reality. The impression they have, and the impression they give to others, is this: religion consists of unintelligible formulae thought out by an authority with a vivid imagination. They have one single purpose, to put our minds and spirits to the test and see how docile we will be.

There is great danger in words. And there is great danger, too, in the ideas and concepts that we formulate about the divine realities. All our representations of God are absolutely inadequate. They are all borrowed, basically, from our human realities. They are on a human scale, not a divine scale. They always lead towards anthropomorphism. They need constant efforts at purification to keep them from lowering the idea of God and reducing it to human dimensions. The idea of God-the-policeman, God-the-giver-of-temporal-goods, God-the-insurance-policy-against-every-risk-of-here-and-hereafter, God-the-avenger, and many others, is only too frequent in certain circles of believers. In fact, one might also say that in their ignorance many unbelievers are closer to a true notion of God than are a very great number of pseudo-Catholics.

We also have to go beyond words and concepts. Otherwise, we shall stop with the concept of God and never reach his reality. His reality is beyond all concept. God cannot be reached except through a very humble and very pure operation of our mind and spirit. The many ways we represent God are all inevitable, but they are not God. We have to learn to avoid all these representations of God and strike out towards the reality of God himself. Otherwise, the most we can arrive at is a conceptual religion, a religion of notions and ideas, but never a real religion, a religion of the real. Otherwise, we can think of God with a greater or lesser degree of success, but we will not be in communion with his Being and we will not enter into his presence.

Reason will be at work, but not the spirit and the heart. That is not religion.

Neither is religion religious science. There is, of course, religious science, the elementary kind that is contained in the catechisms or manuals of religion, and the more profound kind, theology. And there is a religious intellectual culture, which consists in a clear and distinct knowledge of everything that enters into the domain of religion. But confusing religion with religious science would be just as serious a mistake as confusing life with biology, health with medicine, flowers with botany. Religion is a way of life that can be worked into a science, but it is not that science itself. The science is certainly extremely useful as long as its whole aim is to increase the motivation for religious love. But to think that knowing and preserving pure Catholic doctrine is all that there is to religion is a very dangerous illusion.

"Books are not the place to look for God," writes Julian Green. "We must look in ourselves; for God is in us long before he is in books, and much more fully. God is the one whom we must discover eternally. The definitions they give us of God are often really obstacles to the knowledge (knowledge by communion, that is, real religious knowledge) we could have of him. Spiritual books, as rich as they are, set up systems, and none of these systems is God; but they turn into a substitute for God in the minds of many readers. The religious feeling for God that a simple peasant can have is sometimes loftier than what the professors of theology say in their books."[10]

Utilitarianism

Religion is a great force in the world. Even in those social spheres of the world which are actually quite far removed from religion, religion continues to enjoy no little prestige, especially when it is possessed, as is Catholicism, of a strong hierarchical organization.

There is a great temptation to divert this power from its purely spiritual aims and put it to the service of purely earthly goals. And that temptation has often been indulged in. History is filled with stories of annexation or prostitution of the spiritual to the temporal.

This spirit of utilitarianism bobs up repeatedly, without ceasing. And it must be set down repeatedly, without ceasing; for it constitutes a threat to religion that is most apt to conceal its transcendency and purity, its absolute and supreme value, and to turn it into something suspect and even hateful for a great number of men.

The first form of religious utilitarianism is the one which tempts individuals to put religion to use in their own interests, in order to work out some temporal gain or improve their secular standing.

A great many examples could be listed here: the beggar who goes to church in order to get a piece of bread, the workman or employee who makes his Easter duty so that he can find work on the recommendation of his pastor, the property owner who discovers that religion is necessary to maintain order ("One priest is worth ten policemen"), the king who lets himself be converted in order to enlist the support he needs to maintain his throne ("Paris ought to be worth at least one Mass") or the Emperor who gives the Church freedom and then tries to run it in order to put his own power on a more solid footing. Religion is merely reduced to a sort of spiritual spring-board for social climbers. To all appearances, it is the individual who is serving religion. But actually he is only making use of religion. And by his activity he makes the whole of religion suspect as nothing more than a tool for domination and subjugation.

Thus it oftens happens that ill-informed Christians do more harm than good to the Catholic religion when they present it as one of the traditional elements in the soul of a people or a country. They insist so strongly on this point, they join religion and fatherland so imprudently in their speech and song, as to give the impression that the value of Catholicism is essentially based upon the fact that it makes up an important element in the history and character and soul of their nation. This is a new and often unconscious treason against the transcendent character of Catholicism. Catholicism is not French, Belgian, nor Italian, nor Spanish, nor Occidental: it is universal. And it is hard enough to get it recognized as universal without having the work of evangelization further complicated by someone's coming and giving a national or racial cast to the Church.

Neither is Catholicism the monopoly of any one particular social or economic regime. And still Catholicism is frequently enlisted either in defense of what is called the existing order or as the vanguard of a new order. There is no doubt that the religion of Christ does inspire ideals of justice and charity and that Christians in a community have the duty of being dissatisfied with social inadequacies and being vitally interested in any concrete solution that will result in the establishment of a more brotherly society.

But the Church is not only a social technician. "The Church can make infallible promises about the hereafter," writes Duméry in *The Three Temptations of the Modern Apostolate,* "but it has no positive guarantee for temporal welfare. To set up a big poster on a billboard with the challenging dilemna 'Jesus Christ or catastrophe' is really confusing two entirely different planes of reality and reducing the Gospel to nothing more than a charter of social security and prosperity. And to make the people believe that our religious teachings contain ready-made, universal, and infallible solutions for elevating the standard of life and resolving all its economic problems is both naturalizing the transcendence of God and denying that human reflection has any role to play, through the long and laborious medium of experience and trial and error, in reconstructing a better social status."[11]

More apparent, though not less distressing, is the tendency to use religion to the profit of a political regime or party.

Everyone knows how, in the mind of French Catholics of the old kingdom, "religion and royalty" were inseparably linked together. It seemed that one could not stand without the other and that the disappearance of royalty necessarily had to mean the decline of the Church.

But the Church has taken every opportunity to prove the fact that she does not mean to bind herself to any one political regime. Usually—in fact, whenever there is any way to do so—she gives her support to the existing government. This support does not mean that she approves the injustices and even the crimes by which the new government has been set up, that she recognizes the philosophy upon which the government is based, or that she gives her blessing to every act of the government. The support simply means that the Church is willing to live together peacefully with the existing powers and fulfill her spiritual mission in spite of the unjust limitations that are imposed upon her from time to time.

It goes without saying that the same thing is true of political parties. The ideal, from the Church's point of view, would be to see her prerogatives respected by all existing political parties so that Catholics could choose among them solely on the grounds of their different programs of temporal reform. This is the situation in England and America. In many European countries, however, political parties spring from a purely materialistic philosophy or pursue an anti-religious political policy. That is when it becomes necessary for Catholics to join together in powerful political organizations in defense of their religious interests.

This does not mean that the Church controls these parties, nor even that she approves all the points in their program. It is not the Church's place to approve them and she could not condemn them unless they ran counter to the moral law. Nor does it mean that the Church is inseparably bound up with the party. All it means is that the Church sees in these political groups the defenders of her spiritual mission upon earth.

Still, this situation is most regrettable. For there is always a great danger that those who do not reflect—and their name is legion—will identify the Church with politics, religion with one individual party; and the harm that such an identification can do the Church in the mind of the people is only too well known. It is a confusion, however, for which the Church can hardly be held responsible.

There is a further danger for certain political figures who put the defense of the Church's rights on their political program. They might tend to use religious energies for questionable temporal interests or to maintain a social regime that the Church cannot approve of in any way. Once again it is a question of religion being used in the furtherance of purely temporal interests.

In our days we frequently hear the expression "defense of Christian civilization." It is one of the most equivocal expressions of all because, once again, it runs the risk of identifying, in the public eye, two things that are really quite distinct: the actual state of a culture or civilization, which is something essentially provisional and changeable and perishable, and the Church or Christianity, which transcends every limitation of time and space and civilization.

Culture or civilization is something purely temporal. It consists in the development of the whole complexus of human activities, intellectual, technical, social, economic, political, and even moral. It is called Christian when it is inspired by the moral ideals that Christianity proposes as the only ones which correspond to the needs of human nature and permit its harmonious development. These ideals are, basically, the following: freedom of the human person in the face of false pretentions of any kind of purely human authority to control human souls; subordination of human passion and instinct to the clarity of human intelligence and the final sovereignty of human conscience; the rights of the family, one and indissoluble in the face of every other power, and especially the state; the fundamental equality of men and nations; the supremacy of justice over force and power; the commandment of love as a force capable of transforming justice and all social life; the subordination of man and human society to God the Creator.

A civilization is Christian in the measure that it respects these ideals and makes them the principles of its life, no matter what the other elements might be—material, intellectual, social, economic, political—that make up its essence; for these are essentially variable: they change from age to age and country to country. That is why it is wrong to speak of *the* Christian civilization. The correct way of describing it is to speak of a certain particular Christian civilization, or, better perhaps, of certain Christian elements verified in a particular civilization, which might be that of the Middle Ages or modern times, that of the Orient or the Occident, that of yesterday or that of tomorrow.

If we observed these necessary distinctions, we would see everything quite clearly. But most of the time one gets the impression that popular writers who use the expression "Christian civilization" tend to identify it on the one hand with Western civilization as it actually exists and all the elements that make it up, and on the other hand with the Catholic Church itself.

This forces the Church into a position where, quite against her real will, she turns into a defense of situations and interests which are purely temporal, or even into a support for social and economic frameworks that official Catholic teaching has disapproved of more than once.

And all this, once again, is just one more veil, in the eyes of men, to conceal the purity and transcendence of the Catholic Church and the real spiritual character of her mission upon earth.

Imperialism

The Church received from Christ the mission of handing down his message to all men. She cannot refuse to pass it down. She would be failing in her primary duty if she were not primarily occupied with constantly teaching the truth that she has received in sacred trust, defining it explicitly whenever it is necessary and defending its integrity and purity by denouncing every influence that tends to disfigure or corrupt it. Nor is it only the hierarchy that are bound by this duty. Every priest, every Christian who realizes the importance of his Faith, knows that he has, in union with the whole Church militant, the obligation of preaching Christ. "Woe to me if I do not spread the Gospel," he says in echo of St. Paul (I Cor. 9:16).

The question is how. The only way that is in conformity with the spirit of Christ is "bearing witness," that is, living the teachings of Christ as perfectly as possible yourself and then presenting them to other men with sincerity and faith, but without ever losing sight of the need for kindness and infinite respect for every human soul. Works first, and then words—kind, considerate words: that is the law.

A lack of these necessary qualities makes people fall into what we call religious imperialism. It consists primarily in the desire to spread the Christian truth and conquer souls for Christ by force rather than by love, by constraint rather than by an appeal to interior freedom.

It is definitely wrong to look for traces of imperialism in the Church. When the Church defines certain truths as contained in revelation, for instance, the infallibility of the pope, or the Immaculate Conception of the Blessed Virgin, and makes them articles of faith for us, when she vigorously condemns anyone who falsifies her doctrine, such as the Modernists some forty years ago, or those who spread a concept of human nature and destiny diametrically opposed to her own, such as the Communists of today, there are a thousand voices to rise and accuse her of dictating to individual consciences and spreading totalitarianism.

Yet it is quite obvious that this is the very heart of her mission and that it is a very strange abuse of the meaning of the word to call the Church totalitarian. Where are her police or her concentration camps? Her sanctions are purely spiritual. Everyone is perfectly free to disobey and go his own way. But if he wants to remain a Christian, then he has to be the kind of Christian Christ wants him to be, one who listens to the Church.

Now, this does not mean that there have never been, throughout the course of history, examples of moral and even physical constraint, and we should be willing to admit it quite frankly. There are pages in the history of the evangelization and defense of Christianity whose memory still leaves the Christian conscience in a state of real distress and proves to be a very serious check on the Church's apostolate in the modern world. There are forced conversions, the Inquisition, and certain episodes in the religious wars, such as the massacre of St. Bartholomew's night.

We know the type of shaded judgment that is responsible for digging up these abuses and understanding the situations only imperfectly, and we are not unfamiliar with the role played by politics and secular powers in these acts of violence. But this cannot prevent us from admitting that Christians were the ones responsible for these past appeals to force. And that is enough to keep certain men from recognizing the true import of Catholicism.

Another fact to be regretted is that the tone of much Catholic polemics with Christian dissidents has not always been conspicuous for its fraternal charity. The strong language can be explained, of course, by the impetuosity of certain churchmen's temper, by their clear understanding of the need to protect the truth, and frequently by the violence and cunning and obstinacy of their adversaries. But, still, it would have been far preferable to "win souls in patience" (Lk. 21:19) and to "preach the word in season, out of season, reprove, entreat, rebuke with all patience and teaching" (II Tim. 4:2), to have an unyielding spirit but a heart of lasting tenderness.

A great debate has recently begun among Catholic circles. Should the work of Christian evangelization be conceived as propaganda or as an apostolate? But that is a poor way to state the dilemma. The Christian apostolate will always have two aspects, one interior and the other exterior. What it really is, is an "incarnate" apostolate, working among men of flesh and blood, in a world in which matter has a role to play. That is why the apostolate always has to have a certain degree of organization, group effort, writing, public addresses, outward show, in a word, everything that we usually call propaganda. It is a sort of liturgy for the apostolate. For the Christian—the young Christian above all—it is encouragement and comfort. For the non-Christian it is a call, the "Gospel preached from the roof-tops" (Lk. 12:3.)

It goes without saying that this is only one aspect of the Christian apostolate. It is the body, if you will. And if the propaganda apostolate were not animated by the apostolate of love and example, it would certainly lead straight towards religious imperialism. Since this unfortunate result has not been avoided as carefully as it should have been in the past, the stress of the leaders of today's apostolate is all the more emphatically upon the spiritual.

Love is the soul of every apostolate. Propaganda alone treats men like mere numbers, anonymous beings who have to be classified. But love sees every man as a unique and personal being in whose presence it experiences a deep emotional response, a sacred stirring.

Propaganda is out for numbers; it is fond of statistics; its whole aim is gaining followers. Love is interested primarily in spiritual values. It wants to see every man become a Christian, but only by his own personal act of sincere adherence to Christ.

Propaganda is taken up with the outside; it tries to strike the imagination and the senses; it is aimed at the less spiritual elements of man. It tries to take men's souls by sentiment and feeling, by a sort of collective hypnosis. It tends, unless it is carefully controlled, to achieve this adherence to Christ by less single-purposed means which play down the free and conscious self-deliberation of the human person.

The apostolate of love is vitally interested in snatching human souls out of their inertia and putting them on the road towards God, in furnishing them with strength and light, if they are willing to accept. But it is scrupulously on guard not to force souls, not to substitute itself in the place of the decisions upon which everything depends and which they must make for themselves, to wait, prayerfully, for the moment of grace.

The Church is following a purely spiritual mission. In this sense, the Kingdom towards which she is working is not of this world. But she works out this Kingdom through men and in the midst of men. That is why she is also a body, a visible society. Christ has given her a visible hierarchy through which she enters into contact with the world in order to sanctify the world. Always with the same basic religious goal in view, the Church has, in the course of time, developed policies and procedures which were adapted to different epochs and different lands. And in this respect she has proceeded even further into the world, into the temporal. Among other things, she has always striven to assure that the economic, social, and political structures of secular society be in accord with the demands of justice on the one hand, and on the other hand that they be equally favorable to the furtherance of her spiritual mission.

That is the Church's right. But it is easy to see how delicate and dangerous the exercise of this right can become. As a matter of fact, under the pretext of protecting religion or furthering the spread of Christianity, spiritual authority can easily begin to interfere directly with temporal affairs; it can become itself a temporal power; it can protect or promote the spiritual in such a way as completely to lose sight of certain legitimate temporal obligations and thus expose itself to faults against the virtue of justice; it can exploit religion to the advantage of purely temporal ends or in the interests of certain social classes who would like to identify their lot with that of the Church; it can grow into part of some tottering social or political structures and then defend them as if Christianity itself depended upon their very existence.

Everyone is familiar with the dangers of what is called clericalism. There is a good deal of abuse in the application of the word. Certain people accuse the spiritual authority of clericalism every time it has to intervene in problems that also touch upon temporal interests. No matter how obvious it is that the Church authorities are acting solely in the best interests of religion, their adversaries—and sometimes some of her own members —do not take the trouble to distinguish. That is the reason for the summary and unjust criticisms that we shall have to bear with as long as there are people in this world to criticize.

But this is no reason to forget the real danger involved in compromising the purity of spiritual authority or being too deeply interested in the temporal structure of society. The problem is a delicate one for anyone who takes the time to face it with impartiality. It is related to the more basic problem of what means are to be employed in the apostolate, "wealthy" means or "poor" means.

"Wealthy" means are numbers, money, complex organization, projects, and, above all, the support of political powers. Clearly they are not intrinsically wrong, and to repudiate them all would be proof of a sort of disincarnate supernaturalism. But it is true that they belong to the class of earthly riches and, on that account, have to be used with great prudence and selflessness. They have to be constantly "exorcised" in order not to turn into snares set by the devil.

"Poor" means are the forces of an evangelical order, the living energy of religion itself: faith, sincerity, purity, detachment, truth, humility, penance, mercy, charity.

It goes without saying that these "poor" means are the primary requisites. Separated from them, the others, the "wealthy" means, can succeed only in confusing the spiritual element and concealing the real meaning of religion. This is something the Christian must never forget. Christianity will be saved only by Christianity, faith only by faith, the Church only by the Church.

Conclusion

It would be well to repeat here that the disfigurations of true Christianity, whose primary manifestations we have just considered, are absolutely inevitable in a world of space and time, where the divine and the human are intimately bound together. They always infect human institutions and human persons to some degree, and now and then they do real damage.

Pure religion is reserved for eternity. Here below there is always a limit towards which the Church, religious institutions, and individuals must aim without growing weary.

The disfigurations which constantly threaten the purity and transcendence of the Christian religion make up the raw material for the constant efforts at reflection and reform that characterize not only the Church at large but each individual Christian within her ranks.

CHAPTER V

Religious and Supernatural Certitude— Divine Faith

U P TO NOW we have been devoting our effort to the task of freeing the problem of religion from everything that threatens to conceal it and give rise to an initial, unequivocal refusal even to consider its challenge.

We know what constitutes the essence of religion. We also know the place it deserves in the whole scheme of human activities, how it crowns and transfigures and eternalizes all of life. We have a very exact knowledge of the Christian mystery and the response that man is called to make. We have attempted to purify Christian revelation and the Christian religion[1] from the principal disfigurations to which they are subject in the eyes of men. We have tried to present them authentically, as they really are.

But there is one question of the utmost importance still to be discussed.

Is the Christian mystery true?[2]

Is it true not only that God exists but that he has entered into history in a manner that surpasses the exigencies and possibilities of nature, in order to communicate his own inmost life to men, from the dawn of history in an original revelation, which was followed—despite the refusal of men—by the Mosaic and Jewish revelations, then by the revelation of the Son of God made man, Christ, who continues his revelation in this world through the Catholic Church? Is all this true?

The Christian mystery is not presented as a rich array of isolated facts from which we are invited to choose according to our liking, accepting whatever falls in with our own particular temperament and rejecting all the rest.[3] It makes up a unified whole which ranges through the course of human history, transcending, leaving its mark from one end to the other.

This, finally, is the problem we have to solve: How can we be sure that the Christian mystery really comes from God? Or, better, how can we be sure that the Christian mystery is really God himself coming to us, offering himself to us, giving himself to us, through the prophets, in Christ, in the Church? Our individual response to this gift, that is, our religion, our communion with God, will not be valid unless this gift of God is real. How can we find out if it is real?

The answer to this question must not be oversimplified. We know that it is real with a certitude of a very special nature, above and beyond all other forms of knowledge. We call it faith, divine faith, supernatural religious certitude. It is not like any other certitude.

I. The Different Kinds of Certitude

In treating the subject of human knowledge and human certitude, insofar as we can have either one, there is a whole world of prejudices and errors to be done away with first. The biggest single factor responsible for this condition is the spirit of positivism which poisoned the end of the last century and which, despite the efforts of a host of brilliant philosophers and intellectuals, still persists in contaminating a good many minds who otherwise show every evidence of sincere good will.

It is no exaggeration to say that a great number of unbelievers and hesitaters, who now think that they have to remain steadfast in their agnosticism out of a motive of sincerity to themselves, would gladly take the road that leads towards faith if they had a more complete and profound understanding of the office and operation of human intelligence. The role of the intellect in quest of reality is a vital problem.

[178]

A. *The Diversity of Reality—Ways of Access to Reality*

The greatest drawback upon the contemporary mind in its quest for reality is the positivistic preconception which postulates that only one road is open to man in his search, that of positive and experimental science, which takes sense experience as its point of departure. "Whatever is beyond the limits of positive science," Littré liked to say, "is inacessible to the human mind."

This point of view makes man a prisoner within the world of matter, and his very existence is brutally reduced to the material dimensions of time and space. All nature protests against such an arbitrary limitation, and by his very thought and life man constantly gives the lie to this idea of material barriers within which the positivist tries to keep him prisoner.

Human intelligence is quite readily capable of going beyond matter. It is endowed with a great variety of potentialities. It is capable of carrying out the most diverse functions in order to arrive at the most diverse truths and realities. It can serve as the instrument of specifically distinct types of knowledge and certitude which have nothing in common with each other.

When man gives himself over to the free play of all his intellectual potentialities, or, better still, when he gives rise to their free play by creating and establishing within himself the interior conditions that allow each of his intellectual keyboards to sound out with a mounting depth and beauty, that is when he sees new and different planes of reality opening before his startled eyes, worlds which were closed to him before. It was a personal experience of this nature that Faraday was describing when he said that the idea of God and respect for God comes into his mind by channels which are just as sure as those that lead him to truths of the physical order.[4]

Just as sure, just as certain: but totally different.

For his part, St. Thomas has this profoundly wise comment to make. "It is the mark of a well-schooled mind not to seek any other certitude in a given thing than that which the nature of the thing can furnish."[5]

There are basically five kinds of certitude, corresponding to five different levels of reality.

1. Positive Certitude

Sight and the other senses put us into direct contact with the material world. That is what we call sense experience. Without any real effort on our part, sense experience provides us with a large body of empirical knowledge which is very useful for the conduct of our life. Bodies fall; fire burns; water quenches thirst.

On the basis of sense experience, human intelligence consciously and systematically sets about developing a more and more perfect knowledge of matter. This leads to the formation of the so-called positive sciences, the sciences of phenomena. In their research these sciences proceed according to different principles. Sometimes they make use of analysis, for example, to determine the basic composition of a molecule of water. Sometimes they stress simple repetition of the same phenomenon. Finally they discover some law: bodies attract each other in direct proportion to their relative masses and in indirect proportion to the square of the distances between them. Sometimes, finally, they proceed by means of deduction. For instance, if they verify an anomaly in the trajectory of two known planets, they can deduce—without even using their telescope—the presence of a new star in that section of the sky.

The world arrived at by the positive sciences is the world of matter, the world of quantity. It lends itself to exact measure and it is the favorite scientific framework for mathematics, which is called into service again and again to express and symbolize scientific discoveries.

That these sciences furnish us with certitude is a fact too obvious for anyone to deny. Even if it were not obvious, there would be the added evidence of their practical success in many technical projects. In fact, it is this very success that is a source of danger.

They tend to monopolize the use of the word *science*. "Here," they tell us, "you have scientific certitude." What they mean is that everywhere else we have only non-scientific and on that account irrational and uncertain knowledge. "Here," they tell us, "you have the exact sciences." And the underlying argument again is that everywhere else we arrive only at knowledge that is inexact. Our modern world is filled with men who have faith only in the positive sciences and nothing but contempt for every other kind of knowledge.

2. Moral Certitude

In common everyday language, when someone says he is morally certain of anything, he means that he is not completely sure but that the thing in question is more than just probable. He means that he has a strong opinion, not certitude.

The moral certitude that we are speaking of here is a real certitude. It is a certitude which has as its object the moral world, the moral values, the general and particular laws that human activity has to follow in order to pursue its true human vocation. It is a question of the qualities that have to be verified in our free acts to make them correspond to the basic exigencies of our nature and our relations with the world, other men, and God.

Sometimes it is a question of first principles: we must do good and avoid evil. Sometimes it is a particular principle: truth is something good, falsehood is something evil. Sometimes it is a concrete act: for this particular person it is wrong to see this particular film and good to stay away from it.

There is real certitude in a great many cases.[6] But it is a certitude of an entirely different order from the positive certitude offered by the world of the physical and chemical sciences.

There are many ways of arriving at this kind of certitude. By moral intuition or moral sense, by reflection, by reasoning, even

[181]

by observing human conduct and the individual and social consequences of human acts.

3. METAPHYSICAL CERTITUDE

Sense experience and positive science leave unsolved a great number of problems that all men are interested in, to a greater or lesser degree, and which all men make an attempt to answer for themselves, with a greater or lesser degree of consciousness.

It is not hard to distinguish, in our world, the existence of purely material beings and of living beings. What is the nature of the physical world and what is the nature of life?

It is just as easy to discover that visible things are situated in a given section of space at a given moment of time. What is the nature of space and time?

The man of science formulates physical, biological, and psychological laws and he comes up with scientific theories. But what do his laws mean? And what is the value of his theories?

Centering his attention upon himself, man sees a great many things which belong to the world of sense and which define his position in time and space. But at the same time that he thinks of time and space he perceives himself, and thus he is above time and space. He realizes that there is something within him that make him identical with what he was yesterday, something, consequently, that is not subject to time and space. That is a clear indication that there is something more than matter in his make-up, that he is at once material and spiritual, body and soul, on the horizon of time and eternity.

Man sees a great many things in the world. He knows how to study their physical properties. Instinctively, he compares and classifies them and sets up a hierarchy among them, a scale of values. But what is at the basis of this scale?

Man is, he lives; other things are and live; then we all disappear, we die. What does this mean? Does everything have one common source? Is everything moving towards one common goal? Is there any meaning in things?

The world exists, but it is clearly something finite, no matter how immense it seems to be. It is contingent: it did not have to exist, or it could exist differently; clearly it is not absolutely necessary. It is perpetual evolution, constant becoming. Can something like that exist of itself or does it demand another being which is neither finite nor contingent nor changing?

All these questions have been discussed by men either consciously or unconsciously. They cannot be answered by the positive sciences. Only philosophy, or more properly metaphysics, can give the answer.

In metaphysics, human intelligence is based—consciously or unconsciously—upon what are called first principles, that is, truths whose existence is so obvious to human reason that in denying them human reason would be denying itself. There is, for example, the principle of identity: it is impossible for a thing both to be and not to be at the same time in the same respect. There is the principle of sufficient reason: everything that is has to have a reason for being. Finally, there is the principle of causality: everything that exists has to have a cause to produce it.

Even though they cannot be verified by sense and scientific experience, these principles are absolutely certain.

Armed with them, human intelligence is capable of discovering with real certitude the existence of immaterial realities of the greatest importance for the conduct of life: the existence of the soul, the existence of an absolute and transcendent reality, God. It can also learn to understand what things are in themselves, as opposed to their outward appearances, to discover the properties that are common to all things, finally to learn the characteristics of being as such. In the same way, it can become familiar with the respective worth of things and set up a scale of values.

Throughout this whole process, human intelligence proceeds by intuition properly so called, as, for example, when it is engaged in grasping the reality of the fundamental ego;[7] or by intuition improperly so called, as, for example, when it seizes upon a sign or a network of signs and passes, almost without realizing it, to the knowledge of an invisible reality; or by a strict and exacting process of reasoning.

4. Historical Certitude

There is still another order of reality, the series of events and facts whose logical progression makes up the science of history. We cannot arrive at a knowledge of these happenings by experience or by positive science or by personal intuition or by the power of reason.

And still we can have perfect certitude of very many of them, for example, the existence of Julius Caesar and the broader outlines of his Gallic wars.

These considerations force us to admit that there is some other kind of certitude, a type entirely different from those we have been discussing.

The basis for this certitude is the testimony of an authority whom we judge worthy of faith. It is certitude based on natural faith or human faith. We called it historical certitude.

5. Supernatural Religious Certitude—Divine Faith

We said above that human reason can, by its own power, arrive at the knowledge of God. This natural certitude of God's existence is metaphysical certitude. The same can be said of the truths upon which the organization of natural religion is based: spirituality, freedom, individual responsibility.

But if God has communicated himself to humanity in a revelation and gift which surpass the exigencies and possibilities of our nature; in other words, if the Christian mystery is true, then it is no longer by the unaided force of natural reason that we are to discover God and learn to recognize his truth.

Knowledge has to be of the same order as the thing known. Here the object, the fact to be contacted, met with, recognized, verified, is a supernatural visit of God to humanity. That means that our knowledge of the fact has to be supernatural as well.

[184]

The certitude with which we welcome the Christian mystery has to be a certitude which not only calls human intelligence and will into play, but also, above and beyond the natural, calls for a special active participation by God.

This is a certitude which is specifically different from all the other types of certitude we have discussed. It is supernatural religious certitude, or the certitude of divine faith. Any attempt to reduce it to one of the other lesser kinds of certitude is like turning into a dead-end street.

There is a great temptation for many men to make divine faith equal to historical faith, purely human faith. Is the Christian mystery not inscribed upon history? Does it not have a history all its own, overlapping the whole natural history of the human race?

Certainly it does. But it is not enough to learn to know it only in its historical appearances and development. It is necessary to see these events as the supernatural presence and activity of God. It is not a question of learning whether a man called Jesus ever really existed. It is a question of learning if he was really the ambassador of God and God himself. It is not a question of knowing whether the Catholic Church exists. We can see her intimately bound up with every event in history for the last twenty centuries. What we have to find out is rather if it is true, as Catholics claim, that the Church is vitally bound to the resurrected and glorious Christ and that she has the right to play the role of an efficacious instrument in the hands of the living Redeemer.

There is no doubt about the fact that the history of revelation, of Christ and the Church, is bound to have a lively interest for us. It is, after all, in this attention to historical reality that we first discover the clear signs that make us look upon Christ and His Church as transcending history, supernatural, divine. But when we kneel down to proclaim that Christ is the Son of God and that the Catholic Church is Christ spread throughout the world and communicated to all men, then we have left behind the domain of history in order to enter that of the supernatural. We have gone beyond historical faith in order to enter into divine faith.

B. *Intuitive, Quasi-Intuitive, and Discursive Certitude*

There is a second error against which we have to warn the modern mind. It consists in a tendency to demand, always and above all else, a conscious and clearly cogent reasoning process before admitting the legitimacy of any certitude. According to this way of looking at things, we should suspect and refuse any affirmation which cannot be verified, in our own eyes and in the eyes of the whole world, by reasons which are distinct and logically conclusive and perfectly communicable to every other person.

Once again, this is a process that tends to clip the wings of our mind and set undue restrictions upon the potentialities with which nature has provided our intelligence.

1. Intuitive Knowledge

The word *intuition* is used to express many different meanings. We have already seen how Bergson understands it. For him, intuition is that type of intellectual sympathy by which we make our way into the interior of an object in order to fall in with whatever in that object is unique and, for that reason, incapable of being expressed.[8] It is equivalent to what we mean by communion.

But currently the term *intuition* is being used to designate a special kind of knowledge. Sometimes it refers to the knowledge of an evident truth, an axiom, a postulate, a first principle which determines the whole of intellectual life, such as the metaphysical principles quoted above (identity, sufficient reason, causality), or determines the basic direction of the moral life, such as the principle that we should do good and avoid evil. These truths do not have to be demonstrated. And for that matter, they could not even be demonstrated without begging the question, without using them to prove themselves.[9] They are the object of *intellectual intuition*.

Further objects of intuition on our part are the things that make up the visible world and the events that take place before our eyes. This is *sense intuition*. And in a similar manner, as we said in the first chapter, it is through intuition that we become conscious of our personal existence and our basic personality. In that category we speak of *spiritual or metaphysical intuition*.

There is still another type of intuition, the kind we meet with in the case of mystics. Mystics have an immediate experience of God, even though it is an obscure experience without the benefit of discursive reasoning and concepts. They "see" God, not, of course, the way we shall see him in the beatific vision; but they have a direct knowledge of God, analogous to the knowledge we have through our eyes, our ears, our sense of touch and taste and smell. This kind of knowledge is aptly termed *mystical intuition*.

2. QUASI-INTUITIVE KNOWLEDGE: KNOWLEDGE THROUGH SIGNS

There is one other kind of knowledge that we all make use of without realizing it, and it is important to make a careful examination of it because it will be of great importance to us in the analysis of faith. It is knowledge by means of signs.

I see smoke coming out of a chimney. No doubt there is a fire that is causing this smoke. In the walls of some primeval cave I come upon a crude sketch representing a reindeer. No doubt there were men living in that cave at some time. In these cases, I needed only one sign in order to be certain of some truth that I cannot see here and now.

In many other cases, one single sign is not enough: there have to be several of them before the mind arrives at certitude.

Take the case of a man whose acquaintance I make on the occasion of a long voyage. I discover one day that he has told another person the exact opposite of what he has told me. I see him somewhere, and the next day he positively denies that he was there. I loan him a map and, when I ask for it back, he denies ever having borrowed it. Finally, he has promised to get a book for me and, when I ask him for it, he acts astonished and cannot seem to recall the promise. Four separate signs: and they combine to form a sort of certitude in my mind. This man is flighty, forgetful, perhaps disloyal. At any rate, he is not the kind of man that I can count on.

A crime has been committed. The detective arrives. He finds cigarette ashes from a certain brand of cigarettes, a piece of paper typed on a certain make of machine, an odd shaped cap, a shoelace. He evaluates his findings immediately and makes inquiries around the house. He discovers that the evidence all points to one particular person. Perhaps it is still too early to decide anything definite. Then the detective uncovers one or two more pieces of evidence that point to the selfsame individual, even more clearly than the first evidence. And there is no more room for doubt: he has the guilty party.

Then there is the historian who is trained and practiced in what is known as historical criticism. He is examining twelve books which seem to be written by twelve different people, but which show remarkable similarities in content and style. He carries his research to the very bottom of the problem and lines up all the evidence (in content and style) that betrays similarity. Then he can conclude with real certainty that there is really only one author writing under twelve pseudonyms. And then he begins to make a careful reading of an author whose name is known and once again he comes upon certain analogies in thought and style between the known author and the author writing under twelve pseudonyms. He redoubles his attention and follows out his research until he can arrive at the safe and certain conclusion that this is the author who used the twelve pseudonyms.

It is important to realize that, in the cases cited above, each piece of evidence, taken by itself, was not enough to give rise to certitude; for it could always be interpreted differently. For example, it would have been wrong for me to conclude, on the basis of one simple act of forgetfulness, that my travelling companion was "congenitally" forgetful. One individual case might be a pure accident. It is the linking of evidence that makes for certainty.

The objection is often made against this method of procedure that certitude cannot result from an accumulation of probabilities. Probabilities, some people say, can never give rise to anything more than a larger probability. They can never lead to certitude.

This line of reasoning is not quite exact. As a matter of fact, when there is a sufficient weight of evidence, we can legitimately pass over to the realm of certitude, in virtue of the principle of sufficient reason. This means that the only sufficient reason for such complete unanimity in the evidence is the truth of the conclusion to which the individual pieces of evidence, each in its own manner and degree of probability, all bear witness.[10]

In the light of the above, it is easy to see that knowledge by means of signs is a true form of reasoning, and not an intuition in the proper sense of the word. It is an inductive reasoning process which proceeds from a number of particular observations towards the one conclusion that is common to them all.

And still it cannot be denied that in this kind of research the intuitive faculties of the mind do have a big role to play. It is, after all, not really a question of verifying the material existence of some particular piece of evidence, but rather of grasping that object as evidence, as a sign, as bearing upon the thing towards which it points. There has to be a special mental attention for this, a sort of instinct, a flair, something that we frequently call the power of intuition.

Once again, in the actual act of passing beyond the collected evidence to the conclusion towards which it leads, the mind functions with one mighty leap. We call it discovery or even vision, intuition, because of the suddenness and speed with which, at a given moment in the inductive process, the mind grasps the message hidden within the evidence.

That is why it is legitimate to speak of knowledge by means

[189]

of signs as quasi-intuitive knowledge. It actually has something in common both with intuition properly so called and with discursive reasoning.

It is by combining, in a sudden flash of insight, all the slowly gathered evidence of the material signs, that the mind leaps to the necessary conclusion. This very fact explains why this type of certitude is hard to communicate, why sometimes it simply cannot be communicated. It does little good to run through a long list of evidence that has been uncovered, point for point. First of all, it may be that the person to whom we are trying to explain our reasoning is not "attuned" to this kind of thing. He may understand what we are explaining to him as individual points; but he does not grasp their value as evidence, as signs. He is something like a man who does not know Hebrew trying to puzzle out the meaning of a text written in Hebrew. He can make out letters and words; but he does not know what they mean. It is even more difficult for a person to communicate to another mind the flash of insight in which his own mind gathers all the evidence and synthesizes it into a proof. It is a strictly personal operation, and it can easily happen that another person is entirely unaware of the very existence of something that almost cries out loud for me.

There is another phenomenon that is interesting to observe. When I want to make a clear outline of all the evidence that has led me to make a certain conclusion, either to communicate it to someone else or to reorganize it in my own mind, I am forced to divide it and express it piece by piece. Thus I myself lose sight of the original intuition that made me grasp the proving force of each piece of evidence and even more so of the flash of insight by which I suddenly organized all the pieces of evidence into one coherent argument. And my position becomes less sure in my own eyes. It may happen that my conviction grows less, giving rise to hesitation and doubt.

In certain cases doubts can be an invitation to more thorough research. In other cases they are entirely without foundation, unreasonable, and they owe their existence to the psychological law analyzed above, the gradual dissolution to which we subject the evidential value of signs by attempting to analyze and express them and consider them apart from each other. In order to escape these doubts, which are not infrequent in human thinking, and in order to keep from falling into a morbid state of hesitation, we only have to cultivate within our minds the same interior dispositions which made the original insight possible. Or else we can banish all doubts by a resolute act of the will.

3. Knowledge by Means of Reasoning

Quasi-intuitive knowledge already has a touch of reasoning about it. It is built up to a large degree upon the process of induction, which consists in gathering particular observations together and drawing a general law from the combined evidence.

But there is another form of reasoning that is often used, the deductive process. Deductive reasoning consists in passing from a general principle to a particular conclusion by means of one or several other propositions which make the conclusion legitimate in virtue of the laws of logic. For example: an essential attribute of human nature is free will; Christ was a man; therefore Christ had a free human will.

No matter whether it is inductive or deductive, reasoning always points back to what we call a discursive operation of reason. In the discursive process the reason proceeds—briefly—from one fact or idea to another fact or another idea, and at the end of its course it has become enriched with new knowledge.

Important Remark

Many people think that it is impossible to arrive at real, genuine certitude by any means other than the conscious progress of rational intelligence.

This is not at all true. The mind of man is constantly in action. So is every other part of man, for that matter. Man is constantly working out new concepts, formulating new judgments, constructing new lines of reasoning. And all this work remains entirely unconscious most of the time. Or, at the very most, there is a marginal consciousness from time to time. In order to acquire a clear and direct consciousness, there has to be some reflection upon what is taking place within a person and within a person's thought. This happens only rarely.

These remarks are concerned primarily with intuitive knowledge, but they are also valid for discursive reasoning properly so called. Man is a reasoning machine. He reasons without knowing that he is reasoning.[11]

The best thing for man to do is to reason systematically and consciously. That is the way that all the sciences proceed. But it is a mistake to suppose that the surest reasoning is always and everywhere the one that we are most conscious of in our minds. In many realms of human effort—the exact sciences not excepted—there are moments of "distraction" and repose in which important discoveries are made, thanks to what Newman calls the "sense of inference," the "illative sense," by which he means a swift and subtle and subconscious dialectical process.

In every intellectual research, no matter what it is—whether it is a question of the positive sciences, artistic or literary creation, or the moral and religious world—the ideal would be to alternate moments of systematic reflection with moments of passive attention and watchfulness. The first process increases our world of particular knowledge. The second gives our minds time to order and synthesize and strike out suddenly beyond the fragmentary data of the evidence to arrive at the rich discoveries and insights that are the fruit of genius.

C. *Experienced Certitude and Reflex Certitude*

The observations we have just made lead us to a further consideration, the distinction that should be drawn between experienced certitude and reflex or reasoned certitude.

Granted that there is what we might call a constant stream

of spontaneous intuition and unconscious reasoning in our life, we are in possession of a considerable quantity of knowledge without really knowing that we possess it. This knowledge might concern the total and eternal destiny of our personality or, again, it might concern the most insignificant problems of everyday life. This knowledge underlies our behavior, it helps determine our conduct, it inspires our life, it is incorporated into our living in such a way that we are not conscious of its presence, without our thinking about it or formulating it or trying to prove its validity.[12] For example, a child readily understands the way it has to act in order to receive a favor from someone;[13] and every man, even though many deny it, habitually acts like a free being and usually resents being treated as irresponsible. This is an example of what we call experienced certitude.

It is not always an easy task to discover the various paths along which these certitudes have penetrated into our minds. Still, it is only natural for a man to make every conceivable effort because these certitudes are faced by many obstacles and are often called into question.

As a matter of fact, every one is inclined to try to justify his conduct in the eyes of other people and to give reasons for everything he does. When there is question of really important knowledge, knowledge that is of interest to the whole man and his destiny (for example, when there is question of human freedom[14] and the existence of God), men try to make others share their own personal convictions. This gives rise to an analysis of the spontaneous, rapid, subtle, subconscious process through which this knowledge has made its way into our minds. We try to discover each separate link in the chain and to illumine each individual step of our progress with a flash of intuitive insight by our *inferential sense*.

This is how we arrive at clear statements, which we make use of to argue back and forth with each other according to the terms of a rigorous logic. We build up arguments. We set up a solid foundation of demonstrations. That is the source of reflex

certitude, worked-out certitude. It is usually the work of philosophers and intellectuals. But there is not a single man who does
not give himself over, at least summarily, to some such sort of
dialectical exercise in the course of his life.

We have already mentioned that all this work of synthesis
and reason corresponds to a deep-seated natural need in the
human mind. It is natural for man to want an insight into his
existence and into the principles which govern his conduct. It is
natural for man to apply himself to verify rationally his basic
intuitions and the certitudes he has experienced. It is natural for
man to try to justify his behavior, especially in its most decisive
and most essential areas, in everything that concerns the primary
problem of human existence. It is natural for man to communicate these data of self-justification to other persons in an intelligible manner in order to show them the rational character of his
own conduct and to make them share his own concept of life.
If, for example, I believe in the existence of free will and the
reality of God, it is normal for me to try to prove these affirmations by an argument that is well reasoned and communicable
to other minds.

It goes without saying that the value of these rational arguments will vary according to the dialectical progress of the men
who work them out. Some will necessarily be more successful
than others.

It is just as certain that the demonstrations worked out in this
manner all contain less than the certitude that was experienced.
They are clearer certainly, and they can be cast into intelligible
formularies. But they never have the density, the "sap," the richness of a certitude that has been personally experienced.
"Thought-out" is never more than a harvesting from the tree
of "experienced," and "clear" is never more than a gleaning in
the fields of "felt" and "lived." Experienced certitude necessarily
goes deeper than reasoned certitude. The propositions I develop
and string together in order to prove free will or the existence
of God are incapable of adequately expressing the real live certi-

tude that I have of these truths in view of some constant spiritual intuition, even if it is only marginal or through some subconscious inference.

This leaves us open to many errors.

It happens not infrequently that our proof seems weak, or even entirely without validity, to someone who nonetheless shares our basic convictions. His analysis of the problem does not correspond to ours. Differences in race (Oriental, Occidental), differences in mental formation (scientific, metaphysical), differences in intellectual temperament (discursive, intuitive), or finally even differences in intelligence (more subtle, less subtle) are often at the root of misunderstandings and misconceptions. We do not really enter into the reasoning that the other person is proposing. These differences, which can turn into real oppositions, cannot, naturally, have any real effect on the validity of the basic certitude which we have both experienced and which we actually share with each other.

It is not hard to see how the same logical arguments that prove a truth for us can utterly fail to produce an effect on another person's mind, simply because that person denies, at least speculatively, the truths that we are trying to communicate to him. It is not at all rare for unbelievers, before their conversion, to consider the proofs for the existence of God as pure verbal juggling. But once God is discovered by the mysterious ways of the spirit, these same proofs take on a different light. Either they are quite useless, because they are no longer needed; or else they are clear and evident, because now they have been illuminated by a deep and fundamental certitude, though not yet reflex.

Sometimes it happens that the person with whom we are speaking, even though he continues to deny our truths speculatively, nonetheless experiences them more or less intensely in his daily behavior. But when either of us makes any attempt to put them into the form of a proof, he is frightened at the lack of proportion, the poverty, the inadequacy of all the concepts and propositions he lines up and all the words he is forced to use in order to express himself. Thus he is forced to stick to his speculative denial of the truth unless he wants to come to grips with it in full earnest. But it is still a truth that he lives practically in his everyday life.

Thus it is possible that some sincere unbelievers reject God speculatively because the only image of God that they can produce seems anthropomorphic to them and every demonstration of his existence that they hear seems insufficient to prove it to them. But at the same time it is quite possible—and this is a secret that only God understands—that this speculative refusal in no way prevents them from submitting their whole life, in practice, to the same reality of God which they call by other names, such as Duty, Truth, Justice, Goodness. Under these abstract names they recognize, in a confused way, what Maritain refers to as the "absolutely good reality which deserves all love and is capable of saving our life." What actually happens, then, is that they refuse a false, anthropomorphic God and adore the one true God their whole life long, without really knowing it.

Another very typical example is the case of free will. Bergson is right when he affirms that "every definition of freedom is a step towards determinism." And this is why. The intimate relation existing between me and the world—which makes up my freedom—can never become distorted, because it is beyond space and time. But every definition tends to dissect and congeal this spiritual and living relationship. What it tries to express, it ends by destroying. Bergson does not conclude from this that our will is not free. Quite the contrary. But he does conclude that we have to keep in close contact with the certitude we experience, with what he calls the "immediate data of consciousness," if we want to safeguard freedom and really understand what it is. The pure rationalist who is unaware of this profound law which governs the activity of the human mind, would end up denying free will. But once again this denial would be purely speculative most of the time. The most hard-boiled brand of determinism cannot help shouting out the existence of freedom in everything it does. "We can invoke all the philosophical systems we want to," says Jung, "but the feeling and consciousness of freedom will always be present in the human heart, indestructible, laughing at all the systems that deny it, the first principle of human nature."

These observations naturally lead us to a practical conclusion that we shall have to recall continually when we speak of supernatural religious certitude, the certitude of faith.

In every domain, even when it is only a question of natural science, but especially when it is a question of sounding the foundations that touch upon our basic personality and our whole human destiny, it is important for the thinker or the philosopher to steep himself again and again in the certitude of experience, the certitude of his original intuition. There has to be a continual come and go between living experience and the concepts that translate it, between pre-reflex knowledge and rational knowledge.

As we have already seen, in speaking of communion, this come and go is a source of great benefit for each party. Not only that, but it also sets up a safeguard. It keeps them both from losing their way. In the life of knowledge and certitude it is necessary to let *Animus* be discursive sometimes and to let *Anima* sing her song at other times. Progress in knowledge, according to Edward Le Roy, means a sort of oscillating rhythm, dual energy, reciprocal propulsion, alternating between intuitive concentration and mental relaxation.[15]

D. *Speculative Certitude and Practical Certitude*

There is one final difference to be discussed in the field of certitude, the difference between purely speculative certitude and certitude that leads to action, practical certitude.

Simple experience proves that among the many questions which occupy our attention there are some which are of interest only to our speculative reason: such questions, for example, as the distance from the earth to Sirius, the date of Caesar's birth, the author of *The Imitation of Christ*. In order to answer them, all we need is reason, intelligence in its purely speculative capacity. None of the answers produces any effect upon my life.

That is, however, no longer true when we are considering questions which are of profound interest for the orientation of our life, even if only the temporal and earthly sphere of living comes into play: for example, when we have to decide upon a state of life (religious or lay) or a profession, or when we are trying to select a husband or wife. All these problems cannot be worked out like so many algebraic equations. Personal elements come into play and their role is of the greatest importance: grace, personal capability, love. Moreover, these are questions whose solution will produce lasting effects upon the whole human person.

This is all the more true, then, of questions which are of interest to the totality of my existence and destiny, questions which concern suffering, spirituality, freedom, immortality, the truth of the Christian mystery. These questions do not only arouse my intellectual curiosity, they reach deep into the very foundations of my being. Their solution involves the basic and decisive orientation of my existence. In solving them, intelligence is no longer simply speculative. It is more like a man who is waiting for a verdict—life or death. It is like being on the verge of a total commitment to action, or else a total refusal to act, with everything in life depending upon the answer.

That is the basic reason why such vital questions can never be solved by a purely rational effort. They demand the undivided attention of the whole person.

Gabriel Marcel, with good reason, calls questions of this second kind *mysteries,* whereas questions of the first kind are called merely problems. A problem, according to him, is a dilemma which can be got around without the person who is confronted by the problem being part of the solution himself. A mystery, on the other hand, is a problem which a person cannot even pose without realizing that he is caught squarely in the middle of it, a problem that a person cannot hope to solve without figuring himself personally into the solution.

One of the most striking examples is the problem of suffering. As long as it is treated as a purely speculative problem, there can be only partial and unsatisfying answers. It has to be faced as a mystery. We have to enter into its mystery with all our powers of reception, with our deepest attention, with open prayer. Someday we will see the light which scatters the shadow. It is a light that is hard to express and hard to communicate, precisely because it cannot be got at without a giving of self which has to be personal and sincere. In these fundamental and primary questions of life, no one can solve his neighbor's problems for him. The most we can do is to invite our neighbors to follow our example and set out upon the road that leads into the center of their souls.[16]

II. Certitude of Divine Faith

Believing means discovering the Christian mystery. It means meeting with God in the supernatural visit and offering that he makes on earth in the person of Christ and in the Church. It means coming into contact with the reality of this visit and this gift, adhering to it with all our intelligence, with all our will, with all our heart, with our whole personality.

It is not hard to see that such a discovery can be made only at the price of complete general mobilization of the whole being. It is always the whole, entire man that believes or refuses to believe.

In this search, in this discovery, the intelligence plays a role of the very first importance. All the lights of reason and all the intuitions of the mind have to work in perfect harmony.

But here more than in any other form of searching after truth, the activity of the intellect has to be supplemented, stimulated, purified, oriented by the conduct of the whole man and especially his theoretical and practical respect for moral values. The will necessarily has an important role to play.

[199]

But there is more. God himself has to intervene in order to help us recognize him and welcome him. No one ever comes to this faith without recognizing the active and supernatural presence of God in the world. It is supernatural; by definition it is placed beyond the reach of our intelligence as long as our intelligence is left to its natural potentialities. We have to cling to this supernatural gift of God by an interior act which will lead us, through the innate power of this gift, into the Christian mystery, into the reality which radically surpasses all our created capacity. God alone can give us eyes to see him as he must be seen. God alone can make us approach the mystery that reveals him and gives him as a free gift. Grace, the personal and supernatural intervention of God in our human life, is absolutely necessary.

Intelligence, will, grace—these are the three principles of activity in the man who is en route towards faith or who has come to the end of his road.

Faith is an activity of our fundamental personality, that is, of our intelligence as spirit and our will as love, both faculties supplemented by grace which lets us recognize the Christian mystery as true and makes us cling to it as the only reality that is capable of saving us.

Faith is thus an act of knowledge and an act of communion. Although it can exist in us without charity, that is, without sactifying grace, it always implies at least an initial stage of love. The sinner who keeps his faith, still proclaims that God is his all, even though he has turned away from God practically through sin. Only his faith is sick. And since it is easier to study the problem of faith when we are considering faith in good health, we shall generally be considering, in the explanations that follow, the faith that exists in a soul in the state of grace, living in charity.

Next to be examined is the role played by each of these three factors: intelligence, will, and grace. It is the combined activity of all three which gives rise to our basic faith in the Christian mystery.

[200]

But first of all there is one extremely important remark to be made. In analyzing, we necessarily undo things. We separate and take apart, and by that very fact we falsify. In order to understand the working principle of a watch, you have to examine each of its wheels and gears, one by one. And still each individual wheel and gear has no real meaning or value unless it is joined together with all the others in the complete mechanism. The same thing is even more true of the vital act which constitutes faith in the Christian mystery. It is a simple act on the one hand, because it consists basically in one swift surge of union, a total adherence of my whole being to God, who reveals and gives himself to me. But it is a complex act on the other hand, if we consider all the machinery that it sets in balanced motion within the human psyche.

In the course of the analysis that we are undertaking, we must be very careful never to forget for a single moment that all this machinery, the machinery of nature (intelligence and will) and the machinery of grace, is always working in perfect harmony, whether we are dealing with acts that only prepare the way for faith or with the act of faith itself. We must hold fast to our sense of wholeness, our understanding of the simple and comprehensive act that is characteristic of divine faith.

A. *Intelligence and Faith*

1. The Role of Intelligence in Faith

The role of intelligence in faith consists, on the one hand, in taking cognizance of the content of divine revelation, or the Christian mystery, and, on the other hand, in taking up the evidence which proves that God has really manifested and communicated himself to man in this mystery and that it is a legitimate and essential human duty to cling to God with our whole being.

Faith is the most complete commitment of my human person that I can possibly make. It is also the most fundamental and basic homage that I give to God. It is the salvific act *par excellence*. That is why it is necessary, above all else, that this act be reasonable. "I would not believe," says St. Thomas Aquinas, "if I did not see what I should believe."

Still, there are reasons and reasons. Faith finds its justification in what are called the motives of credibility. This certitude by external evidence is the only certitude that the Christian mystery can claim. Methods of approach, we have said, differ according to the different realities that are to be discovered. It would be absurd to demand, by way of proof for the Christian mystery, any demonstration of the scientific or mathematical or even metaphysical type, just as no one can prove the existence of God in the same way that he proves "two and two make four," because God is not a problem in arithmetic. And neither can we prove the supernatural intervention of God in the world by any metaphysical deductive process. If the Christian mystery is authentic, it can be recognized only by means of evidence that portrays it as bearing witness to a supernatural visit by God to humanity. It is a fact unique in history and it needs the support of proofs that go beyond the realm of history.

It is obvious that the two lines of search mentioned above—the one having as its object the content of the Christian mystery, and the other pursuing the reliability and bearing of the evidence—are actually one and inseparable in practice. The signs of external evidence accompany and situate and permeate the Christian mystery in its historical development; or, better perhaps, they spring up from the Christian mystery; they radiate its brilliant light; they are interior, intrinsic within it.

2. EVIDENCE OF THE SUPERNATURAL INTERVENTION OF GOD

It will be easier to understand what has just been said if we keep before our eyes a brief resume of the principal pieces of evidence that are a sort of divine seal upon the Christian mystery, the mirrored reflection of God's presence.

One of the first signs is the internal coherence and unity of the Christian mystery in its historical development. The Christian mystery has a history that ranges through the whole world, a history made up of many individual episodes, all of which go together to make up one single theme which could be briefly put as follows: Christ announced and awaited, Christ giving himself, Christ continued in and by the Church.

In the chainwork of these events it is hard to miss the footprints of a supernatural Providence that leaves the written inscription of its activity upon what would pass for a chaotic jumble of historical facts if viewed exclusively from an earthly point of view.[17]

There is more than history; the essence of the Christian mystery affords a second clear sign. Christianity is a mystery of love, the greatest love, the love of God for man. Anyone who reflects seriously upon the problem will realize that there is nothing greater, nothing more powerful, more absolute, more necessary, more vital in the life of man than love. An immense and inescapable urge for harmony, unity, coherence, communion, sharing, is at work in the bosom of the universe, and particularly in the heart of man. The Christian mystery represents the most adequate response to the most profound aspiration of the human person; for it presents us with a God who "is love" and who gives himself to man so that man can "believe in his love" and "abide in his love."

Then there is the person of Christ himself, the greatest of all signs. When we consider Christ with real attention, we see the clear evidence of his divinity appearing bit by bit until it shines through his entire personality. Here is a man whose balance and wisdom and holiness are recognized by the whole world. But this man makes himself equal to God, makes himself the center of his own religious message. He claims to be the way, the truth, and the life. He performs miracles. He prophesies, and his prophecies are fulfilled. He proves everything that he is, everything that he does, with absolute certitude, absolute security, absolute freedom, absolute authority, absolute love. He does not believe; he knows. He does not hope; he already has possession. He never repents because he is free of all sin. He does not make a single effort towards perfection; he is perfection. Never for a moment can we see him turning aside from his mission, which is a unique and transcendent mission: to save mankind, to reawaken in mankind the inmost longing of their hearts, to make them respond actively to the search for God, to unite them with each other through a bond of charity, to reconcile them to his Father so that they may be one in him, just as he and the Father are one.

Finally, there is the Church; and not only in her earthly successes and visible triumphs, because they are always followed by reverses and persecutions, but in two all-important considerations.

1. The transcendent mission of salvation which she has received from Christ and which she pursues unceasingly in the world: her function is that of savior and sanctifier. She lives within history, but her role is beyond history, spiritual, supernatural, eternal. In her essence and her mission, the Church is always identical with the Church of the Apostles and the Church of every time.

2. The heroic virtues of the saints, as well as the miracles which marked their life or followed upon their death, and especially the complete and total charity which inspired their whole existence.

3. Reading the Evidence

It is not enough that this evidence does really exist. We also have to know how to read and understand it, that is, how to grasp it effectively as proof, pointing out and establishing the supernatural intervention of God.

This understanding of the evidence demands, on the part of the examiner, certain interior dispositions which must be analyzed in their turn.

It is one of the most important aspects of the drama of faith that we are touching upon here, whether we are first mastering the problem of faith, or whether, already possessing faith, we are trying to make it something more living in itself.

A. THE NECESSARY ATTENTION

We are already familiar with the problems connected with reading natural evidence.

Take a farmer, for instance. Without having read the weather reports, he will be able to tell you, sometimes with real certitude, sometimes only with a high degree of probability, what the weather will be like. Now put an intellectual from the university in his place. Most likely he will not only be incapable of predicting the weather, but he will not even care about it, unless perhaps he has planned a day off or an outing.

The difference is obvious. The work of the farmer, the drawing up of his daily schedule, his material interests all depend almost completely upon the weather. His attention is constantly alerted. He grasps even the most insignificant signs and knows how to interpret them intelligently. His long familiarity with nature has developed a certain talent in him. The intellectual's case is entirely different. But put some unknown author's work into his hands and, as he reads it, all his faculties are working, razor keen. He notes a familiar expression here, a familiar thought there. And finally the answer dawns upon him. This is the work of Racine, he will announce, or this was written in the early Renaissance, or this comes from Southern France.

Similarly, when it comes to gathering and interpreting the evidence of the Christian mystery, attention is the first prerequisite. As long as the conscience is not awake to spiritual things, as long as the attention is entirely monopolized by secondary problems such as work, profession, family, pleasure, everything that is, even legitimately, taken up with the here-below of human life, there is no hope of discovering the evidence of the Christian mystery.

In order for the unbeliever to become aware of this evidence, three things are necessary. First of all, he has to cast his life in a

more serious mold. From the very outset he has one fundamental choice to make, one basic condition to fill, one general
orientation to establish: the world is not absurd; it has meaning.
Life is not a gay pastime, but something difficult, something
important, a precious gift that has been offered to us for our use.
The spiritual, no matter how invisible it is, is more important
and more real than the material and the earthly.

Next, his attention has to awaken to the Christian mystery
and its manifold evidence. It is a personal secret of each individual, a secret shared only with God, how this awakening takes
place in each individual life. Converts, in their writings, often
speak of a moment, a sudden impulse which snatched them
from the grasp of sleep into a state of full wakefulness and intense search. For one, it is reading a book, and not always a
Christian book. For another, it is seeing someone perform a
really selfless act of charity. For still another, it is some great
suffering which has entered into his life. For one, it is a consciousness of the limitations of human existence or its moral
weakness. And for another, it is the magnificence of Christian
art. But it is always an important moment, and converts cling
to it with real gratitude; the role it plays in their existence is
a decisive one.

Once his attention is aroused, the unbeliever has to keep it
active and alive within his life. He has to set boldly out upon the
search for the evidence and meaning of the Christian mystery,
by every means that is at his disposal.

B. AWARENESS OF THE EVIDENCE

The greater number of converts give the impression that the
passage from unbelief to faith is like the passage from blindness
to light. After the fleeting moment of their enlightenment, they
are astonished to think they could ever have been blind to realities and arguments which now strike them with the force of
real evidence. For many of them, just as for the eyes of some
fervent religious souls, the moment comes in which the evidence

mounts into an overpowering throng of innumerable details. God shines through his creation, shines into the Christian mystery, and the soul takes the steps that follow, bathed in certitude.

What has happened?

Frequently it is something like this. Moved by a grace to which they have been faithful, they have prayed, they have put forth their efforts at great cost, they have made a real effort to live a more selfless and true and pure kind of life. In all this, they constantly kept adding to their interior capacity for grasping the force of evidence. Perhaps they also began to study about religion, to read, to spend time with sincere Christians, to take part in certain religious ceremonies, to acclimate themselves, in a word, to familiarize themselves with the Christian mystery. They acquired the skill we spoke of in describing the peasant and the university professor.

Anyone who has practiced a science for a long time will readily understand what we mean. Biologists, for instance, will tell you that the proofs and traces of the evolution of species seem very weak to the uninitiated who come across them only occasionally, but that they leave no room for doubt in the minds of those who have observed and studied them for a long time.

The same thing is true of souls who are generous in their search for God. After a cloud-covered path of darkness, they suddenly experience an interior illumination and they see a whole forest of evidence rising up where before they could see nothing but mist and darkness. They begin to be connatural with the supernatural world.

C. FROM SPECULATION TO SYMPATHETIC UNDERSTANDING

In the account he wrote of his conversion, Karl Stern makes the following remark: "There we were sitting, talking away on Kierkegaard, on existentialism, on dialectic materialism, but without the moral decisiveness, the *raison du coeur* which all these questions demand. Most of us lived the same life, a life of libertinism and *laissez faire,* and therefore any subject on which we touched in our intellectual pursuits became equivocal, amorphous and meaningless."[18]

The remark is significant. There are a great many young people, and a great many adults, too, for that matter, who see every domain of human life and especially those domains which are the most crucial and decisive for human destiny as nothing more than subjects for discussion and dissertation and debate. For them, religion is a purely psychological and historical phenomenon which has a certain bearing on reason and culture, but which has no legitimate appeal to the whole of man. They are taken up exclusively with knowledge, not with real discovery. There are university students who devote their whole lives to philosophy or the history of religions. And not infrequently they achieve a truly remarkable competence. They build up purely natural explanations that are often most ingenious and cause no little uneasiness in many souls. But they are all relegated, sooner or later, to the museum of outdated hypotheses. These are great thinkers, people say: there is nothing they do not know about the Christian mystery. But, far from believing the Christian mystery, these men give nearly perfect explanations of its origins and development in the light of purely natural causes.

This is, of course, hardly surprising. One of the reasons that they are blind to all the evidence is their purely speculative and "photographic" bent of mind when they are confronted with any religious phenomenon. They do not try to discover the truth or to give themselves to the truth. They treat truth as the object of study and exegesis and speculative debate.

The attitude of the man who looks for the truth in order to make it his own and to surrender himself to it is quite different. His whole being is awake. He sympathizes, he communicates, he holds his spirit open and ready. He keeps in contact with the whole of the area or of the world that he is exploring. Gradually he learns to develop a sort of sixth sense which lets him grasp the evidence effectively. He turns into a sort of student who has a great love for his master and who, because of that love, tries to acquire the increased intellectual liveliness and readiness he needs in order to grasp his master's thought even in its most subtle nuances and details.

4. PERSONAL SIGNS AND COMMUNICABLE SIGNS

It is the role of apologetics to collect the reasons that lead to faith, the signs of credibility, and to arrange them in logical order so that their proving force strikes the human mind.

This is a very important and, at the same time, a very difficult job. If apologetics, sometimes, is deceiving, then the fault is certainly that of the apologist, or even more it is because people expect impossible miracles from apologetics.

Perhaps apologetics too often confines itself to a didactic exposition of the evidence, without sufficient interest in awakening the spirit of the inquirer and creating within him the interior dispositions that are always prerequisite for any effective evaluation of the evidence. But even when apologetics does make a serious effort along these lines, it must not lose sight of the fact that attention and growing familiarity and earnestness in searching for the truth, as well as the spirit of sympathetic understanding that has just been described, always demand a personal interior effort which can be undertaken and brought to a happy conclusion only by a will that is supported throughout by the grace of God.

The evidence of credibility can be divided into two main categories.

There is some evidence that is personal and incommunicable. And in many conversions it is this kind that plays the decisive role. Frequently it is nothing more than an interior experience in which God reveals himself to a soul as clearly existing and present beyond all doubting.[19]

In other cases, it is a miracle, true and authentic, but with a purely personal bearing.[20] The fortunate beneficiaries of these graces are absolutely incapable of expressing or communicating the reasons that impel them to faith. They have only one answer:

their way of acting, their faith, is to them reasonable beyond all appeal.

Some of the evidence of credibility is universal, adapted to the intelligence of anyone who wishes to examine it attentively. This type of evidence lends itself to expression in the form of reasoning and argumentation which helps the mind to discover the signature of God in the Christian mystery.[21]

But, even granting that these arguments are developed with a maximum of intelligence and clarity, it is no less true that they lose a great part of their value by the mere fact that they are put into words. Words narrow, congeal, circumscribe. And the evidence itself is living reality. It is clear in some of its aspects because it has to be accessible to our intelligence, but in other aspects it is charged with mystery because it is supposed to lead us into a world that is beyond our normal world. Think, for example, of the person of Christ. His person bears within itself, as we said, the evidence of its own divinity and the transcendence of Christianity. The divine can be seen shining through the human. But the human can conceal the divine. Only through a great effort at attention and prayer and a humble spirit of communion can we prepare ourselves for contact with the divine. Only in this same spirit can we give full scope and full attention to the evidence.

All these individual pieces of evidence do not produce any result, of course, unless they are taken together. When we discover that the evidence all points in one and the same direction, taken as a whole, that it all bears witness to the supernatural presence of God in the Christian mystery, then and only then will the Christian mystery appear to deserve the complete adherence of our faith. But apologetics is limited to presenting the evidence step by step. Its task is an important one and cannot be passed over. But, left to its own resources, it can never stir up that mysterious flash of brilliance in the light of which our mind can take in all the evidence at one sweep and pass swiftly on to the hidden reality which, taken as a whole, the evidence all combines to present. All that apologetics can do is prepare the way. This "moment" is something strictly personal in the life of every convert, something bound up with the mystery of his own manifold spirit and the mystery of grace.

Given all the difficulties that have just been analyzed, it is no wonder that the greater number of believers are unable to give an adequate answer to anyone who asks them to justify their faith. Even if their faith has become something very personal and is supported by reasons for believing which were at one time clearly present to their mind, they have long ago left them behind, forgotten, to live peaceably in their faith. No one lives constantly prepared for an examination in apologetics. Moreover, in order to give a convincing explanation of the evidence—to say nothing of merely becoming aware of it even—a person needs a real power of reflection and analysis as well as a solid mastery of the spoken or written word. These are not common gifts. Most men would be quite taken aback if they had to outline and justify the moral pattern even of a person with whom they come into almost daily contact. And still they have a very exact picture in their mind. It is a question of experienced knowledge as opposed to analysis. Only a practiced psychologist is equal to the task of isolating the various traits that make up personality and grouping them into the proper configuration to describe a particular person.

As for believers themselves, they need not be surprised if, upon examination, the reasons behind their faith seem suddenly much weaker than they ever thought possible. There are many things that could explain this situation. One of the main reasons is that any piece of evidence that is analyzed and put into words and isolated cannot help losing much of its real power and meaning. Only a quick reference to the evidence as a whole, together with ready and alert attention, can lead the troubled mind to its security.[22]

5. The Certitude Produced by Evidence

All certitude that is got through evidence has one thing in common: it does not give a direct insight into the reality that is represented by the evidence. This is particularly true in the case of the Christian mystery. The evidence never gives intrinsic proof (that is, the immediate vision without any intermediary and without anything hidden) of God speaking through the prophets, of God incarnate in Christ, of Christ speaking infallibly through the Church, present in the Holy Eucharist, communicating his grace to us through the medium of the sacraments. The whole strictly supernatural content of the Christian mystery is clear and certain for us, but it remains veiled. If it were not for this fact, we would speak of vision rather than faith in describing it. We may say that the Christian mystery has two different faces: one incarnate and visible, and the other spiritual and invisible. They are inseparable, and the one is the evidence of the other. The visible face of Christianity shows us how reasonable it is to believe in its invisible face. And not only that it is reasonable, but that it is a duty; because it is a question of God's will and our whole destiny.

Neither should there by any surprise if the evidence is not sufficient in itself—even the most personally experienced evidence —completely to suppress every hesitation and every fear. The evidence is meant to play a role in a vast and complex spiritual drama. It is strong enough to put aside every prudent and reasonable doubt, but it is not the nature of evidence like this to eliminate, speculatively, every fear of error. We are not at work in a purely speculative order here, but rather in the practical order. The arguments are such that their weight rules out all hesitation and commands our assent. There is always an area of shadow left, but a reasonable man is neither likely to be stopped by it nor even willing to be taken up with it. He surmounts his last hurdle by an act of his will under the powerful influence of grace.

The act, then, with which we give ourselves over to God is at once *reasonable* in that it is based upon sufficient evidence, *free* in that it demands an act of the will in order to overcome the uneasiness of negative doubt, and *supernatural* in that God has to give us special help in every act that leads us nearer to him.

Actually, it could not possibly be any other way. Frequently, unbelievers, and Christians, too, for that matter, demand a more brilliant and obvious brand of evidence, justifying their unbelief or their doubts by appealing to the insufficiency of the evidence upon which the Christian mystery is based. They forget that, between the visible face of Christian faith (the evidence) and the invisible face of Christian faith (the supernatural realities) there necessarily exists a certain lack of proportion which can never be made up by intelligence alone. What it actually involves is passing from one world to another. The evidence can only be an indication, an orientation, an invitation to set out upon the search and never give it up. God cannot want us to cling to him as the result of force or the overwhelming lightning-stroke of his free intervention in our world, reducing us to the state of an unwilling and rebellious prisoner. What he wants is a transformed soul, growing every day in interior dispositions, open and frank and receptive and waiting, a soul that gives itself to him freely, in one great upward surge of love.

6. SHADOW AND LIGHT

There is, thus, a certain degree of shadow left over both the evidence of credibility and the content of the Christian mystery.

That is why it is not surprising that we come upon moments of uneasiness and hesitation, and even doubt.[23] Faith is necessarily a state of waiting, transition and, consequently, of tension. Our intelligence is fashioned to see, and it is never completely at ease in the presence of any reality that wears a mask. It longs for vision.

Besides this, in coming down upon earth and falling in with

the development of history, the Christian mystery could not escape being caught up into the backwaters of human passion and all the chaotic events that follow it in time. It is not of this world, but it *is* in it. This close intermingling of supernatural with natural, eternal with temporal, pure with impure, that which is with that which is becoming, is bound to lead to a thousand anxious *why's,* and there is not, for every one of them, an answer that is really and completely satisfactory.

Finally, since, as we have explained, the evidence itself is closely bound up with the Christian mysteries and their historical development, it can very well be clear enough to justify and even demand our adherence and still leave a wide fringe of shadow before which the human mind stops in hesitant confusion.

This mixture of light and shadow in matters of faith is frequently encountered in life. Moreover, it is a specific characteristic of knowledge by faith and life in faith. Face to face with the problem of light and shadow, the human mind splits into two big families. The one group is particularly taken up with the shadows, the *why,* the *how,* the unsolved questions. They would like everything to be clear and open, and sometimes they suspend their allegiance until they can manage to see through the problem that is disturbing them.

That is a disposition that runs the risk of sometimes, perhaps, not arriving at any conclusion at all. No one will ever finish examining every one of the problems that can be posed. Many of them are far beyond the actual potentialities of our intelligence and they can never be solved unless God himself gives us the key. And if he has not given us the key, it is because he did not come to satisfy the intellectual curiosity of men, but to offer his Being to their being, his Love to their love.

Some other minds travel in just the opposite direction. They try to uncover all the light that is to be found in the Christian mystery and in the evidence that embodies and illuminates it.

They do not discount the objections and the shadows, but they know that "a thousand difficulties do not make a doubt." The shadows they accept as a necessary condition of earthly existence, and they go on boldly in the light they have towards the light they hope for.

B. *Will and Faith*

Faith is a meeting between the whole man and God revealing and giving himself. Even the deepest levels of the machinery of human personality are at work to set the stage effectively for this meeting. The role of intelligence has just been discussed. But throughout the explanation there was constant reference to the very important role which is played by the will in the act of faith.

In every intellectual reflection, be it speculative and abstract or practical and material, the will is always present. It is the will that sustains the mind's effort in the conquest of the real and true. The will has a part to play in the act of faith *a fortiori,* since faith is a certitude of the practical order, a question of learning to know a duty, adherence of our entire being to the supreme reality and the absolute truth, since faith is an act that calls for the activity of the whole man.

This is why the will's share in the act of faith differs not only in degree but also in nature from the will's intervention in the scientific and philosophical activities of the intellect. In these last-named activities the will acts in an external capacity, merely applying and sustaining the attention of reason. But in faith it penetrates deep into the interior of the act. It is incorporated into it as an essential component; it is an intrinsic part.

Nor is this word *will* to be taken in the sense of a faculty that hurls out its imperatives without further interest. There is a mighty, vital surge of activity here, involving every important element that figures in the very roots of human personality. It is the product of the will, no doubt, but there is also free range for generosity and warmth and love. The word *heart* might be substituted for *will* here, provided it is understood in the Gospel sense[24] or Pascal's sense.[25]

In setting forth the reasons behind the will's intervention in the act of faith, we are going to touch upon the most mysterious and decisive moments of all the drama of human freedom. Free will is not always kept in a uniform state of alertness. It has periods of drowsiness and even lethargy. It also has its periods of sluggish and disconnected activity. But at certain moments it is called into decisive action, sometimes warily, sometimes imperiously. Those are the times of important choice, sometimes decisive choice, the hour for *yes* and *no,* the hour that determines the lot of a human life, or, in any case, the hour that settles the question of whether a man will forge ahead with the full current of progress towards the truth or succumb to the ebb-tide and withdraw into doubt and deceit.

These decisive moments of individual choice in life are what stake out the path along the mounting slope that leads towards faith and the life of faith. In its relationship and dialogue with God, human freedom is at the peak of its activity. It does, to be sure, have a role to play in the secondary decisions that are of interest to our temporal life. But when it is face to face with the problem of good and evil, face to face with the choice of giving or refusing self to Absolute Being and Absolute Love, then it has come to the crossroads for which it was created.

Nor is it particularly surprising that Christ, God himself and God's envoy to us, bearing the gift of God, should have gone to such great lengths to remind men of these all-important hours of decision. We mention this only in passing, and not in order to use it as an argument; but merely to show that Christ, in his simple and direct appeal to the hearts of men, was far in advance of the modern psychologists and philosophers of the human will in focusing upon the innermost recesses of human freedom.

The different stages that we present in orderly progression here—it may be well to point it out from the outset—do not necessarily always follow in that precise order in actual fact. Frequently they overlap each other. Nor is the activity of the will always something reflex and conscious. Just like the activity of the intellect, it is lived and experienced by a man who is on the go, constantly in action. It is only later, when he turns back to survey the course he has traversed, that the believer can make out the steps he has mounted and come to understand what turns and detours were the most important.

1. ATTENTION

In order for faith to take root in a soul, to hold its position, or to grow, that soul has first of all to be earnestly awake to moral and spiritual values.

Every conversion—from unbelief to faith or from lukewarm faith to living faith—begins by breaking through the indifference that up to that moment surrounded the foremost problem of human life, the problem of religion.

Too many men allow their attention to be monopolized by secondary values, scientific, technical, political, social, esthetic, even carnal values. At some given moment, all these things, even the most important among them, such as daily bread and the social reconstruction of a more just and brotherly humanity, all have to step back and yield their position. They have to disappear or at least fade into the background. Without really ceasing to exist, they have to be as if they no longer existed, in comparison with a problem that interests the whole personality of every human being. For "what does it profit a man to gain the whole world if he suffers the loss of his own soul?"

The greater part of all conversions begin by a bold and, frequently, quite sudden burst of consciousness: consciousness of self, the presence of self in the world, individual destiny and the destiny of all men, considered now no longer as an impersonal mass—that is an abstraction of the mind—but as individual persons, each with his own particular place and his own particular calling.

Converts frequently recall this moment; it is a decisive one in their evolution. Up to that point, the world was scenery, background, stage; and now it has become a drama, and I realize that mine is a leading role. Life has been a chaotic series of unrelated events; and suddenly it turns into an ordered whole that has meaning, and that meaning depends upon me. The earth has been one huge factory, a colossal business to be organized and managed, a closed system, self-sufficient; and now it has turned into a journey, a road, a temporary shelter.

Or perhaps the problem of religion does not come up precisely at this moment. But it is still there potentially, in germ. Most frequently, a man ceases to be indifferent towards God and religious values at the same time that he ceases to be indifferent to the drama and mystery and challenge of human life.

Once the indifference is broken through and the attention alerted, the will comes into play without hesitation. The will is the subject, finally, of this whole awakening. It is the will, now, that has to prolong this state of attention freely and make it bear its proper fruit. Perhaps our attention was aroused by some force which remains mysterious to us. Was it some outside shock, the voice of our conscience, or grace? No matter what, it is up to us now, up to our free will, to seize the opportunity and intensify our attentiveness. Being attentive is more than just seeing things. There is the same fundamental difference between just seeing things and paying real attention as there is between glancing at something and really examining it, between hearing and listening. Attention implies something more than being awake. It implies a free and deliberate answer to the first call to wakefulness and, then, free and deliberate wakefulness ever after.

This theme of attention has deservedly figured as an important one for everyone who studies the mysterious workings of the human will.[26] In the preaching of Christ it is frequently presented under the form of a passing invitation to watch, to be on guard, to stay awake.[27]

[218]

Experience amply proves how ready we all are to turn our mind away from problems that tend to disturb our mental inertia, our peace and tranquility, our false sense of security. We might say, then, that here we are face to face with one of the decisive moments that life casts before our personal sincerity in the exercise of our free will. Faith, in the words of Duméry, consists in overcoming the temptation to fall asleep.

2. THE SEARCH

Once attention is aroused, if we want to be faithful and consistent, the next step is search. The idea of searching for God is a familiar one in the whole of the Old Testament. "If you seek the Lord your God, you will find him, provided only you seek him with all your heart" (Deut. 4:9). And the same challenge comes from the lips of Christ: "Seek first the Kingdom of God" (Matt. 6:33).

With the possible exception of one or the other extraordinary case, experience shows that unbelievers who come to the faith and believers who have a personal and living faith have been true and persevering seekers after God. They have tried to come to a better and more perfect understanding of the content of the Christian mystery, Scripture, the Person of Christ, the Church in her supernatural mystery and in her organization and history. They have overcome the disfigurations and prejudices that once concealed the real face of truth.

For the successful outcome of this search, two fundamental dispositions are particularly important.

This project must be faced with at least as much care and application and perseverance[28]—even more so, in fact, for there is no proportion between this basic problem and the common problems of life—as a serious man generally brings to bear on the worldly problems in which he is particularly interested, such as passing an important test, overcoming a difficult situation, setting up family life, rearing children. "It would be most strange," writes Malègue, speaking of God, "if precisely that one facet which is the most unwieldy and the richest of all our knowledge should be given to us by some short cut or at a bargain."[29]

Then the seeker after God must set his face firmly in the direction of truth, following all the signs and footprints of God, never letting himself grow discouraged at the shadows that surround them. His progress will be like that of a detective, a hunter stalking his game, an inventor or an explorer. All these men know, as if by instinct, how to read even the most insignificant signs from what, at first, was nothing but confusion, riddle, and obscurity. That is how light grows and finally develops into fruitful discovery.

3. PURITY OF VIEW

Even the most superficial observers are familiar with the influence that passions have upon intelligence. Sometimes they fascinate our minds; sometimes they warp them outrageously; sometimes they darken them to the point of making them completely blind.

The Christian mystery presents itself to us as a spiritual reality aimed at whatever is most interior, purest, most refined in the very core of our being. It comes with moral demands that are categoric and severe. And no wonder that it looks like a threat for the proud and sensuous man who lives in each one of us. It is not hard to see why the passions rebel in face of the imperious call that God makes to humanity through Christ. It is no wonder that they swing into full play in the hearts and minds of men in order to hold them fast to the forces that keep them captive, in order to make them deaf and blind to the more satisfying but too costly values that divine revelation offers and imposes.

That is what causes the great spiritual conflict in the souls of so many converts, a more brutal conflict, Rimbaud says, than any human battle. The purity of heart and openness of view of which Christ speaks can be got only by destroying in ourselves the dark and spiteful powers which hitherto have dominated the whole ambit of our life.

For many, this will mean pride or attachment to self-will. In creating us in his own likeness, God put into us a mirror image of his own freedom and autonomy. That is what makes our nobility. But that is also the source and ground of our greatest temptation. We want to cling to that liberty for itself and make gods of ourselves, turn ourselves into completely self-sufficient beings. This tendency can lead to extremes. "I should much rather suffer than give in to any domination," wrote Rivière before his conversion, "even if the domination were to last but for a moment and then give way to everlasting happiness." Most of the time the biggest danger is that pride will remain unconscious. Man is so kneaded into the spirit of pride that his pride becomes a part of him and turns his will into an unassailable buttress against the truth.

For others, there is a different hurdle to surmount. They are dilettantes. They want to remain open to every current, every diverse phase of human life. They look upon life as a show, a spectacle. And they go through it like the true amateur, sampling and plucking, but never being taken up with any one reality. Religion, then, looks like a shackle, a bond, an intolerable diminution of life.[30]

For many young people, the cult of self takes on the form of an uncontrolled quest for originality. It is not truth they are partial to. It is rather the unheard of, the paradoxical, the eccentric, even the shocking and perverse and monstrous.

Still others—and their number is legion in every society— find their mind's eye clouded by a base and slavish sense of conformism to the prevailing mentality and morals. Their trouble is human respect, afraid to stand out in good, afraid to be judged unfavorably, afraid to be the butt of indecent mockery, afraid to lose control of the situation, afraid to miss an opportunity. There is no counting the number of men who pass through life like this, with half-conscious fear for their only standard.[31]

Others live a life wholly given over to vanity and foolishness, to matters of no consequence and childish curiosity and worldly success.[32]

Others, finally, are the prey of their carnal intoxication, the spirit of greed, or the will to power.[33]

In all this matter, the will has an immense task. It has to heal the whole being, and heal him in such a way that he is no longer anything other than an open, simple, clear, transparent soul.[34] All our most important discoveries, all our most important decisions go essentially to make up the quality of our fundamental personality.

4. Absolute Preference

A clear and simple soul knows how to grasp the absolute value hidden in the Christian mystery. But there is a second interior disposition that is equally essential to religious faith. And that is the will to give self to God without condition, without reserve, above every created thing, just as soon as God's presence is recognized, and in the form that his own presence takes. By way of preamble to our search for God, we have to settle one fundamental question. "If there is a God and if he has revealed himself, then I will give myself to him, no matter what it costs."

Faith, it has been seen, poses a problem of values as well as a problem of truth. And in the world of values we are unconsciously influenced and guided by what we prefer. These personal preferences can often play the role of villain and hold us back in our quest for truth. They like to fix our attention on the immediate, on the here-and-now. They like to cloud our vision and distract our attention. They know how to arouse unreasonable fears and lend weight to shadows which have no body.

No one can arrive at faith unless he is resolved to give up everything, to sacrifice every value of only earthly proportions, no matter how excellent in itself and no matter how worthy of our mind and heart. It is on this score that the cruelest interior battles are waged and free will is called to witness, forced back to its most elementary grounds. Read the Gospel. When Christ comes to the question of absolute preference, he uses words of fire, words that sound cruel. "You have to deny yourself," he says. "You have to pluck out whatever might scandalize you, that is, whatever might prove to be a stumbling block for you. It profits nothing to gain the universe if you lose your soul. You have to be ready to leave"—in fact, he says "to hate"—"father, mother, brother, sister, husband or wife, children, land, home."

This is exactly what has been demanded of many converts, among them the most noble. One is called to sacrifice the warm affection of family ties;[35] another has to take leave of co-religionists who will thereafter look upon him as the worst of apostates;[36] a third has to bid his own country farewell, his own race, and see himself accused of treason; a fourth has to leave behind him the political group for which he worked, perhaps even founded;[37] a fifth has to turn his back upon position, property, and even livelihood.

5. DECISION AND CONSENT

In studying the role of intelligence in faith, we saw that even when a person has sufficient reasons for believing in the Christian mystery, his mind is still subject to hesitation and uneasiness.

This state of mind is the result, first of all, of the very reasons for faith. Proof by external evidence is a kind of proof that can never completely suppress every shadow, every fear of error. The evidence is strong enough to make my adherence reasonable and to justify my acting upon it, but it always leaves a certain area of shadow which remains a source of uneasiness. These shadows do not touch the reasons behind faith nor do they attack the bright central nucleus that is spelled out by the converging links of evidence, but still they envelop it like a hazy mist. To make progress, it is not enough to keep the attention fixed on the evidence and the light that has been discovered. There has to be a bold act of decision to carry the seeker bravely beyond his hesitation and incertitude, beyond what Malègue calls the unexplored and even unexplorable caverns. He cannot allow himself to be intimidated by his fears once he has properly judged them to be empty and unreasonable. Conscious and living faith is always an act of courage, putting a decisive end to a period of indecision which no longer has any solid reason to maintain itself.

On the other hand, even when I have strong enough evidence to believe, the reasons do not make me see, directly, immediately, face to face, the reality to which they summon me to entrust myself, with my whole mind, with my whole heart, with my whole being. I see neither God nor the Three Divine Persons nor the divinity of Christ nor his presence in the Eucharist nor his grace in the souls of the just. I am forced to admit that it is only reasonable to admit all these truths. But I do not have any intrinsic evidence for them. And my mind is made to see. That is why the seeker, invited to believe, always holds back a little, always a bit hesitant and uneasy. He is, despite everything, somewhat taken aback at the prospect of accepting and agreeing to a world of realities that he cannot see.

It might be added here that for human nature in the state in which it is found here on earth, the Christian mystery always involves something paradoxical and ambiguous. It falls in perfectly with certain deep-seated needs in human nature, and it uses them like steppingstones. But it also meets with unwillingness and resistance.

In his being and in his gift of self to us, God shows himself for something superior, transcendent, supernatural. He satisfies the sense of mystery in us, the impression, so strong in all of us, that we are at the crossroads of two different worlds, the created world and the uncreated world, the world of matter and the world of spirit, the world of the relative and the world of the absolute, the world of time and the world of eternity. But, on the other hand, this hidden God and the Christian mystery arouse in us a desire to see, to understand, to control, to use, to shape for our own purposes, in much the same way as we expend our efforts so effectively on the world below us.

The Christian mystery responds to our most deep-seated sense of waiting. It is the bearer of love and peace and joy and freedom. And yet it brings us other things as well, strange things, far different from the earthly, concrete, historical world in which we work out our everyday existence. Phenomena, someone has said, do not look Christian. That is true. There is no yardstick common to the history of the gift of God in the world and the history of earthly events. The history of the world is chaotic, without direction, without obvious meaning. Earthly happenings are the manifestations of the freedom and often the disorder of man. The Christian mystery transcends them, soaring far above and superimposing its own plan and order. It ranges through the whole of history and goes far beyond it, without contempt, but also without complicity or fear. "Fear not; I have overcome the world."

The Christian mystery attracts us by means of the promise it offers: absolute self-realization and achievement, absolute happiness. But no sooner do we welcome this promise than it begins to make us uneasy. Here below we have known only limited happiness, happiness subject to the fluctuation of time, constantly threatened. We cannot picture an absolute happiness, withdrawn from the world of time, effectively protected against every threat of diminution or cessation.

Finally, if faith promises everything, it also demands everything. The Christian mystery is the supreme demand. God wants to be loved above everything, with our whole being. We have to give up everything. We have to lose ourselves. "Let us admit," writes Malègue, "that we are inclined to shudder at the wide range of the moral demands that we foresee will follow, at the unlimited obligations to which we will subscribe, this sort of foreclosure upon the whole of our future. But it is signed and registered. It is all at the disposition of a sovereign creditor. Paradoxically enough, our conquest of the very roots of our human freedom has made us, at the outset, slaves."[38]

If these paradoxes of the Christian mystery are kept in mind, it is easy to understand the hesitation that often holds the unbeliever back, even when he has strong enough reasons for believing.[39] He has a more or less clear impression that the answer he is on the point of making is going to commit him whole and entire, compromise him beyond remedy, and make him "lose his life," in the words of Christ. Despite all the reasons of heart and mind that urge him to give himself to God, he cannot avoid the feeling that he is leaving behind him a narrow terrain, circumscribed by space and time, uncomfortable but at least solid looking, all in order to set out boldly after a reality which is certainly capable of bringing out the full value and meaning of his whole life and personality, but which, nonetheless, is still veiled, shadowy, mysterious, and demanding. He might be compared to a child walking in his sleep and suddenly waking up on top of a high fence. His father is there, standing at the foot of the fence and calling to him to jump down into the darkness. The child knows that his father is there, that he is strong and powerful, that he will catch him in his arms, and that everything will be all right. Still he hesitates, because jumping means leaving behind the narrow but reassuring foothold on the fence and facing the shadowy emptiness beneath. But he has to jump.

Everything urges me onward. And if the God to whom I am to give myself is not to be seen (that would no longer be faith, but vision), it makes no difference. I know he is there and I have to jump.

Writes Malègue: "The man who is impelled by an act of faith in God drives onward with a cry of trust and joy. He realizes that he is abandoning himself to arms that are all-powerful and that, basically, his trust and confidence all stem from God and are God's due. Not only at the final moment of his life, but in every act of faith he ever makes, he commends his soul into God's hands."[40]

6. Living the Faith

The words just quoted above are a powerful reminder of the fact that Christian faith is never certitude, definitively worked out. It always remains active, militant. It is a way of life, and life without activity is condemned to weakness and finally to death.

If it is recommended to the seeker that he "do the truth" which he already has in order to arrive at the further light for which he hopes, the same invitation must be made to the man who has found the light. Hereafter he must live his faith.

Living the faith means adapting mind and heart and action to the Christian mystery. It means becoming what Christ wants us to become, doing what Christ and the Church have ordered. The life of faith, the Christian life, the true life which is concerned primarily with its own growth and spread as the most important thing in the world, necessarily mobilizes the free will of man and makes an earnest and repeated appeal to his creative powers.

This life of faith is known as the Christian life, the interior life, and also religious experience. For a long time, writers were wary of that last expression because of the abuse it suffered at the hands of Protestants and Modernists, and because of the ambiguity that ensues whenever the word *experience* is used.[41]

Independently of the mystical states, the term *religious experience* can be applied to the life of any Christian who makes a real effort to live up to his calling and who, with the help of grace, makes a continuous and increasing effort at interior communion with the hidden realities which the Christian mystery holds open to his mind and heart.

It is legitimate to speak of experimentation in the religious life. It differs, naturally, from the experimentation that figures so prominently in the positive sciences in that it has to do with spiritual and supernatural realities and, even more so, in that it demands a radical commitment of the whole person and is not satisfied with the simple curiosity of the amateur. We do not live a Christian life in order to see what effects it will produce in us and whether it will make our life succeed.[42] We live it because we see it as a duty that cannot be got around.

But all this does not keep the Christian life from being accompanied, generally,[43] by happiness and joy and assurance and light. It does not keep it from leading to the discovery of new and personal evidence to serve as a powerful confirmation of Christian truth.

III. Grace and Faith

"The man who is impelled by an act of faith in God drives onward with a cry of trust and joy. He realizes that he is abandoning himself to arms that are all-powerful and that, basically, his trust and confidence all stem from God and are God's due."

Faith is a duty. In the spiritual evolution of a man, there comes a time when he has the feeling that if he does not take a decisive step he is no longer squaring with his conscience.

It is a reasonable duty—that we have demonstrated.

And, lastly, it is a duty in whose final accomplishment God himself mysteriously mingles his own activity. Faith stems from God; faith necessitates grace. Faith is a gift of God.

Let us avoid, from the outset, a dangerous equivocation which serves as a pretext and false assurance for many minds. When we say that faith is a gift of God, this does not at all mean that it is nothing more than a gift of God and that, as a result, we are dispensed from any intellectual search to clarify, in our minds, the evidence and content of the Christian mystery, or that we are exempted from the moral effort which is supposed to acclimate us to the values that the Christian mystery presents. After what has been said above, it is quite clear that I cannot be satisfied with a slothful attitude and say that, since faith is a gift of God, it will be offered to me when God wants to offer it to me, and that if it is not offered, it is only because God thinks it best.

When we say that faith is a gift of God, we mean grace is also necessary for faith to come to life and grow and develop in our souls.

"No one can come to me unless the Father who sent me draw him" (Jn. 6:43). And when Peter, near Caesarea Philippi, made his solemn declaration of faith, "Thou art Christ, the Son of the Living God," Christ answered, "Blessed art thou, Simon Bar Jona, for flesh and blood has not revealed this to thee, but my Father in heaven" (Mt. 16:17).

Grace, that is, the supernatural activity of God in a soul, is, together with the intelligence and the will, an indispensable element, an essential ingredient of faith.

A. *Why Grace Is Necessary*

In order to understand the necessity of grace in faith, it is sufficient to recall the role of faith. Faith is not simply a matter of recognizing the existence of God. For that, reason alone would be enough. It is a question of learning to pick out the supernatural activity of God in the history of the world, the supernatural presence of God in the Christian mystery. It is a question of welcoming him into our heart, of—and it is much the same—going into him, abandoning ourselves to him, delivering ourselves to him. But neither this knowledge nor this giving can be accomplished in us without the supernatural help of God.

Grace is first of all necessary for an effective reading of the evidence that accompanies the Christian mystery. It is not enough merely to look at the evidence. We have to grasp its meaning, and its meaning is supernatural.

A simple comparsion will make all this easier to understand. An animal can see the letters and words printed in a book. But it is incapable of grasping their meaning. For an animal to understand, it would have to have the gift of intelligence. Now, the gift of intelligence would not dispense the animal from the job of using eye and brain to read the letters and words; intelligence would merely allow it to understand the meaning of what it always could see.

The same thing is true of grace. It helps our intelligence grasp the supernatural meaning of the evidence it sees. Grace does not suspend the role of intelligence; it perfects and elevates it.

Above and beyond this, as we have seen, faith is really effective only when the entire being enters into the Christian mystery, following deep into the bosom of God himself, passing completely from the natural plane to the supernatural. To achieve this, our spiritual faculties have to enter into action. But their activity is not enough. The Father has to draw us. Only God can lead us into God. And when he does, when his divine activity comes to supplement and support our own activity, that is what we call grace.

B. *When and How Grace Acts*

There is one thing we can always be sure of: God never refuses anyone the grace he needs to arrive at faith—at least to that measure of faith in the basic truths that is necessary for salvation, the propositions that St. Paul reduced to two: that God is, and that to those who seek him he gives a reward.[44]

Another point to be noted is that grace is never directly discernible in itself because it belongs to the supernatural world. There is no reason to be surprised if faith makes us perceive the value of the evidence without being perceived itself. A similar phenomenon can be discovered in the natural order. The human eye sees without seeing itself: it adapts itself to a close or distant range without our being conscious of the fact. And the human intelligence understands without understanding itself.

Just as the human eye and human intelligence can be known by their exercise—I know that I see and I know that I understand in the very act of seeing and understanding—even so, the presence of grace can be detected by living experience, by seeing it in action, by the fruits it produces in the human soul. Thus we can speak of a sort of experimental knowledge of grace.

It is safe to suppose that grace is secretly present in the man who is sincerely looking for God, in all the efforts that he makes to find the truth, and that his intelligence is enlightened and his will strengthened by God, along the whole length of his path.

In examining the manner in which grace acts in the soul, one is struck, from the outset, by the unimaginable richness and variety of the divine plan. It is a splendid proof, at one and the same time, of both the liberality and the liberty of God in the way he uses his gifts. Our sense of equality is hard put to fathom it all. But no matter. In this whole question we are standing close to the very heart of a conversation between two persons, between two freedoms, between two unique beings. No wonder that each case is something strictly unique, like a vocation, health, or the spiritual life of any soul. "He has loved me," says St. Paul. *Me,* singular, individual. For God, there is no such thing as a mass of men; each single man is a unique, individual being.

Still it is possible—if we remember that any classification is the result of our own personal need to analyze and compare— to distinguish one or the other particular patterns in which grace is offered to the soul.

In certain cases, the convert has the impression that he is acting all by himself. There is no trace, it seems, of those interior lights which, all of a sudden, lift the soul out of itself and, in a free and perfectly unrequested gift, flood the soul with the understanding it was looking for without success short moments before. Reason remains cold. The heart remains dry. There is no emotion, either sense or spirit. God, it seems, is not speaking.

But if we examine the matter a bit more closely, we can see that he is powerfully at work in the soul. For who besides God is keeping this soul in a state of alert and uneasiness and searching? The interior conversation that often rises to dramatic heights is not being carried on with self after all; it is with another, *the* Other, "who is in us more than we are in ourselves," who is not only our Creator, but also our love, all-powerful, drawing us to himself.[45]

In other cases, grace acts with the suddenness of lightning and in a tangible way, triumphant and sovereign from the outset.[46]

Most of the time, though, the activity of grace is one of delicate but intermittent influence. And yet it can be felt and known by the person who is being acted upon. This is how Father Brunhes describes it: "In place of the blinding flash of quick conversion, a gradual increase of light steals over the soul to fix its attention, to teach it the deeper meaning of a truth already known, to make it appreciate an argument that seemed plausible enough up to that point, but lacking in real conviction. In place of a sort of *coup d'état* suddenly seizing control of the will, it is a progressive conquest, characterized first of all by uneasiness, by desires apparently without a solid object, then by a better defined attraction which leads the soul onward gently but firmly towards its goal. Each of the lights taken individually, and each interior inclination taken individually, and each feeling of remorse taken individually, could never give rise to the categoric and indisputable statement that God is at work here. But the sum total, the whole balanced network of spiritual ascent, the peace of conscience in obeying the mysterious inclinations and the remorse of conscience in resisting—all this is a powerful influence upon the mind. The ordered sequence of interior experiences points to the intentional working of some plan. It is proof positive, in the happy expression of one philosopher, of the 'workings of the invisible educator.' "[47]

C. *Grace, Freedom, and Secondary Causality*

While placing due stress upon the importance of grace, most converts also insist upon the freedom in which grace leaves their human activity. God calls; he does not force. He helps, but he does not excuse man from doing what he can himself. God may stir up a tornado of love that bears a soul along almost irresistibly to the bosom of his own great love. But even then there is still freedom. In fact, it is in circumstances like these that human freedom finds its most perfect exercise. Freedom was not given to man for him to refuse the Source of all love and to sin against his Creator; it was given to man to drive him forward towards him who is love and peace and happiness and eternal freedom. What good is love if it is not free?

"We cannot overemphasize," says Malègue, "the enormous and almost respectful place in the scheme of things that the sovereignty of God freely allows to the autonomy of his creatures. It should really surprise us, and make us not a little afraid. God accepts and directs this little bundle of free causality which is our soul, its spontaneous workings, the organs of expression which it has developed for itself and upon which it has stamped the seal of its own actual, historical personality."[48]

Just as he does not annihilate freedom, God does not suppress the intervention of secondary causes, that is, the external created agencies whose influences all help, each in its own way, to keep man aimed along the path of truth—the example of a Christian life lived to the full, a striking act of charity, a book, a sermon, a trial, or any event which points a finger at the weakness and emptiness of human life.

On his road towards God man is not an abstract being nor a monad set apart from everything that surrounds him. He is freedom making his way through a confused medley of external influences.

Since the role of freedom and, even more so, the role of the visible exterior influences upon life are more readily accessible to the examination of observers than is the mysterious and interior working of grace, naturalistic psychologists claim that they can find in these purely human factors the complete and exhaustive explanation of conversion, without any appeal whatsoever to the activity of grace.

[233]

Here again we are face to face with one of the many attempts at reduction which positive science is so apt to foist upon every phenomenon that goes beyond its sphere. Living solely on the level of sense perception, it denies everything that goes beyond sense, obstinately bent upon explaining the higher in terms of the lower. It has been compared to a mineralogist who would consider the Cathedral of Cologne as nothing more imposing than a cross-sector of mineralogy, pretending that there was nothing there but ordered layers of marble, glass, iron, and limestone. Malègue, in his turn, says "If the material of which these things are made were conscious of itself as material, its wrong side would imagine that it was alone in the world and that there was no right side."[49]

D. *Grace and Prayer*

Grace is God at work in us, supernaturally. It is God offering us his hand. But we have to grasp that hand. We have to obey grace. And we have to ask for it. We have to cry to God. We have to pray.

Even the unbeliever. Yes, even the unbeliever. And he can do it in all sincerity. It is enough for him to pray conditionally, as Father Sertillanges invites him to do in his *Catechism for Unbelievers:* "Our Father, if you really are our Father, then I turn to you. If you really are, your name is holy: hallowed be your name. If you really are, your kingdom is order and glory; your kingdom come. If you really are, your will is the law of worlds and the law of hearts; your will be done in everything, on earth as it is in heaven. Give us, if you really are, our daily bread, the bread of truth, the bread of wisdom, the bread of joy. If you really are, then I have debts to pay; forgive them, just as I myself forgive those who owe me debts. For the rest, do not lead me into temptation, but deliver me from every evil. Amen."

But this is more than an invitation. He *has* to pray. He is in a state of not knowing. When we do not know, we ask, we seek, we call and see if there will not be some answer. If the unbeliever does not do this, then he is not playing the role of a man lost upon the lonely planet. He is not living up to his first duty. He is refusing to be a question mark and a challenge to himself, when, basically and essentially, he realizes that he is both a question and a challenge.

Prayer, then, at least conditional prayer, is a part of real sincerity. It fits naturally into the life of the man who refuses to lie to himself. It is confused at the outset; and perhaps it is identical, at first, with open attentiveness to the fundamental self and a spirit of waiting and attention. But it will grow more and more precise in the course of discovering God.

This role, this necessity, or, more exactly, this natural presence of prayer in the life of the man who is sincerely looking for God has been admirably described by Edward Le Roy. He sums up masterfully, not only what we have already said on the subject of faith, but even the predominant ideas which have inspired this whole book:

"The search for God, the very first moment of interior experience, is something far different from a scientific investigation on some matter of free speculative curiosity. Here the problem is set up in advance by the very fact that we are born into life, and our very living solves the problem, well or poorly. Moreover, in this work of seeking we are not abandoned to the unaided powers of our own individual intelligence. We are set to our task. The inspiration and direction of our labor is clear to us, first, in the guise of an innate demand, hidden in the secret bosom of our will. It grows clearer and clearer, constantly more urgent and impelling, but always respecting our autonomy, so that by our own free response we learn, gradually, to answer its advances.

"Answering its advances means nothing more than being open to them, finding our position in the growing sense of perfection that they give us, making a free gift of ourselves to the prime mover of our heart who calls to us and draws us toward himself. This attitude is *prayer*. And what ensues is this: there can be no real search for God except through prayer joined with the earnest efforts of reason. Any other way is atheism from the outset; for it reduces God to an inert thing, either material or abstract, which we like to think we can possess without his cooperation, something to hunt and capture. We are treating God like an idol, as Blondel puts it so well, if we do no more than make him the object of our knowledge, if we fail to keep alive the activity that began with his first movement in our heart by our own activity in cementing all the relationships that bind our hearts to his. That would mean denying the existence of God by the very act in which we claim that we are looking for him.

"It goes without saying that this prayerful search is not merely something to be dreamed about; it must be lived. It is never enough to admit, in an abstraction of pure intelligence, that it is an obligation, that it is just and for our own welfare. No; at some given, concrete moment in time, recollected and in full and deliberate possession of the depths of our conscious soul, we have to make that act a reality. Only upon this condition will our search for God really be sincere, and not an empty mirage, the mere ghost of honest searching.

"This prayer has nothing to do with ritual and gesture and many words. Nor, on the other hand, is it to be mere emotion or theory. And finally it has to be acted upon, turned into effective practice. Set your sights upon the best and highest in every order, believe speculatively and practically in a spiritual hereafter, with all your soul work towards that hereafter, try constantly to outstrip everything you have accomplished in the warmth of a love that is always growing. That is prayer put into action. It means working, as long as you can, to establish the primacy of the moral in your life, the Kingdom of God. And the very practice of searching will raise up within your soul clearer light to see the truth, and new strength to keep on searching. Trials purify and illuminate. Living today to its fulness the light that yesterday's religious experience makes possible, prepares the way for a fuller and a brighter life tomorrow.

"All who have really practiced the spiritual life in this way join in unanimous chorus to declare that persevering prayer is answered. You may refuse to follow their example; but that does not give you any grounds to deny what they say. Nor can you escape by saying that you cannot pray. That only proves that you know nothing of the real meaning of prayer, especially the prayer of a beginner. Just as it is not made up of the anti-intellectual meanderings of a very naïve anthropomorphism, neither does it demand a premature ascent to metaphysical heights, where the atmosphere is too rarefied for the beginner to breathe unless he has had time to get acclimated by degrees. Prayer begins at the lowly and familiar level of everyday life and simple love. No one can find these things beyond his grasp.

"Only after you have entered into this path does the problem of the Divine Person begin to take on a bit of its real meaning. I have had the experience myself, and I shall be the first to admit that the Person of God is in danger of being understood, most of the time, in a very wooden and anthropomorphic way, too much influenced by the imagination. Still, I cannot pretend that, even with the aid of experience and warning, it will be any easy task to escape the sway of the imagination and the harm it works. But gradually, eventually, under the external trappings of images of every kind, the basic, experienced truth begins to make its way. Even the least philosophical souls have a real and tangible share in it, granted that they could not even begin to translate it into words. If you are more philosophically inclined, you will do better at the attempt to put it into your own language; but the experience itself, for one and the other, is not essentially a different one. Here, finally, at long last, is the one human preoccupation that can satisfy the problem of the Divine Person: intimacy is the answer, heart to heart."[50]

Notes
to
The Living Religion

Chapter I

1. "These thoughts and feelings," writes Jacques Rivière, "are comfortable and reassuring; everyone has experienced them. We know where they lead: no one has ever come to grief through them. They bob up all of a sudden in my heart with all their calm assurance. I do not even think of doubting whether they are true or not; they are so useful. They have just the right slant I need to put myself on the same plane as someone else and fall in with his own thought process. They are calculated to facilitate conversation. But, for all their usefulness, they can never really get at my soul, no more than any standard conventional expression of courtesy." Jacques Rivière, *De la sincérité envers soi-même,* pp. 22 f.

Gustave Thibon joins him in lamenting the way we abuse our social ego to the detriment of our fundamental self. "How simple, these people of Roman-Russian extraction. Their most weighty plans, their most solemn resolutions they change in the course of a commonplace everyday conversation. Their most intimate and secret life falls in perfectly with their social life, with an ease and natural spontaneity which, in the case of persons who did not know each other perfectly, could only be taken for joking and pretense. The Latin temperament is bound up with futility and artifice. Truth and real depth are embarrassing, and even the most seasoned conversationalist is at a loss when it comes to putting his naked feelings into words. We stop being natural when our nature begins to speak. We are born men of the world in which we live. . . ." Gustave Thibon, *Le pain de chaque jour,* p. 142.

2. We all know that, when we focus on any given point, besides the object that is in the direct focus of our gaze, we also see, to the right and to the left, in a vague and less distinct manner, all the other objects that are within a certain radius. This section of space and the objects it contains make up what we call our marginal vision. The same thing is true of our psychological consciousness. Side by side with the thing that holds our attention directly—we might say that it is in the focus of our clear consciousness—there are a great many other things which enter into our consciousness without attracting our direct attention. They are what makes up our

marginal consciousness. One of the most common examples is the case of distractions in prayer.

3. "I maintain that it is better to know about them than not to know about them. A really big soul cannot bear to be noble if all that nobility means its being blind. I think that the most shameful vice of all is this interior make-believe, this art of self-delusion that many people like to pass off as the greatest virtue. I hate self-fear. I can never begin to have any real worth unless it is built up upon myself, unless I look at everything that I am as the raw material of my efforts." Rivière, *op. cit.*, p. 31.

4. "If someone loves me for my judgment or for my memory, does he really love *me*? No; I can lose all these qualities without ceasing to be myself." Pascal, *Pensées*.

5. "It is in virtue of a spiritual intuition experienced by my soul . . . that I come face to face with myself in my human acts as their conscious source: active, autonomous, responsible." N. Balthazar, *Mon moi dans l'être*, p. 45.

6. "Intuition of my ego is truly explicit. I come to grips with substantial wholeness as something experienced, incompletely understood no doubt, but still immediately present, like a whole that is experienced and tasted all at once." N. Balthazar, *op. cit.*, p. 47.

7. "I can," in the sense "I have the power to"—not in the sense "I have permission to," "I have the right to."

8. "This is the mystery of auto-determinism. No man ever faces it without a certain momentary terror, without the anguish which Kierkegaard, with good reason, treats as one of the most important aspects of human consciousness. This anguish, moreover, springs not only from the mystery that the intelligence uncovers there, so close because it is within us and so far away because it eludes every attempt at exact expression, but also, and even more so, from the atmosphere of aloneness which all of a sudden overcomes the consciousness. Being free means being alone in the precise measure that you are free. It means having to bear the whole responsibility of your acts." L. B. Geiger, O. P., *L'existentialisme de Sartre et le salut chrétien*, in *Délivrance de l'homme*, Part VII of *Jeunesse de l'Église*, 75.

9. Instincts are not evil in themselves. They are part and parcel of human nature. Together with other energies, they go to make up the

most basic of its vital activities. But they are blind and blinding forces. They need to be clarified, purified, controlled, regulated.

10. We say "to the call of the fundamental ego," and not "to the call of nature." Nature is made up of an unordered throng of aspirations, impulses, and needs which are far from being all of the same value. It is a shadowy and chaotic world, and the only way it can be put into any kind of order or hierarchy is by bringing it into contact with the fundamental ego.

11. We are thinking here of the truth about man, that is, the sum total of all the individual data which concern his nature and destiny.

12. We are thinking not only of unbelievers in writing this; we are thinking of the numerous Christians who live in a half-conscious Pharisaism and false security which assures them that they have the truth—a truth which they have never dared to look in the face.

13. Cronin's hero in *The Keys of the Kingdom* makes several remarks on this subject which are both humorous and to the point. "No one in good faith is ever lost. No one, Buddhists, Mohammedans, Taoists . . . the blackest cannibals who ever devoured a missionary. If they are sincere, according to their own lights, they will be saved. That is the splendid mercy of God. So why shouldn't he enjoy confronting a decent agnostic at the Judgment Seat with a twinkle in his eye: 'I'm here, you see, in spite of all they brought you up to believe. Enter the Kingdom which you honestly denied' " (pp. 215 f.).

14. There are many examples of this in literature: Maxence van der Meersch, for example, in *Corps et Ames,* and Daniel Rops in *L'épée de feu.*

15. J. Malègue, *Pénombres,* p. 145.

Chapter II

1. In the same way we will be able to understand the tremendous unbalance which exists in our civilization, no matter how brilliant it looks from the outside. We overfeed the secondary activities and starve the essential ones: that is the tragedy of our civilization. We are a body looking for a soul.

2. A. D. Sertillanges, *Science et scientisme,* in *L'avenir de la science,* pp. 65, f.

3. *Ibid.,* p. 38.

4. *Ibid., passim.*

5. *Ibid.,* p. 68.

6. *Ibid.,* p. 70. On this whole question of the relationship between technology and humanism, and more precisely Christian humanism, we recommend the important work of Jean Laloup and Jean Nelis, *Hommes et Machines* (Casterman, 1953).

7. Lecomte du Noüy, *La destinée humaine,* p. 29.

8. Saint-Exupéry, *Citadelle,* p. 113.

9. On this subject see A. Eymieu, *Le gouvernement de soi-même, I. Les grandes lois.*

10. See J. Payot, *L'éducation de la volonté.*

11. Attention is one of Simone Weil's favorite themes. She sets it up as an essential condition of study, love of God and neighbor, and moral progress. See for example *Gravity and Grace* (Putnam, 1952).

12. It goes without saying that in the eyes of the Christian there is another extremely important element in the moral life: grace, that is, the activity of God himself coming to strengthen and supernaturalize our own personal activity, without in any way suppressing it.

13. *Inform* here means to give a form. The sculptor gives a form to the marble when he fashions it into the figure of a saint. A person gives his act a form when he performs it according to some particular intention and purpose.

14. This refers to communion as well, which will be treated at greater length later on.

15. This is not to say that in certain cases here on earth the same act cannot be accompanied by anguish and suffering, as in the case of a mother who has to watch her child suffer.

16. See R. Guardini, *Pascal.*

17. See Lalande, *Dictionnaire philosophique;* Canon F. Gregoire; *La collaboration de l'intelligence et de l'intuition selon Bergson* in *Revue*

internationale de philosophie, X (1949); or *L'intuition selon Bergson: Étude critique* (mimeographed), fascicle I (Louvain: Nauwelaerts, 1950), pp. 35-43.

18. Bergson, *L'évolution créatrice,* p. 217.

19. Edward Le Roy, *La pensée intuitive,* (Paris: Bovin, 1929).

20. An analysis of this parable, together with many other considerations which bear upon the subject we are treating here can be found in H. Bremond, *Prière et poésie,* ch. 12.

21. Maurice Zundel, *Recherche de la personne* (Paris: Desclée-de Brouwer, 1938), p. 19.

22. *Ibid.,* p. 20.

23. A. Valensin, *François* (Brussels: University Press, 1946), p. 19.

24. Zundel, *op. cit.,* p. 47.

25. Christian Mathioly, *Notes sur l'expression de l'Absolu,* in *Etudes carmélitaines,* 1947, *Ma joie terrestre, où donc es-tu?,* p. 298.

26. Edward Le Roy, *Revue de métaphysique et de morale* (1899), p. 726.

27. *Ibid.,* p. 721.

28. Alexis Carrel, *Prayer,* pp. 17 ff.

29. Etymologically, *religion* means to bind, to tie together, according to some authorities; according to others, it comes from the word *re-legere,* to re-read, to review seriously, to meditate upon.

30. Alexis Carrel, *Prayer,* p. 25.

31. E. Boutroux, *Science et religion,* p. 375.

Chapter III

1. On this question see De Lubac, *De la connaissance de Dieu* (Paris: "Christian Witness," 1941); *L'incroyance des croyants* (Part VI of *Jeunesse de l'Église* (Seine, Petit-Clamart); and the always opportune remarks of Jacques Rivière, *À la trace de Dieu* (Paris: Gallimard).

2. Every philosophy has its own way of working out the proofs for the existence of God. Chapter five will explain why there is no need to be alarmed at this. On the whole problem, see Franz Grégoire, *Questions concernant l'existentialisme,* Part II, *Essai d'une phéno-ménologie des preuves métaphysiques de l'existence de Dieu* (Louvain: Nauwelaerts, 1953).

3. On this question see Karl Adam, *Jésus Christ;* and our pamphlet, *La personne de Jésus.*

4. This idea is developed with great skill by H. Delsaute, *Le mystère de l'unité et du retour* (Tournai: Casterman, 1952).

5. It would be very useful to read C. S. Lewis on this question: *The Problem of Suffering.*

6. A. Letousey, *L'Évangile, règle de vie,* p. 240.

Chapter IV

1. "This has no value; this is very valuable; he is a valuable man." Or simply the word *value:* moral values, spiritual values, economic values; to evaluate, to value.

2. One of the best studies on this subject is by Louis Lavelle, *Traité des valeurs: I—Théorie générale de la valeur* (Paris: University of France Press, 1951). It has an excellent bibliography.

3. The hierarchy of values is described with real insight by Pascal in Fragment 793 of his *Pensées.* "The infinite distance that separates the body from the mind is only a shadow of the infinitely more infinite distance between the mind and charity; for charity is supernatural. . . ."

4. It is just as interesting to observe the life cycle of values in the course of history. Frequently there is a predominant value that determines the specific form of a civilization and creates the type of man that is characteristic of an era: the Roman citizen, the medieval knight, the humanist of the Renaissance. It is easy to follow the history of the values that have left their stamp upon each generation from the end of the seventeenth century down to our own times: freedom, glory, nature, science, life, activity, technology, community. We can see how certain values are born, how they develop, and how

they are displaced by others, how values become unbalanced and go astray and split off from each other.

5. For example, concerning the Immaculate Conception of the Blessed Virgin, which he confuses with the virginal conception of Christ by the Blessed Virgin.

6. "Lower values are degrees of the higher values and have to be integrated into them. . . . When they begin to be sought after for their own sake, they turn into an obstacle instead of serving as the steppingstones for our spiritual ascent to God." Lavelle, *op. cit.*, p. xiv.

7. Lecomte du Noüy, *op. cit.*, p. 134. This whole chapter, devoted to superstition, spoils what would otherwise be a very interesting and thought-provoking piece of work. The idea of seeing in superstition an insufficiently developed form of religion or a regressive stage of religion can, of course, be defended. But in illustrating this thesis, he could have come up with a good many examples, even from Christian terrain, instead of presenting as superstitious the dogma of the Immaculate Conception—which the authority whom he follows did not understand at all—or the veneration of the saints—in which his authority had eyes only for the abuses he had encountered.

8. On this whole question of "spiritual sensitivity" the work of Jean Mouroux can be read with profit: *L'expérience chrétienne* (Paris: Aubier, 1952).

9. L. Kammerer, *Obscurcissement de la notion du salut*, in *Délivrance de l'homme*, Part VII of *Jeunesse de l'Église*, p. 104.

10. Julian Green, *Journal*, IV (1943–45), 109.

11. H. Duméry, *Les trois tentations de l'apostolat moderne*, pp. 53 f.

Chapter V

1. It is important to use the terms correctly here. Revelation is God's part; it comes from God. Religion is man's part, man's answer to God's revelation.

2. The Christian mystery and Christian revelation are both the same thing. We prefer the term *Christian mystery* here, because the word *revelation* has too intellectual a ring. It suggests the idea of a pure

communication of doctrines, whereas revelation is actually the activity of God working supernaturally in all of human history.

3. This is the frame of mind which is often met with in the intellectual milieu of those who are taken up with what they call "free examination." Everyone can choose his own truth, they say, and they set up an eclectic religion according to their own individual lights and preferences. Man creates a religion according to his own image and likeness and no longer according to the image and likeness of God. This "free examination" has no meaning except in a loyal and unprejudiced search for objective truth. And once this truth has been discovered, there is no longer any room for "free examination." It is time to cling to the faith.

4. Quoted by Pasteur in his address upon his reception into the French Academy.

5. St. Thomas, *In Ethic.*, I, 3.

6. Not always certainly. Some acts, in the concrete, present such a complexity that we have to give up the idea, in examining them, of ever having any real certitude. We live in probabilities then and we keep our freedom of action.

7. Bergson, together with many other contemporary philosophers, uses the term *metaphysics* in a still different sense. It consists in the concrete and primary knowledge that is had through the direct intuition of things, as opposed to the abstract knowledge that is the result of discursive thought.

"If there exists any means of possessing a reality absolutely instead of knowing it relatively, of placing oneself within it instead of looking at it from outside points of view, of having the intuition instead of making the analysis: in short, of seizing it without any expression, translation, or symbolic representation—metaphysics is that means. Metaphysics, then, is the science which claims to dispense with symbols." Henri Bergson, *An Introduction to Metaphysics,* Tr. by Hulme (New York: Putnam, 1936), p. 9.

Obviously, the word can mean whatever a person wants it to mean, provided he is consistent. The reader will recognize in this "metaphysics" what we have been calling "communion" and considering as an activity distinct from both philosophy and metaphysics properly so called.

8. Bergson, *Introduction à la métaphysique* in *Revue métaphysique,* January, 1903.

9. "The first beginnings, the principles, the sources can only be the object of direct intuition, which can be contemplative or practical, but always it has to be directed." Le Roy, *Introduction à l'étude du problème religieux,* p. 204.

"No one can prove a judgment of value or obligation unless he bases his proof upon another judgment of value or obligation. If someone refuses to admit any affirmation that contains the terms 'this is better than that' or 'you should do this,' what kind of proof could you give him? It is just like the case of a man who is asking his way and admits that he does not know where to go or whether he wants to go there." Laland, quoted by Le Roy, *op. cit.,* p. 205.

10. An excellent development of the proof from the convergence of evidence is to be found in H. Pinard de la Boulaye, S. J., *L'étude comparée des religions,* II, 517–564.

11. "All men reason . . . but not all men reflect upon their reasoning. . . . Even less so are they all capable of justifying their own way of life. In other words: everyone has a reason, but not everyone can give a reason." Newman, *Universal Sermons,* XII, "Explicit and Implicit Reason."

12. The same thing is true of certain emotions. Love, for example, can spring up in a heart without the heart's being able to perceive it there. But then something happens, for example, the loved one falls into a serious sickness, and the love suddenly becomes felt and conscious.

13. See what has been said about empirical knowledge in Chapter II.

14. The word *liberty* is polyvalent: it is a real "tangle of equivocations." It is used to mean *instinct,* which can be found in animals as well as man, which propels each individual person to flee from every law and rule, every subjection and dependence and domination. It is also used to mean the *rights* that the law allows us (and this refers to any law, natural, positive, religious, civil). For example, I am free to walk about the streets at any hour of the day or night; but at certain hours I am not free to make a disturbance on the streets. In the third place, it can mean *free will,* that is, a power which is proper to spiritual creatures, angels and men, which consists in this that they can freely determine some things for themselves on their own responsibility. Finally, we use the word *freedom* to describe the state of a man who has used his free will correctly

and arrived at a more secure and natural self-mastery and a more perfect feeling of interior detachment and security and joy. This is what we call *interior* or *spiritual freedom*. It is a conquest, whereas free will is a gift. It is one of the goals of human life, whereas free will is only one of the means. In the pages that follow, it is freedom as free will that we are speaking of.

15. Le Roy, *La pensée intuitive,* I, 52.

16. Cammaerts' excellent book, *Upon This Rock* (Harper, 1943), illustrates this point very well. A professor of French at the University of London, Cammaerts had the misfortune of losing his only son shortly after the outbreak of the war in 1940. His book reproduces his long and poignant dialogue with himself and his surroundings, with his missing son, with God, shortly after the great shock that so disturbed his soul. And since he tries to understand with his whole being, he sees the light by slow degrees. Finally the whole story closes on a triumphal note.

17. Newman seems to have been especially struck by this evidence, the appearance of "Him whom the very history of the Judeo-Christian religion, from its distant preparation in the Old Testament down to its final development in the history of the Church, clearly points to. In his opinion, the discovery of this powerful network which binds the whole ensemble of facts together to make them into a real unity in the midst of a great many historical events that unroll without any obvious order, gives rise to a reaction that is not unlike the experience of seeing a figure gradually produced upon a tapestry: you realize that there has to be an intellect at work, setting up the whole machinery in advance." R. Aubert, *Newman, Au seuil du christianisme,* Lumen Vitae IV (Paris: University Press, 1952).

18. Karl Stern, *The Burning Bush.* A German Jew, he was a doctor and a convert to the Faith.

19. The case of Claudel is famous: Notre Dame in Paris, December 26, 1886. "In an instant I believed. I believed with such force and strength, with such an uplifting of my whole being, with such a powerful conviction, with such a degree of certainty that there was no room left for even the slightest doubt, so that, afterwards, all the books, all the reasoning, all the hazards of a troubled life were not enough to shake my faith, not enough, for that matter, even to touch my faith." And suddenly some great thoughts flooded into his consciousness: "How happy are those who believe! If only it were all

true. . . . But it *is* true. There is a God. He is present. He is Some-one. He is a personal Being just as I am a personal being. He loves me. He calls me."

20. Such, for example, is the conversion of the Jew Ratisbonne who, when he was still hostile to the Church, was favored with a vision of the Blessed Virgin in a Roman church where he had gone to wait for a friend.

21. These have all been mentioned above.

22. On this whole question, and for the whole problem of Faith, see the important work of R. Aubert. *Le problème de l'acte de foi* (Lou-vain: Warny, 1945).

23. This is a case of frequent occurrence, especially among young people who are subjected to the de-christianizing influences or even merely the scientific studies of the universities. We might recommend to them the small pamphlet of J. Leclercq, *Le problème de la foi dans les milieux intellectuels du XXe siècle* (Paris: Casterman, 1948) as well as the work of Xavier de la Bonnardière, *Devoir de croire et sincerité intellectuelle* (Paris: Aubier, 1949).

24. "Blessed are the pure of heart."

25. "The heart has reasons that the reason does not know."

26. We quote Malebranche: "If men are not equally enlightened, it is because they are not equally attentive." And William James: "The most voluntary kind of will is realized essentially in attention. . . . Attention is the essential act of the will." And P. Ricoeur, *Philoso-phie de la volonté,* Ch. III, art. 3. Let us refer once again to Simone Weil and the importance she attaches to attention—above all, passive attention—in intellectual research and literary creation, in the love of God and neighbor.

27. Compare the appeals to watchfulness in Mt. 24:42; 25:13; Mk. 26:41; 13:35; the parables of the servant waiting for his master in Mt. 14:46; Lk. 12:37 and 43; the appeals to attention in Mt. 11:15 ("Let him who has ears hear"); 13:43; and the significant text in Mk. 4:24-25: "Take heed what you hear. With what measure you measure, it shall be measured to you, and more shall be given to you. For to him who has shall be given; and from him who does not have, even that which he has shall be taken away."

28. We do not say "time," since that is impossible for most men.

29. Malègue, *op. cit.,* p. 15.

30. This is the attitude of Gide, irreconcilably opposed to faith. We can find it, for example, in the case of Peter Van der Meer de Walcheren. "What a terrible yoke all these ideas are for me who want to be open to every current, to every form and shape of life, for me who admire the terrible loneliness and sacrilegious boldness of Nietzsche every bit as much as the charity of a St. Francis. For me religion is a shackle, a bond, an intolerable diminution of life."

31. Claudel himself, sincere and restless Claudel, had to admit that the strongest sentiment keeping him from declaring his convictions was human respect. "The thought of telling everybody about my conversion, of telling my family that I would be abstaining on Friday from now on, saying publicly to all the world that I myself am one of the Catholics they make fun of—the thought always made me shudder."

32. Think of the case of Eve Lavallière before her conversion.

33. The examples are well known: Coppée, Claudel, Psichari, Louis Bertrand, R. Leyvraz.

34. "The lamp of the body is the eye. If thy eye be sound, thy whole body will be full of light. But if thy eye be evil, thy whole body will be full of darkness. Therefore if the light that is in thee is darkness, how great is the darkness itself!" (Mt. 6:22–23).

35. This was the case of Newman. He felt very strongly attached to his mother and sisters and to the Anglican friends with whom he had begun and organized the Oxford Movement. Yet, despite the pain and disillusion it would mean for all of them, despite the deep pain that it would mean for himself, he did not hesitate to join the Catholic Church as soon as he understood that "it would be a grave sin" not to join it.

36. This was so with many Jews, for example Bergson, who was prevented by his scruples from making public profession of his new Faith till his death. That was in 1939, during the persecution of the Jews under the Nazi regime. The same was true of Karl Stern and Edith Stein.

37. R. Leyvraz, a Swiss, Douglas Hyde, an Englishman, and Marchant, a Dutchman, are examples of this. Marchant, Minister of Public Education and head for thirty years of the Democratic Inde-

pendent Party he had founded, addressed this communication to the press on May 1, 1935: "Monsieur Marchant, Minister of Education, announces that he has joined the Catholic Church and that he is leaving the Democratic Independent Party. He has requested Her Majesty the Queen to release him from his duties in the Ministry."

38. Malègue, *op. cit.,* p. 86.

39. Two examples: "I clearly saw," writes Thayer, a German Protestant minister, "that the truth of the Roman Church was based upon many clear proofs. I saw that her answers to all the Protestant objections were solid ones, satisfying ones. . . . But I did not have the courage to join." And Miss Baker, an English Protestant, writes: "Even though I knew that Christianity was the divine religion in the only full sense of the word and that Catholicism is the only logical form of Christianity, I did not become a Catholic."

40. Malègue, *op. cit.,* p. 93.

41. On this subject see F. Grégoire, *Sur les termes intuition et expérience,* in *Revue philosophique* (Louvain, 1946), pp. 411–415.

42. That is what makes Sartre's hero in *Le diable et le Bon Dieu* so absurd. He commits himself to live a holy life merely for the sake of experience. His life is vitiated from the very outset. You cannot experiment with God. You give yourself to him. The experience is something secondary.

43. We say "generally" because it is not impossible that life in faith, even in the case of fervent Catholics, even in the case of saints, should undergo periods of great struggle, doubt, and anxiety. This state of mind can have natural causes, such as a nervous temperament or scruples. Thus it can be a trial sent by God to purify the soul and test its faithfulness. In addition to this, the lives of many of the saints pass through three stages which have been described by the Fathers of the Church: the struggle between flesh and spirit, the meeting with God accompanied by joy and happiness, the resumption of the journey again in the light of new certainty but also in the realm of the purely spiritual and frequently in spiritual aridity.

44. See what has been said about atheists in good faith in Chapter I, article 2.

45. The conversion of Hugh Benson is a good example.

46. This was the case of St. Paul. Among the converts closer to our own times we might mention Ratisbonne, Herman Cohen, Paul Claudel. By way of example let us examine the case of an Anglican, Robert Bracey: "When I try to figure out the way that I was led into the Catholic Church, I do not have to work my way through the history of any complicated intellectual evolution or any painful struggle with difficult problems. If it is allowed to compare little things with great and heroic things, then Faith came to me just as it came to St. Paul, by means of a sudden illumination, without any struggle or effort on my part. . . . One day which I shall never be able to forget—I was sixteen years old—I went to the oratory at Egbaston for Mass. I had been there once or twice before, principally out of a desire to see Newman, and I had not been particularly struck by anything about it. I well remember, on this occasion, my contempt for all these things that I could not understand and my complete ignorance of what they all meant. It so happened that that particular morning the sermon was perfectly miserable: the preacher ranted and raved on and on. And yet it was in the midst of this sermon that faith came to me. I suddenly felt—how, I do not know—that I believed in this religion which I so little understood; to my great unhappiness—for I could forsee the hardships and difficulties that such a change implied. I discovered that I was a Catholic. I left the Church that morning with all these ideas in turmoil in my mind, but still just as certain of the truth of Catholicism as I am today, and ready to give up everything else for it. That night, for the first time since I was eight years old, I said my prayers. The next morning I bought some Catholic books and began to study them. The more I read, the more satisfied I became. And soon I felt that I was capable of giving good arguments for the faith that was in my soul. But the firm conviction was there before I began the reading."

47. Msgr. Brunhes, *La foi et sa justification rationelle,* p. 114. There are two good examples of this. The first one is from J. K. Huysmans, in *En route:*

"When I was alone in churches I often heard unexpected voices, mute counsels; and I declare that it is a most frightening experience, feeling, deep in your heart and soul, that an infinite Person is coming down to you, knowing that this Person can turn you out of the comfort of your own personality. But really it is more than this. My own will is not replaced by another will from the outside: my freedom remains essentially intact. It does not present anything like the irresistible impulse that many sick people think they can experience. Nothing is easier than to resist. Even less is it a suggestion. No; it is the incessant influence of the power of some outside Personality. It is the implanting of a desire that is clear and impelling without importuning, a firm and at the same time gentle impulse in the soul. You just begin hoping that the impulse will come again and it is gone already. You are left alone; you are free to obey or not to obey. There is no forcing your will; that you know. But you also know, and you know it without any doubt, that you are taking a big responsibility upon yourself for the future if you refuse this in-spiration. In a word, here is some divine impulse at work here . . . something like the famous interior voices of the mystics. Only it is more complete, more precise, and also more certain."

For his part, Julian Green proposes a very exact analysis of his refusals in the face of the "invisible Educator."

"On this certain day of your childhood [God is speaking to him] when you were playing all by yourself in your mother's room and the sun was shining brightly through your fingers, this thought came to you first, fitted out like a king's envoy, and you were happy to take it; but since then you have refused it. Still, it did not leave you; it was with you, sustaining you. When you were walking along this avenue in the shade of the plane trees and your cousin said these words, you knew at once that they had come from me, but once again you forgot them because there was something in them that said no to your thirst for pleasure. That letter you tore up and threw into the fireplace to burn, it could have kept you from that other difficulty; it could have given you back your faith. But you did not want to give me that little bit of freedom that I go about begging from men while they are on earth." *Journal,* Vol. II.

48. Malègue, *op. cit.,* p. 99.

49. *Ibid.,* p. 100.

50. Le Roy, *Introduction à l'étude du problème religieux,* pp. 211–214.

Index

Activities, irrational, Carrel on, 56; moral, 39–45; scientific and philosophical, 26–33; technical, extent and limitations of, 36–39; technical, vast field of, 33–36

Affection, as disfiguration of religion, 155–156

Aim, Le Senne on, 42

Alain, 20

Anima, Claudel on, 55

Animus, Claudel on, 55–56

Anti-chance, du Noüy's use of term, 140

Attention, Weil on, 48–49; and will, 217–219

Awareness, ordeals of, 82–84; religious, 81

Bergson, H., on creators, 35; on freedom, 196; on intuition, 55

Blondel, M., on knowledge, 55; on need for prayer, 236

Bonnard, Abel, on love, 60

Bossuet, J., definition of Church, 102–103

Boutroux, Emile, on religion, 79

Brunhes, on activity of grace, 232

Camus, Andre, 20

Carrel, Alexis, on irrational activities, 56; on neglect of moral sense, 26; on prayer, 69–71; on spiritual atrophy, vi; texts of, 47–48

Catechism for Unbelievers (Sertillanges), 18–19, 234

Causality, secondary, and grace, 233–234

Certitude, different kinds of, 178–199;

of Divine Faith, 199–228; experienced, 192–197; historical, 184; metaphysical, 182–184; moral, 181–182; positive, 180–181; practical, 197–199; produced by evidence, 212–213; reflex, 192–197; religious and supernatural, 177–237; speculative, 197–199; supernatural religious, 184–186. *See also* Knowledge

Chain-letter prayers, as superstitions, 143–144

Charity, Christianity as religion of, 122–127

Childhood, virtues of, 108–109

Christ, religion of, 97–101

Church, function of, 103

Civilization, as Christian, 168–169

Clarity, 11–12

Claudel, P., distinction of, between *anima* and *animus,* 55–56; on illumination of spirit, 51

Clericalism, abuse in application of term, 173–174

Collaborating, variation in meaning of, 140

Communion, 45–68; different names for, 53–56; objects of, 56–61; as role of spirit, 52–53; science and, 61–68

Community, Christianity as religion of, 127–130

Consolation, religious meaning of, 156

Conversion, Rivière on, vi

Comte, A., as autonomous skeptic, 22

Creators, Bergson on, 35

A NOTE ON THE TYPE

IN WHICH THIS BOOK WAS SET

This book has been set in Granjon, a lovely Linotype face, designed by George W. Jones, one of England's great printers, to meet his own exacting requirements for fine book and publication work. Like most useful types, Granjon is neither wholly new nor wholly old. It is not a copy of a classic face nor an original creation, but rather something between the two—drawing its basic design from classic Garamond sources, but never hesitating to deviate from the model where four centuries of type-cutting experience indicate an improvement or where modern methods of punch-cutting make possible a refinement far beyond the skill of the originator. This book was composed by Progressive Typographers, Inc., York, Pa., printed by Wickersham Printing Company of Lancaster, Pa., and bound by Moore and Company of Baltimore. The design and typography of this book are by Howard N. King.